P9-CDI-891

❧

SEVEN DAYS OF POSSIBILITIES

❧

Seven Days
of Possibilities

∽

ONE TEACHER, 24 KIDS,

AND THE MUSIC THAT CHANGED

THEIR LIVES FOREVER

∽

Anemona Hartocollis

PublicAffairs

NEW YORK

BOOK DESIGN AND COMPOSITION BY JENNY DOSSIN.
TEXT SET IN ADOBE MINION.

Library of Congress Cataloging-in-Publication data
Hartocollis, Anemona.
Seven days of possibilities : one teacher, 24 kids, and the music that changed
their lives forever / Anemona Hartocollis.— 1st ed.
p. cm.
ISBN 1–58648–196–7
1. School music—Instruction and study—New York (State)—New York.
2. Grussner, Johanna. I. Title.
MT4.B7574P3 2004
372.87'044'0974747275—dc22
2004044721

FIRST EDITION
1   3   5   7   9   10   8   6   4   2

To Josh, Daphne, Dove, and Daisy
who have taught me so much about life and love.

CONTENTS

❧

PART TWO

Aland, Finland

Who can sail without the wind?
Who can row without oars?
Who can be separated from a friend
Without shedding a tear?

I can sail without the wind.
I can row without oars.
But I cannot be separated from my friend
Without shedding a tear.

Vem kan segla forutan vind?
Vem kan ro utan aror?
Vem kan skiljas fran vannen sin
Utan att falla tarar?

Jag kan segla forutan vind.
Jag kan ro utan aror.
Men ej skiljas fran vannen min
Utan att falla tarar.

ALAND ISLANDS FOLK SONG

PROLOGUE

⁄⁄

Slouching in the front five rows of graffiti-scratched wooden seats in the cavernous, sloping school auditorium, sixty fifth- and sixth-graders fidget and chatter as they wait for Johanna Grussner, their chorus teacher, to begin rehearsal. They are bored. They make fun of the luxuriant vowels of Johanna's Swedish accent and titter at private jokes.

In an echo of a more dignified time, the auditorium walls are painted sky blue above their granite skirts. Art deco brass and opalescent glass chandeliers hang heavily from the 40-foot ceiling, though they are illuminated only for special occasions (cheap modern track lighting substitutes at other times) because the custodial workers don't like climbing up to change the light bulbs. Blue velvet draperies shroud the towering procession of windows.

But even in this sanctuary, it is hard for the children to shake off the jangle of the Bronx—the video arcades, Laundromats, bodegas, Korean bazaars hawking athletic socks by the dozen, plastic flowers, and $7 knockoffs of the robot dogs that command $300 at FAO Schwarz. They worry about the surly teenagers who congregate just down the street at the local junior high school, a place where boys become more proficient at fistfights than at algebra or literature, where parents despair of sending their children, but send them anyway because they have no other choice.

Then the accompanist at the grand piano tucked just below the stage leans into the keyboard and softly plays a few bars, and the mood changes. Sixty 10-, 11-, and 12-year-olds snap to attention, the molded plywood seats in the first row flipping up like a volley of machine gun fire as their occupants rise. Their eyes fasten on Johanna, standing facing them in her jazz siren's tight black slacks over skinny legs, her V-neck sweater cut nearly to the breastbone, blue eyes widened like searchlights. As she signals the harmony, starting pitches, and breathing, the children burst into an old Negro spiritual "Come and Go With Me," and the ones standing in front swing into the hip swiveling and hand clapping accompaniment Johanna has taught them. ("If you happen to bump into anybody right now, it's because you're going in all directions, so watch my legs. Step together," their teacher coaxes.) Vincent Maldonado's black smudges of eyebrows knit together sadly, and his mouth widens like a mask of tragedy as he sings. Pierre Marquez could be at a revival meeting, the way his elongated El Greco face looks transported with joy. In the halo of the music, Paloma Perez's limbs shed their stubby awkwardness to take on a comforting solidity.

Their voices swell jubilantly at the crescendo, "Come and go with me to that LAAAAND . . . . There's no suffering in that LAAAND," and just as suddenly hush at the diminuendo, "where I'm bou-ouund."

"Freeze!" Johanna cries, silencing them. "Don't lean back. Hold the last phrase. I don't care if you turn green in the face and are going to faint right in front of me. You have to hold the last word, because that's what's going to make them cry."

By the time their voices well up into the last phrase, "HALLELU-JAH! HALLELUJAH! We are going to seeee the kiiiiiiiiiing," a knot of teachers, aides, and a security guard have been distracted from their errands and are gathered at the far end of the auditorium, peering through the doors down the sloping aisles, transfixed.

The children are angels. They are the Select Chorus of Public School 86, and many of them had never carried a tune before Johanna Grussner discovered them.

They had worked together for three and a half years, building their voices and their bonds to one another. It was a measure of the strong, if unlikely, identification between the teacher and her students that Johanna had become determined to take them to her hometown in Finland. She wanted to show them the scene of her idyllic childhood filled with everything the children lacked: the warm embrace of a tiny school, frequent doses of fresh air and play, and music lessons for every child.

Just as fervently, she wanted her hometown to meet the children. She wanted her parents to finally see that she had been right to leave her tiny archipelago of Aland on this madcap trip to America, and to meet these children she had been telling them about for so long.

For at least one brief moment, the experience transformed the school, and the lives of everyone in it—the children, the teachers, the principal. For some of the children, Johanna's song meant more than that. The greatest adventure in Vincent Maldonado's young existence, the one thing that convinced him he could rise up in life, began in the cold granite corridors of P.S. 86.

PART ONE

❧

The Kingsbridge Heights School, P.S. 86
The Bronx, New York

CHAPTER ONE

❧

Looking for Paradise

When she was 9 she asked the barber to cut off all her hair. She had taken the bus from Palsbole to Godby, a 6-kilometer ride, with her cousin. She was well armed with pocket change caged from her father. She always had money in her pocket. Even at a young age, she was an entrepreneur, a schemer. She ran a lemonade stand, Johanna's Sommarcafe, in front of her house, and gave her little sister Bodi the privilege of washing up in a bucket, while she collected all the earnings: 50 penni for lemonade, 1 mark for coffee. She brought home a pile of maps of Aland that her father's tour bus company gave out for free and sold them for 5 marks each at the corner grocery store. Whatever project she came up with, her father, a self-made businessman, was one of her best customers. He was her co-conspirator. When she defied him, he was secretly tickled by her ingenuity. Like the famous beer party.

"Pappa, I need to buy beer for the party," she begged.

"No, Johanna, you know you are too young."

"I'm 18," she protested.

"I'm not talking about the law."

So she sold ads for his bus fleet—to a beer company. In payment, she took kegs of beer instead of cash. Her sisters helped her stash the kegs in the root cellar next to their house. The night of the party, 200 people got wind of the beer and flocked to the root cellar from miles around. Her father was upstairs sleeping, her mother out. Before it was over, the neighbors had complained. Mamma was furious. Pappa kept his counsel; this was one of those times when Mamma's reaction counted for two. But Johanna could tell her father was impressed.

So by the age of 9, when it came time to do something for herself, like buy candy or cut her hair, she could take care of it.

"Cut it off," she told Sickan, the family hairdresser, settling into the high vinyl chair. "About an inch long."

"You'll look like a boy," Sickan warned.

"I don't care."

When she got home her father tried to conceal his horror at the sight of her, shorn of her long blond tresses. Her mother only laughed. "You look like a little hedgehog," she said, running her hand over Johanna's bristly scalp. From then on she called her Kotte, the hedgehog.

The nickname, Kotte, stuck. Twenty years later, her mother keeps it programmed into her cellphone. But you hardly ever heard anyone say it out loud, except in lamentation. If she broke a glass or came in late, it was "Oh Kotte." If she cried for a lost romance, it was "My little Kotte." Can you blame her if she felt slighted? Her sisters got their nicknames, Cocki and Bodi, when they were infants. Meaningless nicknames, nonsense, baby-babble, what her mom and dad would say when they tickled their little bellies—kooki, kooki, kooki or boodi, boodi, boodi—the way Americans would say coochie-coochie-coo. The whole world calls them Cocki and Bodi even now that they are full-grown women. How could she not feel left out? Nobody thought to give her a nickname until she was 9, and then they hardly ever thought of using it. She was born Johanna, a grownup name, and that's the name she's lived with ever since. Cocki, Bodi, and plain old Johanna. Only her father makes it sound special, hurrying over the first two syllables to bear down on the n's like a caress, Yo-ha-nnna. Even her own family treats her warily, as if she might be hot to the touch or shatter like glass.

Johanna is the middle of three sisters. You know how the middle child always feels the most neglected? That is her. She works hard to overcome her sense that she is always a step behind where she needs to be, running to keep up. Maybe she's spent her life imagining this handicap, but whether real or an illusion, it haunts her still. Age doesn't take the sting out of it. She sometimes imagines that, because she is so much like her father, she has been his clandestine favorite. Despite that fantasy, she often feels small and unloved. She is not fearless and breathtakingly beautiful, like her younger sister Bodi, who was three-quarters-blind at birth and now deploys keen 20-20 vision under her coquettishly batting eyelashes, as if by a miraculous visitation and cure. She is not studious and domestic, like her older sister, Cocki, the Madonna, who is raising three perfect children. She is the ordinary one, the one with the average looks, middling grades, sure that the door is about to shut in her face, sweating every step of the way as she strives for extraordinariness, or at least for a ticket outside the confines of her little town.

From an early age she worked hard to be noticed, to get the attention she craved. She was the charmer, the flirt, the class clown, the skinny blond pied piper, all sharp elbows and skinned knees. She was not naturally courageous, but whenever a risk presented itself, she closed her eyes and tackled it. She had to ride her bike faster than anyone else, climb to the highest branch of every tree, willfully ignoring the fact that the branches were too green to hold her. On snowy days in winter, she pushed her wooden kick-sled to school down the slippery street, heedless of the drivers struggling past on their way to work.

She discovered her gift in music and acting. If the teachers wanted to put on a show, she would not stand for anything less than the director's job. When they had a school circus, she had to be the ringmaster. They obliged. No one had the stamina to cross her. She was unstoppable. She and her partner stayed in the eighth-grade dance marathon until there was only one other couple left, and she collapsed from exhaustion. "*Herregud*, my legs," she groaned. The cramps rose up from her calves and squeezed her thighs like a steel vise.

As a teenager, she thrived on melodrama. She rebelled, ate little, became light as the wind and never slowed down. Her scrapbook is the proof. Here's a picture in the local paper, when she and her girlfriends were plucked off the street for a consumer survey of push-up bras. Here's another one, of them taste-testing crayfish. That's a big summer activity here. You drink Schnapps and gorge on crayfish. You end up with a tummy like a beach ball, drunk and singing. Singing is a big thing here. She sang old Motown ditties with four friends at a school show. She played in a middle school rock band.

She was always a performer. The year after she graduated from high school, she didn't know what she wanted to do with her life. The school asked her to stay on and teach music. They had never had a teacher so young. She wrote and directed the high school play, a musical called "The Mirror," about a girl who runs off to the big city and joins a gang. A show with an edge. You know how it is in a small town; even high school theater is important enough to rate a review in *Alandstidningen*, the local paper. It was a hit. She sold the show to six or seven other schools for $300 a pop and the class took a trip to Sweden. She was outgoing, popular, but still thought of herself as a misfit, the ugly duckling hoping to discover that she was a swan.

Everyone predicted that she would go far. She took them seriously, and their conviction became an inspiration and a curse. If you are the temperamentally contented type, a small town will hold you in its warm embrace like a mother's arms. For some people, to venture even a few kilometers from home is unthinkable. Home, school, church, the corner store, a job—those are the touchstones of life. You marry your high school sweetheart, settle down, start a family, and never worry about whether you belong. You just do.

But the Aland Islands have always attracted their share of restless souls, Johanna's family among them. To understand why, it helps to know something about the islands. Neither completely Finnish nor Swedish, they were historically part of Sweden, which gave them their language and culture. They are just two and a half hours by ferry from Stockholm, but subject to Finnish currency, and foreign policy. Geography and geopolitics have shaped their character. As island people the Alanders are farmers, fishermen, or seafarers. Their connection to the sea has made them more open to foreigners than mainlanders tend to be, and more peripatetic. Like their Viking ancestors, they are not afraid to go out into the world. But they always long to come back.

As if Aland's endemic sense of being betwixt and between were not unsettling enough, the Grussner roots are less firmly entrenched than they might be. Johanna's mother is Swedish by birth, a high-bred colonel's daughter from Stockholm; her father's paternity is German, and rumor had it that her German grandfather was a spy. Her paternal grandmother, though, is an Alander to her bones, and everyone says Johanna takes after her. In her father's first-floor study, on the right-hand wall facing the desk, is a black-and-white photograph of her father's mother as a young woman, a ferociously determined young woman, her arms thrown over two little boys in knickers. Those are Johanna's high, flat cheekbones, her long slightly crooked front teeth in the big flashing smile. That is her dimple screwed as firmly as a bolt into a washer in the middle of her chin. They have the same sinewy washboard build, though Johanna has never done the heavy labor, taking in laundry, baking bread to get by.

They are an outsized family in an undersized town. Yet some of them have struck a truce with Aland. Johanna's sisters are happy here. Her father can't bear to leave his herb garden and his wildflowers, even for a few days. Her mother, well, her capacity for agitation matches her husband's penchant for tranquillity, so they are two interlocking halves of a whole. As for herself, Johanna can only say that she had an idyllic childhood. But of course she didn't know that at the time.

When Johanna was 18, she called a family meeting to decide her future. Everyone gathered, obedient, at the old scarred wooden farmtable in the cavernous kitchen of her parents' beloved eighteenth-century house. Without thinking, they took their places in the usual constellation of stars around her father's sun. Her father, Ulf, whom everyone called Uffe, took up his position at the head of the table facing the kitchen door. The slate-gray evening light poured over his shoulders from the two tall windows behind him, the light reflecting off his shock of snow-white hair and the white half-moon beard covering his chin, which he has grown, perhaps deliberately, to look like one of his Viking heroes, the poetic and battle-wise Rode Orm, the Red Snake. To his right, poised gingerly on the straight-backed wooden chair, ready to rise whenever someone needs a glass of water or wine, more butter or bread—or when she imagines they do—her mother, Lillemor, a faded beauty in her loose bohemian tunics from Marimekko. On Lillemor's right, the oldest sister, the ever-composed, straw-blond Cocki. On Uffe's left, their last and youngest, the one to whom all transgressions are permitted, flame-haired, snub-nosed Bodi lounges on the carved wooden bench. Then Johanna, the farthest from everyone, on the bench next to Bodi.

"Sweden or Boston?" was how she posed her dilemma. "I'm so confused." She had been accepted to a conservatory three hours outside of Stockholm, Orebro Musikhogskola, which was very tough to get into. She viewed it as a Scandinavian Juilliard, prestigious, the type of place whose name you would append to your own with a coy flourish for the rest of your life; therefore, admission was hard to turn down. She also had a scholarship to Berklee College of Music in Boston. Maybe not as well known in Aland ("Hhhhun," the corner grocer had said noncommittally, with that polite Finnish intake of breath), but still a feather in her cap. She listed the pluses and minuses. Her family listened patiently, but they knew, even if she didn't, that she had already made up her mind. They knew that whatever she might pretend, she was not going to make a purely rational decision, the kind of conclusion you would arrive at by reading "So and So's Guide to the Best Music Schools in the World."

"I'm going away" is what she was telling them. In every immigrant story, the process of selection is never accidental. Those who leave are always different from those who stay behind. They are refugees of the soul. Something is pushing them, something they can't resist. It could be a crime, a family feud, a guilty secret, a thwarted love, a broken heart. Maybe nothing so definite, nothing you can put your finger on, but a force nonetheless like a firm hand against your back. Maybe all it takes is a nagging sense of dissatisfaction, of being a misfit, of dreaming that there is a place for you, as the song says, a time and place for you. That doesn't mean you give up all hope of coming back. But you know that if you return, it will be because you are different, stronger, ready to stand on your own. You must return triumphant, with something to show for your trouble. Otherwise, you are only running away from home. Like the fabled Vikings, you would not reappear without a trophy, a few stanzas of verse, composed during the voyage, commemorating your adventures in faraway lands. At the time, she didn't actually think these things, let alone say them out loud. She concentrated on the sheet of paper in front of her, squinting to read her notes in the pale light filtering through the opalescent lampshade over the kitchen table. Such an impractical light, an 1860s brass candelabra, with a ball-and-chain counterweight to lower the kerosene base and candle branches when they needed to be lit or extinguished. The church custodian, the previous occupant of the house, had left this relic behind, and despite its dim, now electrified, light, her mother treasured it. In her mother's house, character and art—whether of the furniture or the people in it—always ranked more highly than convention or utility.

Johanna was under the illusion that she had defied her upbringing to become the practical one. Staring into the romantic pool of light in front of her, she considered the pros and cons. In their stark black and whiteness, the facts were easier to grasp and harder to dispute than motives, emotions, the big and shadowy truth of life. Stockholm: Cheaper. (Free tuition.) Boston: More expensive. Boston: New language, culture. Stockholm: Easter in Sweden. Stockholm: Near. Boston: Far.

Who was she kidding? Of course she was going to go, the farther away the better.

CHAPTER TWO

❧

The Accidental Teacher

She spent three happy years at Berklee College of Music in Boston, never losing her accent but learning hundreds of American jazz songs by heart. Internally driven as always, she wasn't content to take the prescribed courseload, but had to adopt a condensed schedule, with the excuse that by transferring credits from courses in Sweden she could save money.

Every summer, she returned to Aland. She raised money for tuition by renting out her father's café for $4,000 for the summer and managing it herself with two friends. They did everything—cooking, cleaning, waiting tables, running the cash register, ordering and bookkeeping—then kept the profits. She always brought along her boyfriend, Gary Heckard, a Coloradan and classmate at Berklee. In her hometown, Johanna was cast as the prodigal daughter, and with typical showmanship, she embraced the role. A reporter from *Alandstidningen*, her hometown paper, visited her in Boston, dutifully photographing the apartment building where she lived with Gary and recording her 19-year-old aperçus about street beggars ("If you don't give them money they can be quite unfriendly"), American attitudes toward blondes (men will try to take advantage) and what she missed most from home (Muesli. American breakfast cereals, she lamented, were little better than sugar-coated paper).

After graduation, Johanna and Gary packed up a U-Haul and headed south to New York. They planned to pursue their master's degrees together, at the Manhattan School of Music, a stone fortress at 122nd Street and Claremont Avenue, just north of Columbia University, in a neighborhood dominated by students, academics, and musicians. After that . . . who knew?

In the winter of 1998, as Johanna was entering her last semester of graduate school, earning a master's degree in musical performance, Rudolph W. Giuliani embarked on his second four-year term as mayor, knowing that it would be his last, by virtue of the city's term limit laws. Reviled by some, admired by others, Giuliani was at the height of his power. After cracking down on the city's notorious crime rate in his first term, he was gearing up for a new target for his prosecutorial zeal in his second. The murder rate was on a downward spiral, dropping to levels that had not been seen since the 1960s, and that some had never expected to see again.

The mayor could now turn his attention to what political polls typically showed to be New Yorkers' next biggest concern, the woefully neglected state of the city's public schools. Although derided by some as a cynical gesture, Giuliani's education policy would shape Johanna's future.

଼୨ଡ଼

Johanna was in the kitchen cooking dinner one winter night when the telephone rang. Dropping her fork on the stove, she reached for the receiver on the wall.

"Hello," said an older woman's husky voice. "Could I speak to Johanna Grussner, please?"

"Speaking!"

"This is Margaret Bartelme, the arts coordinator at P.S. 86. I got your number from Education Through Music. I understand you're interested in a part-time position."

"Yes, definitely."

Tucking the receiver under her chin, Johanna walked back to the stove and stirred her pasta. Pasta, boiled potatoes, Chinese—her diet had suffered since she left her mother's house.

"Have you ever taught before?"

"Not exactly. I did some student teaching my last semester up in Boston. But I really love kids."

"We've been looking for someone all fall, but. . . . "

"Could you hold on a second? I'm having trouble hearing. . . . "

Johanna waited for the rattle of the elevated subway, which ran outside her window, to fade. She realized that the woman had kept on talking. Who had she said she was? Margaret somebody. The principal?

"Sorry?" Johanna said. "What was that?"

"My own background is in visual arts," Margaret was saying. "I'm afraid I don't know too much about music. We're looking for someone who can build the program."

"What kind of music are you looking for?" Johanna asked.

"Oh, I don't know. Fun songs. Children's songs. Whatever feels right to you. Use your judgment. Could you come up to the Bronx? For a demonstration lesson?"

"Of course. I live in Harlem. It's not far."

"Is there any grade you'd prefer?" Margaret wondered.

"Fifth?"

"Fine. Is there anything you need?"

"Will there be a piano?"

"I'll try to get you one."

Margaret told Johanna when to be there and gave her directions to the school.

Johanna wrote down her full name: Margaret Bartelme.

℘

She hung up the phone and plopped down on a kitchen chair, feeling less certain than she had sounded.

The woman on the other end had been nice, but vague, formal, a little distant. Who was she, anyway? The principal? A teacher? A secretary? Johanna couldn't remember what the woman had said. The assistant principal, probably. She obviously knew very little about teaching music, though to her credit, she hadn't tried to pretend otherwise. Johanna thought about canceling; there was just something so unfocused about the whole conversation. Student teaching was different from having a class to yourself, all the responsibility for whether kids learned. And Margaret didn't sound like she was going to offer a lot of direction.

Johanna had one semester left before graduation. At this point, she would be able to teach music only two days a week while taking college classes during the other three. As an international student, she was entitled to a one-year work visa, with which to put her music training to some practical use. She thought she should take advantage of that, while earning some pocket money.

She had tried out for two other jobs, and there was still a chance she would get one of those. Both had the advantage of being in Manhattan, within easier range of her apartment. One was on the Upper East Side. The students had been well dressed, well behaved. They had struck her as affluent, or at least comfortably well-off. She had noticed a pretty Petit Bateau shopping bag in the classroom, casually used by a child to bring in something from home, the way another child might bring in a plastic bag from C-town supermarket. Within walking distance of the Metropolitan Museum, you couldn't beat that. A few blocks from Madison Avenue, too, though she didn't see much Prada in her future, not while she was stuffing a measly couple of $50 bills in her jeans after singing her lungs out 'til 2 A.M. to a crowd of sleep-deprived New York University students and junior advertising executives at a West Village cabaret. The other was on the Lower East Side, a little more bohemian, the post-hippie kids, but a comfortable, homey school, with a community garden nearby and murals on the walls. She had loved getting off the L-train and walking through the funky East Village, the vacant lots sprouting zany welded sculptures, the raised beds covered with soggy, decayed winter remains of tomatoes, string beans, and black-eyed Susans, the spunky little boutiques. She had stopped at a hole in the wall to buy a pair of earrings, silver filigree with little blue beads, for Bodi. How many piercings did Bodi have these days? Bodi would fit right in on Avenue B. Nothing like plain vanilla Johanna, settling for just a pair of pierced ears.

Jesus. Who was she kidding? Neither tryout had gone too well. She might not be a professional teacher, but she knew what a good performance should be like. She had tanked at those schools. The principals there had known exactly what they wanted, and Johanna didn't have the background. They wanted Dalcroze or Eurhythmics, gimmicky programs, which, in her opinion, had more to do with educational fads than with music. She had boned up on them a little, but she came across as phony. Hell, the programs were phony. Music as therapy. Music for tin ears. Rhythm as formula. Why aim for the lowest common denominator? Every child, every human being, has a song in his heart. What was wrong with Frank Sinatra, Ella Fitzgerald, Tony Bennett, Glenn Miller? The great singers and band leaders in Pappa's record collection. Musicians who could swing. Musicians who were happening. Those were her idols when she was in grade school. She had pictured herself as the blonde bombshell in the slinky gold lamé sheath, kissing the microphone while eighteen horn players sat behind her in straight rows ripping jazz licks.

You didn't get that from Dalcroze. . . . Never mind. What a stupid childish dream. She wasn't going to grow up to be Ella Fitzgerald, and not just because of her blue eyes and blond hair. She wasn't going to be hired as a music teacher, either. She had screwed up. She had forgotten

everything her father taught her about running a business: The cus-
tomer knows best. And she had ignored the cardinal rule of performing: Know your audience. You've got to give them what they want.
Don't cry over spilled milk, she told herself. Johanna had shed too
many tears too easily in her life. She cried over the smallest things. But
the one thing she wouldn't do was cry over not being hired. From the
first time she skinned her knee, her father had taught her to stand up,
brush herself off, and try again.

Arrgh. The pasta. She hoisted herself out of the chair and dumped
the bloated spaghetti into a colander, then went to her bedroom for her
bag. She opened her black book, the big solid planner she had bought
at Wilson's leather store, as if its very weight assured her of a secure
future, and made a note of the appointment with Margaret Bartelme.

For Johanna, the coincidence in timing between her graduation and
Giuliani's new agenda could hardly have been more felicitous. With
New York City sharing in the national boom-times, this seemed an
especially promising moment for an aspiring jazz singer to take the city
by storm. The money was easy and people were spending it on good
food, drink, and music. The moralistic mayor might be cleaning up the
peep shows and topless bars in Times Square, but the legitimate clubs
were packed. The stock market seemed to be going nowhere but up.
Everyone was in a party mood. New York was on a roll, and so was
Johanna, who could whisper a ballad by Antonio Carlos Jobim, her
favorite Brazilian composer, one night and surprise you by growling out
the blues like Bessie Smith the next. She found inspiration in the hypnotic click-clacking of the subway, the babble of languages on the
street, the excitement of other twenty-somethings who lived on air and
a prayer in the conviction that someday, by dint of raw talent, they
would rise from the gray masses of wanna-be's and morph into the next

Keith Haring, Savion Glover, or Melissa Etheridge. Every day in New York tested her in a way that made her music richer. "In New York you have to struggle to survive," she would say. "You have to be aggressive. Everyone here has an edge, which is something you need as a jazz singer." But in the age-old tradition of the small-town girl trying to make it in the big city, she needed a day job. A few years before, she might have waited tables or temped in a law office, but now she wanted something more and her timing was perfect: New York schools were looking for a musical renaissance.

By many measures, New York's public schools had never recovered from the city's brush with bankruptcy two decades earlier. In the fall of 1975, the city appealed to Albany and Washington to bail it out of fiscal ruin, but President Gerald Ford declined, inspiring the infamously bitter tabloid headline "FORD TO CITY: DROP DEAD." It was the teachers' union, among others, that came to the rescue, however reluctantly. The municipal unions agreed to use their pension funds to contribute to billions of dollars in emergency financing. Despite these efforts, more than 14,000 teachers would be laid off. Art, music, and athletic programs would be decimated. The middle class abandoned public schools in many neighborhoods. The most affluent New Yorkers sent their children to exclusive private schools; police, firefighters, and civil servants turned to more economical Catholic schools; and after accounting for white flight to the suburbs, public schools in large parts of the city became the province of low-income black and Hispanic children with few, if any, other options. They were schools of last resort, and the establishment perceived them, with a certain sense of noblesse oblige, not as a middle-class amenity but as a service to the poor, like welfare and Medicaid.

Mayor Edward I. Koch took steps to repair the damage in the early

1980s, working with an aggressive and independent chancellor, Frank J. Macchiarola. Macchiarola was able to leverage his good relationship with the mayor into better financing for city schools. He offered summer school for children in key grades—fourth and seventh—who were falling behind. He experimented with reducing the number of children in early-grade classes to as low as fifteen—private-school size—from twenty-five or thirty, after persuading the city's budget staff, which had to pay for the extra teachers, that this was the optimal number for learning. Koch's successor, Mayor David N. Dinkins, continued the upward trend for a time. He forged strong ties with the chancellor who took office when he did, Joseph Fernandez, a Puerto Rican high school dropout, a school of hard knocks graduate who had shot heroin growing up in Harlem, then gone on to become a charismatic symbol of how far disadvantaged children could go.

Fernandez teamed with teachers, parents, and community groups to create networks of small schools, organized around inviting themes like music or public service, to combat the numbing anonymity of the big factory–type education that had prevailed for most of the twentieth century. "Let a thousand flowers bloom" was the unofficial motto. But during the recession of the 1990s, Dinkins made crippling cuts to the school system. Crime had risen through the late 1980s. In a spate of random shootings in July 1990, innocent children had been cut down by gunfire in their own homes, making average New Yorkers cringe in fright as they stood by their own windows. Dinkins focused what resources he had on beefing up the police force.

After taking office in January 1994, Giuliani continued the trend, reducing spending on the city schools while building up areas, like the Police Department, that he considered a priority. He decried the city's tax burden and complained about the Board of Education's bloated bureaucracy, constricting the flow of money to the schools more than any other mayor since the city's fiscal crisis. When the chancellor, Ramon Cortines, resisted, the mayor derided him as "precious" and jeered him out of town. But Giuliani was shrewd enough to recognize that for his core constituency—conservative white ethnics in Queens and Staten Island—public schools were an important attribute of the quality of city life. By his second term in office, Giuliani had crime under control and was ready to tackle education.

Giuliani's early education agenda was twofold: to reintroduce the arts to city schools and to improve reading skills in the early grades, a strong predictor of future success. It was a less than sweeping agenda. But arts and reading had sex appeal, and they could be targeted with relatively modest resources and without running the risk of political opposition.

Giuliani and his immediate advisors had little inside knowledge of the public schools and how they worked. When parents and teachers complained about how difficult it was for children to learn in classes of thirty-five, Giuliani retorted that he remembered going to school in a parochial school class of fifty-two children, and he "hadn't suffered." He did not mention that his children—like those of many other public officials—attended private schools, which typically had classes of eighteen or fewer. His son, Andrew, attended a $13,000-a-year parochial school with regular classes in art, pottery, and woodworking, two literary magazines, and a glee club. His idea of school reform was to offer publicly financed vouchers to students who wanted to go to private and religious schools, which he argued would drive reform by fostering competition, while giving the children in the worst schools an immediate out. Most middle-class parents, legislators, and the teachers' union opposed vouchers, making their chance of being adopted almost nil.

After hounding out Cortines, Giuliani needed to burnish his image on education and could not afford to alienate the next chancellor. Rudy Crew took over the school system in September 1995, at a low point in the mayor's popularity, when the public had doubts about his ability to unify the city. As an African American, Crew could help solve the mayor's political problem. Although the chancellor was accountable to a seven-member Board of Education, with only two members appointed by the mayor, Crew was shrewd enough to forge a cordial relationship with Giuliani, recognizing that the mayor employed not just the bully pulpit of his position at City Hall, but most of the time, an effective majority of the seven-member board. The five board members not under the mayor's direct control were appointed by the borough presidents. Queens and Staten Island, Giuliani's electoral strongholds, could be counted on to give the mayor a bare four-member majority when he needed it, in exchange for services to their constituents.

Crew's press secretary assiduously built up a mythology around the relationship between the pugnacious mayor and the chancellor, who had blown in from small-town Tacoma, Washington, declaring that reforming New York City schools was not for the "faint-hearted." New Yorkers were told that this unlikely pair were so chummy they enjoyed private meetings over whiskey and cigars. In hindsight, the syrupy sentiment behind those stories came to seem largely apocryphal. Crew's turn came on December 23, 1999, when he was ousted by Giuliani's allies on the Board of Education after threatening to resign rather than permit the school system to experiment with private-school vouchers. Looking back later, Crew might have been forgiven for wondering if he had made a pact with the devil, in which he had been forced from the beginning to curtail his own educational agenda in deference to the mayor's political imperatives.

The Giuliani administration inaugurated Project Read and Project Arts, as they were called, in 1997, a mayoral election year, with modest allocations of $25 million a year for three years. Project Read offered after-school remediation to children who had fallen behind in reading. Project Arts was designed to bring musicians, actors, and dancers as well as museums and other arts organizations into the schools for workshops. Critics argued that the arts program was more of a boon to arts organizations than to students. By subsidizing professionals to give performances and demonstrations in schools, some said, the program was raising a generation of children trained to be passive audiences rather than independently creative artists. Still, after years of cultural deprivation, the schools were hungry for whatever they could get. In a little-noticed coincidence, the teachers contract also played a role in supporting the new mandate for the arts. The contract had been rene-gotiated to increase the number of prep periods—time outside the classroom during the day—for teachers in many schools to three from two. So-called cluster teachers had to be hired to cover those periods, and some principals had the imagination to supplement Project Arts by hiring cluster teachers who could teach art or music or dance.

There was an inherent tension, however, between the two prongs of Giuliani's initiatives—reading and the arts. Despite the arguments of arts advocates, there was little evidence that music or art or dance helped children learn to read or do math. Ultimately, schools like P.S. 86 would be judged not by the artistic sensibility of their students but by their standardized test scores.

It was into this hothouse atmosphere of political ferment around education that Johanna plunged as she went looking for a job.

Margaret had been right to be apprehensive about the commute. The northwest Bronx was a long way from Manhattan, even the upper reaches of Manhattan. The street grid that had steered Johanna faith-fully within the tight orbit of her life in New York—the hulking stone edifice that was the Manhattan School of Music, her apartment, the clubs where she sang, the Norwegian Seamen's Church, where she sought solace from homesickness—this logically engineered map all fell apart in the Bronx. Margaret had recommended the No. 4 train. But Johanna had done some research since then and discovered that there was no reason to endure a slow bus ride across 125th Street to the Lex-ington Avenue subway. Just outside her apartment door, she rode the clackety old escalator up to the familiar subway station, its wooden floors oddly reminiscent of a beachside boardwalk, at 125th Street and Broadway.

Feeling as if she were going the wrong way, she headed to the uptown platform instead of the downtown one. At least traveling against the morning rush she did not have to stand. She sat nearly alone in the slippery orange bucket seats, gazing out of the Plexiglas windows at the industrial flotsam of West Harlem unfolding below the train trestle. First came the old warehouses divided into cheap metal storage lockers stuffed with the couches and rugs of people who had had the misfortune of being evicted, or whose stingy apartments could not begin to contain the accretions of a normal life. She looked down on gas stations, the U-Haul rental, African CD vendors camped under a plastic shed pitched against the facade of El Mundo, the discount department store selling calico housedresses, polyester quilts, and gaudy wineglasses. In a few short blocks, Johanna had crossed the demilitarized zone of 125th Street, and the landscape had changed radically, from college-town shabby chic to inner-city ghetto. Like a roller coaster, the train dipped and roared underground again at 135th Street. Closing her eyes in the yellow glow of the tunnel, lulled by the hypnotic swaying of the subway car, she surrendered to the journey and whatever it might bring.

At 225th Street Johanna picked her way down from yet another elevated platform and stepped onto solid ground in the Bronx. She could walk up the winding road to Kingsbridge Heights, or take the bus. The walk looked arduous, uphill all the way. She chose the bus. The route had a certain bedraggled charm. Instead of apartment buildings, two- and three-story brick and clapboard houses lined the road on one side, giving it a curiously small-town feel. Not like New York at all. So this was the Bronx. The sight of those houses tugged at her heartstrings. She imagined domestic scenes unfolding behind the blank windows and wooden porch railings. Families watching TV in the living room, fathers in their underwear, mothers leaning over the hot stove.

She got off the bus at Kingsbridge Road and Jerome Avenue, in a surprisingly pretty neighborhood of mostly low-rise six-story buildings, well shaded by tall trees. It must look green in spring, Johanna thought. The next thing she noticed was the Kingsbridge Armory, a turreted red-brick castle, looking mysteriously medieval against the gray winter sky. Behind it loomed the five-story bulk of P.S. 86, covering nearly a half city block. "It's so big" was all she could think.

P.S. 86 was not an opulent school. The exterior was a plain rectangular box, made of gray brick. A portico of fluted Greek columns guarded the front door, like a gateway to democratic values and ideals. The name was chiseled into a stone banner across the front: PUBLIC SCHOOL 86.

It lacked the Gothic grandeur of the H-plan schools built by Charles B.J. Snyder, the architect for city schools from 1891 to 1922, the closest the New York City school system ever had to a Roman empire builder. Those early schools, with their gargoyles and turrets, conveyed grand visions of the transformative power of education. They were havens for the wave of immigrants who reached New York in those years, for the huddled masses yearning to be free.

But what P.S. 86 lacked in flourishes, it made up in gravitas. Completed in 1928, on the brink of the Depression, it was conceived as a dignified laboratory for the next generation. Immigrant craftsmen had built it with nearly indestructible materials meant to last the ages: brick, granite, marble. It conveyed a belief in the value of utilitarianism and an appreciation of the classics.

Nearly identical Greek-revival schools, called E-type buildings, overseen by William H. Gompert, then the Board of Education's chief architect, could be found all over New York City. In the early 1920s, Gompert announced plans to build more than fifty E-type buildings, which were designed to be constructed rapidly and economically, and to be easily expanded as the student population grew. Gompert said the exterior of these buildings exemplified the theory that: "an American school should be of a purely American style of architecture." With that philosophy in mind, he said, "the facades and interior of the building will be in the Colonial style."

They were planted in once-solid middle-class Irish, Italian, and Jewish neighborhoods, inhabited by merchants, small-factory owners, and civil servants who had not gone on to higher education but whose children would. Even the floor plans were mass-produced. Teachers or principals who had been to one such school could navigate any other one with their eyes closed. In a ghostly twist of history, John F. Hylan, the city's mayor in the 1920s, once had grand plans to make P.S. 86 part of a "Music and Art Centre" for children in the area of Jerome Park. But until Johanna came along, those plans turned out to be little more than castles in the sand.

Seven decades later, the custodian of P.S. 86, Ted Pannullo, called the building his "stately old gal," noting proudly that "back then, things were done right." He had brought his own tiller from home in New Jersey to plant perennial flower beds around the towering red maple on the front lawn—wild tiger lilies dug up near his backyard, flats of pansies from Home Depot, and fifty rose bushes bought at fire-sale prices from a garden center that was closing down. Old women, some new arrivals in babushkas from the old communist bloc, would walk out of their way just to admire them. "I want to leave a legacy," Pannullo once said, poetically. "As the kids grow, the flowers grow too."

To Johanna, who knew little of New York City schools, P.S. 86 was not just another cookie-cutter building. As far as she could tell, it was unique, imposing, portentous. Looking up at the massive brick walls, she felt both intimidated and comforted by their rectitude. But in spite of the custodian's touches of color, she couldn't help being disturbed by the prison-like grates on every ground floor window. And where, she wondered, was the playground? She had seen only a parking lot in back, and no sign of slides or swings or climbing equipment for the little children to play on.

Pulling open the heavy metal front door, she found herself in a kind of inner atrium, two stories high. Railed staircases, one for going up and one for going down, the gunmetal gray banisters worn smooth by countless hands, rose on either side to a mezzanine balcony, like a quaint interior widow's walk, a perch where the principal could stand to observe people coming and going. Shoved underneath the treads of the up staircase—on her right—was an old metal desk, the security guard's station. Next to the desk she found a gaunt woman in a loose-fitting pantsuit waiting. The woman had straight, shoulder-length auburn hair that was parted severely in the center and fell in two sheets over her face like blackout curtains, as if she were guarding her privacy, or at least preferred to keep her thoughts to herself. "I'm Margaret Bartelme." Belying her reticent posture, Margaret's voice was direct, throaty, and soft. Her smile was wary, but her crinkly eyes were warm and penetrating. Her plain style—no makeup, earth-colored clothes—communicated an understated elegance.

"There's been a change of plans," Margaret said, shaking Johanna's hand. "I have to teach a second-grade art class this period and I couldn't find a substitute." Johanna absorbed the news that Margaret was a teacher, not an administrator. She wondered when she would meet the principal and if Margaret had the authority to hire her.

"Is it OK if the kids sit in on your demonstration lesson?" Margaret asked.

"Yes, of course. That's fine. Just bring them along," Johanna replied. Margaret waited patiently as the uniformed security guard demanded Johanna's identification, and Johanna signed the visitor's ledger. Johanna felt as if she were crossing the border from Finland to Russia, getting her passport stamped. What were they afraid of? P.S. 86 was a tight ship, Margaret explained. Not even parents were permitted to enter without signing in.

These were the Board of Education's rules, not the school's. The bureaucracy took the dimmest possible view of the families it was meant to serve. Parents were treated like adversaries, not allies. Fathers were potential kidnappers, mothers were a drain on the teachers' time. Even the best principals and teachers often let the rules go unchallenged because keeping the parents cowed made the staff's job easier.

The tone was set from the very top. To get to the office of a petty bureaucrat at central, let alone the chancellor's office, every principal or teacher and their belongings had to pass through metal detectors. Not even books were exempted from the airport-style security at 110 Livingston Street, the Board of Education headquarters, the symbolic implications of X-raying books being lost on the system. The system was not set up to encourage communication between schools and the bureaucracy. In fairness, it was a very big system. No chancellor could hope to become intimately familiar with 1,200 schools. So sometimes for better and sometimes for worse, schools became little fiefdoms. On a day-to-day basis, a school like P.S. 86 was largely left to its own devices.

The demo lesson was on the third floor. There didn't seem to be any elevator. Johanna followed Margaret upstairs in the cool granite and tile gloom, marveling at the empty hallways, the orderly atmosphere.

They found the fifth-graders sitting expectantly in groups of four at small worktables. Margaret must have brought the second-graders in ahead of time. They were crammed on the floor at the front of the room. There were more than thirty fifth-graders in the room, and another two dozen second-graders. A piano had been pushed against the wall.

Johanna didn't want to turn her back to the children, so she pulled the piano out at an angle.

"My name is Johanna Grussner. I come from another country. From Europe. Do any of you come from other countries? Puerto Rico, maybe? Or the Dominican Republic?"

Nearly half the children, it seemed to her, raised their hands.

"How many of you speak Spanish at home?" she asked. Almost as many children raised their hands again.

"English is also my second language," she said, trying to establish a bond. "In our house, we speak Swedish."

Noticing a roll-up map above the chalkboard, she pulled it down and pointed out Finland and Sweden. In between, she told them, were the Aland Islands, her native land.

The room was so cramped that the second-graders were practically touching her ankles with their little knees. They looked so lost and confused. She felt bad. They didn't know that she was trying out for a job. All they knew was that she was ignoring them.

She looked at Margaret, who had taken a seat among the children.

"Is it OK if I change my plan and involve the second-graders?"

"Just do what you want."

She remembered a bike-riding song she had learned while student-teaching in Boston, an Aline Shader composition. One part was really easy; the little ones could handle that. The other part was trickier. She would teach that to the older ones. It was a silly song, a Dr. Seuss–type ditty in which the same few words were repeated over and over again. "Riding, riding on my bike, is the finest thing that I really like."

The kids were restless and Johanna knew instinctively that they needed to move. If only they had a little more room to move in.

"Let's pretend that we're bicycles. Make your hands into fists and churn them around like this. See? Those are the wheels. Now raise your arms like pistons. What else could we do? You decide. What movement can we do for the word 'bike'? How about riding, riding?"

When it was over, she had a gut feeling that it had gone well.

The next day, Margaret called to tell her the job was hers. When could she start? Johanna paused. There were no other offers. "Right away," she replied.

CHAPTER THREE

࿐

Location, Location, Location

Sheldon Benardo, the principal of P.S. 86, had not immediately been convinced that hiring Johanna was a good idea. Nothing personal, he had never met the girl, the bottom line was that he had reservations about hiring any kind of music teacher at all. He was not a Philistine. He had traveled widely during his vacations—not during the school year, for he was obsessively dedicated to his work. He wanted no less exposure to the wider world for his students, and growing up in a place like New York City, they had at least a fair shot of achieving it. There were museums, libraries, and concert halls galore, but none of them would matter if these children did not start life with a firm educational foundation. His job was to recognize potential, nurture it, and nudge as many of his students as possible into top-flight middle schools, their means of escape from the dead-end Bronx streets. Some of these schools were a long subway or bus commute away, in Manhattan or other parts of the Bronx, but he knew there would always be a few children willing to go the distance. It was one thing for a child to go to the neighborhood elementary school. But middle school, when their hormones and peer pressure kicked in, was a minefield. Most of P.S. 86's graduates went to the zoned middle schools, the closest schools to their homes. If they did not make honors classes, they were likely to be sucked under by a riptide of class-cutting, petty vandalism, marijuana smoking, schoolyard fights, and then, who knew? Drug dealing, theft, murder, prison. Every principal had seen it happen. A strong educational foundation was the antidote.

But more than that, he had to cater to the systemwide imperative. It was no longer enough for principals and teachers to follow their own internal compass, to rely on the accumulated wisdom of their years in education school and the classroom to arrive at a freely chosen educational destination. The pressure to show improvement in reading and math scores had become a steady drumbeat, drilled into the superintendent by the chancellor, the principals by the superintendents, and the teachers by the principals.

Chancellor Crew, who liked to extol a business model of education, was even talking about rating principals and granting bonuses based on performance. Differential treatment of principals and teachers had been anathema in the city's unionized school system, but the unions were feeling public pressure to yield, and such projects were moving forward on a trial basis.

The state Education Department seemed to be finding ever more sophisticated ways to parse the scores and determine targets for improvement at each of the city's 1,200 schools. The targets were calibrated based on an intricate formula that took into account a school's past performance and the performance of schools in similar peer groups—that is, with students of similar demographic background. But in a kind of Sisyphean agony, once a school met its target, the bar was raised, and you could hardly rest before you had to push forward again.

There wasn't much room for sentimentality in Mr. Benardo's line of work. He had grown up in this neighborhood and could find his way around in his sleep. He had graduated from this very elementary school nearly four decades earlier. He came from a family of educators, some in prominent positions. When he put in his papers to become a principal in 1991, there were ten or twelve vacancies in district 10, the northern Bronx, where he had grown up, learned his craft as a teacher, and lived still. He never imagined that by some spin of the roulette wheel he would regress to the place where he had started out. So when Shelly Benardo was assigned to P.S. 86, he would later recall, he "wasn't thrilled."

He would have liked to start his administrative career without preconceptions, without the burden of nostalgia, without encountering his past every time he walked through the schoolhouse door. He also knew that there were schools where the job was inherently easier, where the children came with more advantages from home. Not that this school was any more of a dumping ground than many others, but New York City schools were severely stratified by race, income, and class, reflecting the equally segregated neighborhoods around them. Ninety percent of the students at P.S. 86 met the poverty standard that entitled them to a free school lunch, far more than the 76 percent average citywide. Though there were few foreign-born students, about 80 percent of the children were of Hispanic background, from the Dominican Republic, Puerto Rico, Central America, and the Caribbean. Many spoke Spanish at home. Though fiercely protective of their children, many parents struggled to make ends meet, working long hours as car service drivers, home health aides, nannies, and factory workers.

But Mr. Benardo had inherited a stable, committed staff, and he could take pride in the fact that it had remained that way during his tenure. Despite the seven security guards in the building, or maybe because of them, it was a safe place. He never had to call the police, in contrast to some of his colleagues at other schools, and the Board of Education's incident records reflected that. There was an esprit de corps that retained effective and well-trained teachers, the vast majority with at least five years of experience and master's degrees.

When it came to attracting talent, being in the northwest Bronx had certain advantages. Not that teachers would necessarily choose to live there. But in hiring teachers, as in selling real estate, a principal quickly learned that there were certain immutable properties that mattered as much or more than safety, building condition, and collegiality. The big one was location, location, location. Good shopping and restaurants were a plus. Proximity to subways and highways—a quick commute— was another big advantage. Here he was in luck. The Lexington Avenue subway stopped a couple of blocks away. The Major Deegan offered quick escapes to suburban Westchester and even Rockland counties, just as schools in eastern Queens attracted teachers who lived just over the border on Long Island.

As alluring as the location might be, the test scores were nothing to brag about. The annual school report issued by the Board of Education showed that in 1999, just over a quarter (26 percent) of the students at P.S. 86 met standards on the state and city English tests, and even fewer (17 percent) met standards on the state's tough new fourth-grade reading and writing test. In the suburbs, or in the more affluent Riverdale section of the Bronx, where Shelly Benardo lived, those scores would be grist for a revolt against the public schools. Even for Kingsbridge, P.S. 86's achievement level was slightly below that of its peer group of schools, defined by the Board of Education as those with similar proportions of immigrants, non–English speaking students, and low-income students. It also put P.S. 86 well below the already abysmal citywide average of about 38 percent meeting standards in reading. Some schools in this position liked to brag that at least they didn't have a lot of children scoring rock-bottom on the tests. Mr. Benardo could not even say that, for at P.S. 86, there were slightly more students (about 28 percent) scoring at what the school report card called "far below standards" in English than there were students who met or exceeded the standards.

But schools, like the people in them, are not monolithic. And in even the worst ghetto school, there were always some students who performed above the averages, even brilliantly. The reaction had been to mercilessly track classes, segregating the best students, the middle students, and the worst students. Some more progressive educators might say this was a draconian solution. Once children were aware—and they were, despite coded room numbers—that they were in the bottom class, it was hard for them to overcome the blow to their own self-esteem. And surrounded by other poorly performing children, they had little opportunity to be challenged, or to learn from children who were better in school than they. Being a bad student became a kind of self-fulfilling prophecy. Once consigned to the dumb class, a student, however innately bright, might never have the opportunity to rise above that stigma. But therein lay the dilemma: Whose needs should be sacrificed, those of the students at the top or at the bottom? For the good students, tracking was all too often an advantage. Removing the stragglers from a class only made the learning go faster. Principals like Mr. Benardo often felt that they owed it to the children and families who cared about education to give them a chance to learn in the best possible environment, surrounded by other motivated students.

But that didn't mean Mr. Benardo wouldn't have liked to do things differently. Like any self-respecting veteran of the New York City school system he knew how to finesse the system when necessary. He was quick to volunteer his students for a drowning prevention program at Lehman College, forging a crucial alliance with the ambitious local councilman, Adolfo Carrión Jr., who financed the program. Partly, his ability to work the system was a matter of temperament. He played a mean hand of pinochle, was good with a bluff. When confronted with someone he didn't know, he held his counsel until he had psyched out the other person's point of view, and then echoed it back. Partly, too, his style reflected the culture of his generation within the New York City school system. Like many principals who had come up through the ranks, he thought of the school as a surrogate family, and ran it with a certain amount of benevolent paternalism. He liked to welcome important guests to his office with a small gesture of hospitality, if only a spread of bagels, cream cheese, and whitefish from the local deli.

What the outside world didn't understand was that no one cared about P.S. 86 and these kids more than he did.

On some level he identified. He had never been cool; he was constitutionally a nerd. Not smart enough to get into the Bronx High School of Science, but close. He had gone to DeWitt Clinton (Class of '68), the rival high school down the street, even if it was the neighborhood school. Public education meant something to a striving Jewish boy like him. And he firmly believed that it meant just as much to the Dominican, Puerto Rican, and Caribbean immigrant families who sent their children to the school all these years later.

Were the public schools worse in 1999 than in 1949 or even 1969? There was no way to compare them. New York had changed so much; society had changed so much. The Jewish, Italian, and Irish immigrants who used to populate the sturdy Kingsbridge Heights apartment buildings had moved on to suburban tract houses in the newly cleared farmland of Long Island, Westchester, and New Jersey. Since then, the skinny little saplings in those suburban subdivisions had grown to solid elms. In the city, the number of single mothers had burgeoned. Poverty was second- and third-generation. Families came from countries, like the Dominican Republic, El Salvador, and Albania, where education was rudimentary.

And of course, the culture of the schools had changed too. Women who once became teachers now became lawyers and stockbrokers. Teaching had always been a route to upward mobility, but in generations past it had attracted idealists as well. Now in some parts of the city it had become the equivalent of a working-class job, a secure paycheck with good benefits, factory hours, and long summer vacations. Like working for the post office. It was no longer a job for the smartest kid in the class. P.S. 86 still embodied the American dream of education as the road to success, but it was a scaled-back version of the dream.

What Mr. Benardo needed was not an art or music teacher but more math and reading teachers. He liked culture as much as the next guy. But music and art mattered little to these children if they could not read or do sums. He did not believe in noblesse oblige. The arts grant sounded glamorous, was designed to win votes from the Manhattan elite, but would not fix what ailed the system in any fundamental way. It was more tinkering around the margins.

Mr. Benardo was endowed with a healthy skepticism about the ability of the central bureaucracy to make decisions in the best interest of individual schools. It was only natural for him to consider Project Arts from all possible angles. For one thing, he was expecting a windfall, between $80,000 and $90,000, depending on student enrollment that year. Project Arts grants were being disbursed using a per capita formula. With nearly 2,000 students, P.S. 86 was one of the biggest elementary schools in the city and the nation. What would be the most effective use of his share? There wasn't a lot of discretionary money in his budget. With that amount he could hire two bushy-tailed young teachers or run a decent test-prep program in reading and math.

It wouldn't have been the first time Shelly Benardo had disobeyed orders. And who would notice? The New York City school system had a million kids, 70,000 teachers, and 1,200 schools. He was a speck of dust. Hell would freeze over before the chancellor, or even a deputy chancellor, walked the halls of P.S. 86.

"The reaction of any principal when you get that amount of money is how can I take it from what it was intended for by central and use it for the school's own needs," he admitted.

But however cynical he might be about the system, he knew that within the smaller universe of his own school, he needed the support of parents and teachers to function. So he put together a committee to consider how to use the allocation.

Within the committee, Margaret Bartelme carried the day. She had worked with arts education programs at museums in California, Minnesota, and Scarsdale, as her husband, a TV news executive, moved his family around. Now she taught art at P.S. 86. Given the resources, she knew how to network with cultural organizations. This was the chance she had been waiting for.

Mr. Benardo was outvoted. Test prep would have to wait. "We'll give it a shot," he said.

∽

CHAPTER FOUR

"Call Me Miss Johanna"

There were no music books, no instruments, no practice rooms. There was a dusty old grand piano in the auditorium, but no one used it. Anyway, Johanna couldn't very well carry a piano from classroom to classroom on her back, like an itinerant peddler. There were signs that P.S. 86 had once been alive with the sound of music. As she made her rounds from class to class, Johanna counted seven pianos scattered throughout the school. Seven old ghosts, seven old shipwrecks. Seeing them, she imagined a golden age at P.S. 86 when proper lady teachers in seamed nylon stockings, pleated skirts, and white blouses, hair tucked into a neat chignon, pulled out their sheet music and led their classes in a brisk round of "Frère Jacques."

She hated the atmosphere at the school. Teachers used whistles and megaphones to control their students, as if they were running a penal institution. Security guards stood sentry at the doors. Students played in the school parking lot during good weather, chasing balls between the cars of teachers intrepid enough to arrive by 7 A.M., before the spaces were filled. They sat in the auditorium during bad weather. In Finland, the teachers used to say: "There is no bad weather, only bad clothes."

The school was so big that students had to rotate through the cafeteria for lunch. For efficiency's sake, one class would eat, while the other went outside or waited in the auditorium. If the weather was bad, which tended to be much of the winter, the children would watch movies instead of going outside. To call watching *Titanic* educational struck her as a cruel joke.

All the female teachers were addressed formally as "Miss," as if they were forever spinsters pledged to their school like nuns to a convent. It didn't matter whether they preferred "Mrs." or "Ms." in the rest of their lives. "Miss" it had always been and, apparently, always would be. All the male teachers were addressed as "Mr." Only the principal called teachers by their first names. But the teachers, in turn, called the principal "Mr. Benardo." A school, it seemed, was not an egalitarian society, no matter what the Constitution might say about all people being created equal. Even Margaret, who was sixteen years older than Benardo, observed this custom, Johanna realized, bemused.

In Finland, children addressed teachers and principals by their first names, and nobody ever worried that this would foster disrespect.

"Call me Miss Johanna," she told her students, in the first of many small acts of subversion, and they did.

She tried to tell Margaret how oppressive the atmosphere felt to her, but was met with incomprehension. "This is a good school," Margaret demurred, even though Johanna had not meant to imply that it wasn't. Johanna, Margaret scolded, did not understand what a massive undertaking it was to ensure order in a school this size. From then on, Johanna tried to swallow her distaste.

This job might not have been her first choice, but Johanna threw herself into it. She thought of each day as a command performance. She wore her jazz singer's uniform of tight black spandex slacks, v-necked blouses, and high-heeled boots or strappy sandals. Every morning, she applied a frame of black mascara to the big orbs of her sky-blue eyes, flecked with black; a singer needed to be able to reach for the audience with her eyes as well as her voice. Her one workaday concession was to brush her ash-blond hair smoothly back from her forehead into a demure ponytail, tucking back the wisps of stray hair.

At first, Johanna borrowed a guitar from Frank, the heavy metal–playing custodian. After a couple of weeks, Margaret bought her a guitar at Sam Ash. Nobody asked Johanna what songs she would teach. They seemed to take it for granted that she knew what to do. Actually, she hadn't the faintest idea. As a newcomer to American culture, she didn't know nursery rhymes or traditional children's songs. Margaret gave her a music textbook series, but that wasn't enough. In a panic, she called up Aline Shader, a songwriter she had met while at Berklee, when Shader was teaching in suburban Boston schools. "You have to help me," Johanna begged. "Send me your songs." Shader was curious about the school, and Johanna invited her to New York. Johanna told the children that a composer was coming to visit. They were perplexed. They had heard of composers, but in their minds, anyone who qualified as a composer had to be male and dead.

Shader left behind a bunch of sheet music, all her own compositions, songs like "Grandma's Song," "Smile," and "Una Luna Brilla." Johanna loved those. Others she found in the textbooks that Margaret had bought for the Project Arts program. Some songs—the alphabet song, the days of the week—were strictly didactic. But how proud the children were when they could recite their letters and days, their memories jogged by the music. One of her favorites was the sinister-sounding "Spaceworms." She liked the bluesy melody, and she knew that although adults liked pretty sentiments, children would rather sing about dirt and worms and other gross stuff.

Spaceworms, crawling in the night.
Spaceworms, crawling out of sight.

Spaceworms, love to talk,
And they love to do the spaceworm walk.

Out in space where the stars shine bright, hither and thither they slither
all night. Now and then you can hear them kiss, and their
kissing sounds like this: kiss, kiss.

The first-graders spat out the consonants and gyrated like belly-dancers; then they all sent air-kisses to one another, or their teacher.

At the beginning of class the children were as squirmy as worms. She didn't blame them after being trapped in their seats all day. Music was often their only chance to let off steam, so Johanna made her lessons as physical as possible. She choreographed Motown–style movements with every song, sometimes asking the children for suggestions.

Many of the children found it easier to remember the pantomime than the words. They retained a kind of nervous system imprint of the song, and once they started moving, their actions triggered the word memories, too. Coming up with the right pantomime became an important part of her technique.

Some of the kids seemed to think it was her job to entertain them.

"You sound so good that I feel very sad when I see you just sitting and watching," she would say to the ones who refused to participate. "I think about television. Do you think I am a television? Do you think it's important that you just sing well, or do you have to look good too?"

She tried to shape their technique. "Take a big step forward. Cock your hips. Put your hand forward and make a show for the rest of the class. There's the word that's called 'exaggerate,' which means you do it even bigger."

She noticed that the better-dressed, better-behaved children were often the most passive. She felt drawn to the ones who acted out, who wouldn't line up properly, who pinched the children in front of them, then acted aggrieved when they were punished. They put so much passion and energy into their singing. They reminded her of herself at that age.

∞

Soon, Johanna was teaching more than 600 children a week, 4 days a week. Her day started at 9:55 and ended at 3, with a 50-minute break for lunch. To her dismay, the students cycled through in an anonymous blur, so many she could hardly remember their faces, let alone their names. Except for the ones that gave her trouble. It was unfair, she thought to herself. "You always have to learn the names of the little brats that you have to yell at."

She taught the youngest ones in the annex, a former synagogue several blocks away, or in the cafeteria of the minischool, a corrugated metal structure behind the main building. Hour after hour, day after day, she perched on the edge of the lunch table, guitar on her lap, as the children cavorted in the open space around her, singing the songs she had taught them. In the kitchen, she could hear the clattering of dishes, the sound of running water, the whir of a small machine, a can opener, maybe. Sometimes a custodian mopped around her while she taught. Once in a while, a kitchen worker clad in a white uniform and hairnet would come out to listen. Sometimes, one of the kindlier ones would sneak her a banana.

For the older kids, she went from class to class, trudging up and down the five stories of the main building, lugging her guitar.

Maybe it was her Cinderella-like banishment to the cafeteria, but she felt strangely isolated from the life of the school. Many of the classroom teachers handed over their students and fled to the back of the room to correct papers. Johanna tried to get them to participate, and occasionally one would. Rob Pape, a fifth- and sixth-grade teacher, kept several keyboards, which he had purchased himself, in his classroom and taught the children the notes. He encouraged his students to play the keyboards, wearing headphones, as a reward for finishing their classroom work. Pape liked to have Johanna in the class, and would often sit and gossip with her afterward. He was a character, and so well ensconced in the school that nothing intimidated him, not even Benardo's tirades.

Often, Johanna would tell him about her latest heartache, a boyfriend, a run-in with another teacher. Rob would commiserate and, in the process, spilled out his life story.

Rob was 46. He had grown up in working-class Rome, New York, where he had set his heart on becoming a teacher while a student at Rome Catholic High School. The school was allowed to bus public school children in once a week for religious instruction, and the high school students were allowed to do some of the teaching. Rob was one of those student-teachers. "I taught fifth grade and I loved it," he recalled. "Until then I was interested in accounting and math. After that, I decided to be a teacher."

The road was not easy, though. His father, a factory worker at Revere Copper and Brass, died while he was in high school; his mother never worked. After graduating from the State University at New Paltz in the late '70s, as public school enrollment was declining, Pape was unable at first to get a teaching job and became the manager of the toy department at Caldor's, a job he despised.

In 1980, St. Anselm's, a Catholic school in the South Bronx, then still an impoverished ghetto, hired him for a starting salary of just $5,000 a year. To make ends meet, he moonlighted for the *Gannett Journal-News,* in suburban Westchester, selling classified ads and taking death notices, a job that he gradually expanded into writing obituaries. He also worked as the superintendent of his apartment building in Yonkers, mopping floors and hallways, shoveling snow, changing lightbulbs, in return for free rent.

Teaching hardly brought with it the dignity and security he had imagined in his youth. Desperate for a living wage, he called Maria in personnel at the DO, shorthand for the district office. "Why don't you call 86," she suggested. "That's a big school. They always need somebody."

He called Ray Osinoff, then the principal, and told him he had four years of experience at a Catholic school in the South Bronx. How many kids in a class? Osinoff wanted to know.

"Forty-five," Pape replied.

"You're hired," Osinoff told him. "You start tomorrow. Bring your references with you." Pape was over the moon.

P.S. 86 felt like a huge promotion. The neighborhood was affluent compared to Tinton Avenue in the South Bronx. The buildings were in better condition; there were more two-parent households. The parents of his students stopped him to talk as he walked down the sidewalks. He even enjoyed the restaurants, the diner on regular schooldays, Caridad or Montezuma on report card days or professional development days, when the teachers could get away for two-hour lunches.

But more than the neighborhood, Pape adored the kids. Every year, he walked into class one day dressed as the freakish Phantom of the Opera. "I was born ugly," he would declaim, then read the entire 120-page play without stopping. The children were riveted. He would take them to see the matinee on Broadway the next day.

Pape kept order through peer pressure. He would nominate a slate of students for class president, rewarding those who set good examples for the others, and then the rest of the class would vote.

Johanna enjoyed Pape's conviviality. But she had the impression that many of the teachers saw her as a convenient babysitter, not a colleague.

The only way she could remember what class she was teaching on any given day, at any given time, was to consult the black-and-white grid she had fashioned for herself and carried around in her purse.

Looking at Wednesday, for instance, she saw: 9:55–10:45, M. Hyams; 10:45–11:35, J. Ciardullo; 11:35–12:25, L. Kyprios; 12:30–1:20, Lunch; 1:20–2:10, W. Herman; 2:10–3:00, A. Rosen. Her day was tight as a drum, always on, almost no time to rest.

She tried eating lunch in the teachers' lounge, but it was hard breaking into the cliques, understanding the shoptalk. Margaret was always busy, and didn't seem to think about food. After a few weeks, Johanna discovered the New Capitol, the white brick Greek diner on Kingsbridge and Jerome. It was a typical boxcar-shaped diner, outfitted with red vinyl booths and fake Tiffany lamps. Decadent whipped cream, chocolate, and strawberry desserts beckoned from the refrigerated glass display case near the door. Johanna always sat in a booth by the front door, and her favorite waiter brought her a Greek omelette or pancakes with bacon and eggs. She almost always sat alone. She needed the time to unwind.

Margaret told her that she was a big success. Teachers were beginning to ask to have their children participate in her class. The kids came back from music calmer, more connected. Margaret's words were reassuring.

She got home exhausted at 5, and flopped across her bed, sometimes falling asleep for a few hours. By 9 or 10, she'd be off to a gig, at Toast, the student hangout near her apartment, or Cornelia Street Café in the Village where she'd be lucky to earn $20 from the cover at the door.

Thursday nights, from 8 to 11, she sang Jobim at a Spanish restaurant in Hoboken with her Brazilian trio—herself, a guitar, and a bass. They collected $50 each, which wasn't too bad, and the restaurant fed them.

She'd come home at 1 A.M., and wake up six hours later, aching to stay in bed. There were many times when she went to school tired or totally uninspired. The trick was to pretend to be motivated.

Kids sensed every mood. She couldn't show them, with the slightest hint of body language, that she didn't want to be there. That would be suicidal. She had to perform. "Oh, I have this song for you," she would say brightly. "It's the best song you've ever heard."

She could go to school feeling devastated about life on the whole, and then being around the kids who loved her, and loved music and loved what she did with them, gave her so much energy and happiness. She would go home feeling better. But mornings were always tough.

⊘⊘

She realized that without the income from her teaching, she would starve to death. It was a hard lesson, which six years in music school had failed to prepare her for. "I was 25," she recalled. "I'd been a student all my life, and suddenly you're thrown out into the real world and supposed to make a living, supposed to be able to take care of yourself, on what you studied in school. I was one of the lucky ones who had a job when I graduated."

Unlike many friends, she wasn't doing temp work, stapling papers, or typing meaningless words into a computer at an office. Still, it wasn't the job she had dreamed of. There should have been a course in the last semester, she thought, to prepare you for real life, "to sort of warn you" how different it would be. No more jam sessions with friends every week in a school rehearsal room. No more student loans and financial aid. One day, you were just out on the streets of New York, surviving.

In the fall of '98, just after she began teaching at P.S. 86, she noticed an ad in the newspaper seeking depressed people to experiment with Prozac. She cut it out and taped it to her wall, thinking she might call.

What was happening to her dream of making it big as a jazz singer?

She had never thought of teaching as a permanent vocation. Now she resented the toll it was taking on her life.

Yet she thought about those children all the time, more than she wanted to. As she ate a bowl of Muesli before bed, the comforting taste of it making her nostalgic for her own childhood, the children's faces floated up in front of her eyes. As she dropped off to sleep, she saw them sitting cross-legged on the cafeteria floor, staring numbly at her with their TV zombie expressions. She was obsessed, haunted. She had never expected to bring them home with her like this.

❦

CHAPTER FIVE

Dear Fingerprints

"Good morning, staff," said the disembodied man's voice over the loudspeaker. "Good morning, students. Today we will respect the teachers. There will be no walking in the hallways and no going to the nurse unless you have a serious problem. . . . This is Mr. Benardo, signing off."

He always ended his morning messages the same way: "This is Mr. Benardo, signing off." Like an airplane pilot, Johanna thought, amused.

He was like an invisible father, rather stern, reminding them of the rules of the house. What did he look like? Did he ever come out of his office? She, for one, had not had the privilege of meeting him before being hired. Was his message, delivered deadpan, intended to be absolutely serious, or a little jocular? She couldn't tell.

Johanna knew enough about schools to understand that the principal set the tone, and certainly she was aware of Shelly Benardo's existence. But not much more. In those early days, she knew that Margaret reported back to him; that he had signed off on her hiring; and that half the staff—the younger ones, mainly—were terrified of him, and the other half—the grizzled veterans—were not intimidated by anyone. To her, he was no more real than the Wizard of Oz, the man behind the curtain who made things happen but who could just as well have been made of smoke and mirrors as flesh and blood. He seemed to have little time for someone like her, and she didn't blame him. In a school this size, who would? He was at the top of the pyramid. Under him there were four assistant principals and 200 other teachers. At that point, she was an incidental member of the staff, working only two days a week teaching a subject that, in the scheme of things, was off the radar.

She had been lugging her guitar from class to class for two or three weeks before she and Margaret ran into Mr. Benardo in the hallway.

She felt Margaret pause expectantly.

A wiry man in his late 40s loped toward them, bouncing on the balls of his feet like a runner. He was about 5-feet-7-inches tall, and had a defensive stoop to his shoulders. His coke-bottle glasses magnified his blue eyes. He was balding, which lent all the more prominence to the bushy, graying mustache that covered his upper lip like a waterfall.

"Mr. Benardo," Margaret said. "This is Johanna Grussner, the new music teacher. Johanna, Mr. Benardo."

Mr. Benardo stuffed his hands in his pockets and looked down his nose at Johanna with his cartoonish gaze.

"Pleased to meet you," Johanna said, in the bright tone of an ingénue. She stretched out her hand.

Mr. Benardo withdrew his hand from his pocket and clasped hers briefly. Despite his detached manner, he had a firm grip. "I've heard you do good work," he said.

"You're welcome to stop by whenever you want," she said.

He studied her for another second, and then looked away, as if distracted by a matter of more importance that only he could see. Margaret recognized the shift in his attention as Mr. Benardo's customary cue that the conversation was over, and she led Johanna away.

Soon after, Benardo sent a letter praising Johanna to her parents' home in Aland. Johanna was astonished, but pleased—so proud that she had the letter laminated. Then Margaret told her that Mr. Benardo always sent flattering letters to new teachers after a few weeks of work, as a morale booster. Johanna buried the laminated letter in a cardboard box where she did not have to look at it.

From then on, Johanna thought of Mr. Benardo as kind of an absentee father, someone whose permission had to be sought out on important matters, but who was better approached indirectly than directly. She realized that gestures that in one context seemed touchingly personal, in another context could be interpreted as little more than management tools, straight out of Employee Relations 101. He rarely wished anyone "Happy Birthday" in person. But somebody kept track of teachers' birthdays, because Mr. Benardo liked to send out public birthday wishes over the loudspeaker during his morning broadcasts.

"Today Miss Coca is 25 years old," he would announce. "Could we please sing Happy Birthday to Miss Coca." (Emily Coca was much older than 25, but he always subtracted a few years.) Yet he could shift in a flash from his solicitous persona to his intimidating one.

The teachers joked that he was Dr. Jekyll and Mr. Hyde. You never knew for sure whether he liked you or, if he did, whether he was going to like you that day. You could never relax, because you didn't know which Mr. Benardo was going to come to work that day.

Margaret became her conduit, confidante and protector. They felt an intuitive bond, in that both of them held themselves apart from the everyday life of the school. They were each there for their own private reasons, and did not see themselves as career teachers. The only thing Johanna did not reveal to Margaret was her illness, the muscular dystrophy that she expected to leave her in a wheelchair some day. Already, stairs were a chore. Getting into a car, she had to clasp her hands under her knees and hitch up her legs, as if they belonged to a rag doll. Johanna hid these problems as best she could, and most people didn't notice that there was anything wrong with her. If Margaret noticed, she never asked about it. Margaret's discretion only made Johanna trust her more.

But other teachers tended to interpret their distance from their colleagues as a sense of superiority, and resented it. Margaret was part of the old guard at the school, hired in 1984 by the previous principal, Ray Osinoff, and as such she had a kind of seniority that even Shelly Benardo deferred to, most of the time.

Osinoff had been a legendary principal of the old school, an intellectual, a child of the Depression, who went into teaching because it was a secure civil service career. Had he been born in a different era, or to a more entitled family, he might just as easily have become a stockbroker, dentist, or lawyer. But Jewish boys from City College in the '50s, like him, faced a quota system in higher education and the professions. His Bronx accent and style of dressing stymied his half-hearted attempts to find a job on Wall Street. As it was, he never thought of education as anything less than a noble profession. He was liked and respected by his staff, skilled at conflict avoidance, someone who ruled through the lavish dispensation of compliments and flattery rather than through criticism and reprimand.

Despite its sclerotic union rules and bureaucracy, the school system is as incestuous as any large organization, and Margaret had come to P.S. 86 through a back door. Both she and Osinoff's wife, Fran, were civic volunteers in Scarsdale, where they lived. Margaret and Fran had met as adult education activists in Scarsdale, and hit it off. Margaret had stopped working full-time to raise her three children while her husband, Joe, rose through the ranks at NBC, successfully revamping the *Today* show in the late '70s, then going on to run the network's domestic news coverage. As the family moved in deference to Joe's job,

Margaret had found work in the education departments of the Walker Art Center in Minneapolis and the Pasadena Museum of Modern Art.

When she told Fran that she had taught sixth grade in Minnesota before the kids were born, Fran offered her a way back in. "If you ever want to go back to teaching, let me know," Fran said. Their home neighborhood of Scarsdale had been a fertile recruiting ground for her husband over the years, filled with accomplished, able women who viewed work as a matter of personal fulfillment as well as financial support.

As Nicole, the youngest of her three children, was finishing high school, Margaret foresaw a future when she might want to be a breadwinner again, and she took Fran Osinoff up on the offer. Ray Osinoff invited her to tour P.S. 86 to see how she liked it. Margaret was constitutionally dour. Not only that, but she had grown accustomed to cushy volunteer jobs at museums, where she could set her own agenda while rubbing shoulders with creative people. He could tell she might be a tough sell. But he had a brainstorm.

He walked Margaret up five flights of stairs to a corner room and gestured toward the shimmering surface of the Jerome Park reservoir in the distance. "Doesn't this look just like Miami Beach?" he asked, grinning. It was a corny line, but Margaret fell for it. She went home chuckling and took the job.

Osinoff assigned Margaret to one of the toughest jobs he had, teaching remedial reading to children in the so-called Promotional Gates program who had been held over because they were not performing at grade level. She was undeniably rusty, and she felt that Osinoff was testing her. If she got through this, she figured, she could do anything. But her career took a turn for the better after she befriended one of the assistant principals who, like her, had a strong interest in the arts. Within a few years, Margaret had become an art teacher. True, she had no classroom of her own, and was forced to drag her supplies around in a cart that she stored in a corner of the cafeteria. At that point, the school had been denuded of whatever art and music it had in the past.

Margaret had heard rumors that there had been a fully equipped orchestra on the premises at one time.

Joe Bartelme died of lung cancer in 1991, the same year that Shelly Benardo became principal. By that time, Margaret was well into her second career as a teacher, and the change in administration did not mean much to her. She was a fixture in the school. Her spirited daughter, Nicole, was about to cruise the Caribbean on the crew of a sailboat. Her older sons were living at what seemed like opposite ends of the earth, Tony in Charleston, Peter in San Francisco. Margaret had been left alone in her big Moorish-style corner house. By the time Johanna came knocking at her door, fifteen years after Margaret had been seduced by Ray Osinoff's sense of humor, she was feeling, frankly, a bit burned out, a bit bereft.

Johanna turned up just in time. She was a vibrant young woman who reminded Margaret of her own early years as a teacher. Maybe Margaret was living vicariously through Johanna; maybe her maternal instincts were aroused. At any rate, she felt a proprietary interest in making Johanna's music program a success. Margaret might not know much about music, but she loved the arts, and Project Arts had given her a vehicle to exercise her administrative ability. Mr. Benardo had assembled a stable of young teachers whom Margaret sardonically thought of, behind his back, as "the girls." They were strikingly young, attractive, and eager to please. She was happy to have a protégé of her own.

Johanna, for her part, so admired Margaret's patrician style that she believed it when the other teachers gossiped that Margaret was working for free, donating her salary back to the school. Margaret laughed when she heard that. Despite all her years at P.S. 86, Margaret had remained a little bit apart, viewed by the other teachers as a wealthy, if capable, suburban matron who was slumming, rather than a widow trying to make ends meet, which was closer to the truth.

∞

Within a few months, Johanna had made herself indispensable. Mr. Benardo agreed to bring her back in the fall, and arranged for her to be cleared as a substitute teacher. On May 26, 1998, he drafted a three-sentence letter to the New York City Board of Education.

Dear Fingerprints:

I anticipate a teaching vacancy at PS 86 for the school year 1998–1999. Please allow Ms. Johanna Grussner to be fingerprinted so that she may be cleared for work in the fall.

Thank you for your kind attention and assistance.

Respectfully,
Sheldon Benardo
Principal

He initialed the letter, gave it to Johanna, and directed her to go to the board's employment office at 65 Court Street. She was struck by the letter's smart-alecky salutation: "Dear Fingerprints." Mr. Benardo was not in awe of the bureaucracy. No doubt he had written countless letters just like this one. Despite his off-handed little joke, it was strictly pro forma. But studying it, Johanna felt a glow rise through her ears to the top of her head. For her, the letter was an important moment of confirmation. Teaching was no longer just a day-job, a lark, interchangeable with waitressing or hat-checking. She was about to become the real thing, her name, social security number, fingerprints, and file number irrevocably registered with the Board of Education. She might never become a famous jazz singer—well, she still hoped she might—but she had managed, without intending it, to become a teacher. Only a provisional teacher. Not a full-fledged certified one. But a teacher nonetheless. She never expected to feel this way. But she was thrilled.

❧

By the next school year, Johanna had increased her load to 1,000 children a week. She might as well be manning the assembly line at the Aland potato chip factory. So many raw potatoes tumbling through chutes of water into the vats of hot oil. So many voices chirping, "Baby Beluga in the deep blue sea, swim so wild and you swim so free." The plan was for her to teach half the children in the school the first semester, and half the second. By the end of the year, they would all have received one day a week of music instruction for one semester. Hardly enough to encourage a budding Raffi, but more than many other public schools had to offer.

It was hard not to switch to automatic pilot. She fought mental duets. Between measures of "Baby Beluga" her mind wandered to the Brazilian bossa nova she would be crooning that night in Hoboken. Her lack of concentration reminded her of how, when she was a little girl, her mother would read Astrid Lindgren to her at bedtime. Johanna was transfixed by the story of Pippi Longstocking—the superhumanly strong 9-year-old enfant terrible—and Lillemor Grussner was a great reader. At her best, she did all the voices and inhabited the characters. But some nights, after a hard day at work, she read robotically, mouthing the words while her mind was far away, choosing passages for the final examinations at Aland Lyceum, the accelerated school where she taught English language and Swedish literature. Her mother's inattention had angered Johanna, who swore she would never do anything like that.

She needed a mental challenge.

Johanna began to think about how to make music more than a fly-by-night program she carried around in her backpack. She knew so many talented people who could enrich the program. She had connections. Couldn't she invite her talented but struggling musician friends to help bring real music, challenging music, to the classroom? In a few years, these guys would be big, the next John Cage and Les McCann. For now, they needed pocket money, and the kids needed more energy and variety than Johanna could give.

With much fanfare, Margaret put out a memo announcing the visiting artists. Nobody needed to know—although in the end many did, since it was an open secret—that Nick Mancini, the adorable vibraphone player, son of a policeman from upstate New York, was Johanna's boyfriend du jour; that Justin Hines, the percussionist, was her classmate at Manhattan School of Music; and that Aline Shader, of course, had been one of her mentors at Berklee. Soon enough, they added Christof Knoche, Johanna's friend the saxophone player, and Bob Bowen, on bass, to the roster.

There were no empty rooms available, so Johanna coaxed the librarian into letting her friends conduct workshops in the library, among the stacks of books.

From the beginning, Johanna wanted the children to understand that music was more than a classroom activity, that part of the fun was performing. She also wanted them to understand the value of teamwork. With that in mind, she tried to organize as many concerts as possible. In a concert setting, one good voice was not enough; every member of the group had to support the others. Given her dependence on Aline Shader's songs, it seemed only natural that her first concert, in the spring of 1998, featured an all-Shader repertoire, and was called the "Composer in Residence" concert. She invited Shader to return, this time as a member of the audience.

The next winter, with the help of her musician friends, Johanna staged an even more elaborate concert, displaying a new and shrewdly multicultural mastery of American children's songs.

The day of the concert, she folded her favorite red velvet dress into her backpack. Anything velvet was high on her list. She hated ironing and velvet was crush-proof. Mr. Benardo had offered to let her dress in his private bathroom. She couldn't very well wear an evening gown on the subway during rush hour. She put up with enough ogling and cat-calls as it was.

That night, the auditorium was packed. There must have been 600 people in the audience. No one could say the parents at P.S. 86 didn't support their children.

The fifth-graders sang "Happy Hanukkah, My Friend," with Rickey Colbourne soloing. Rickey had volunteered to sing the song, telling Johanna that he was Jewish. She didn't question it, although she knew his father was Antiguan. Sometimes it was best not to ask too many questions. More in tune with the predominant culture, the kids also sang "Silver Bells," "12 Days of Christmas," and "Rudolph the Red-Nosed Reindeer."

Her friend Justin directed a group of kids playing percussion instruments in "The Bronx Boogaloo."

Rob Pape had always fantasized about conducting, and Johanna let him conduct a piece of his own choosing, "Heal the World." Rob was incurably sentimental.

When it was over, the audience burst into a standing, whooping ovation. Mr. Benardo, still wearing his red Santa hat, grabbed the microphone.

"Our music teacher is also a professional jazz singer," he said. "Now we will hear her sing a song of her own."

Johanna hadn't expected this. She swallowed hard, then cued the band for "Chestnuts Roasting on an Open Fire."

∞

The winter concert was a turning point. She could no longer be disparaged as a babysitter. She had shown what she could do, and the children had lived up to her expectations. She had seen the glow in their parents' eyes. They were ready for more and so was she.

A few days later, she flew home to Aland, and that's where the inspiration struck her. Visiting friends, she realized that she had met most of them through Lembote, the summer music camp that she started going to when she was 6 years old. When she started high school, Guy Karlsson, the director of the camp, formed a gospel chorus, Intermezzo, and she joined. The group had stayed together through high school, college, relationships, and careers, performing at churches and festivals and becoming well known in Aland. Now in their 20s and 30s, most of the others had married, had children, and settled into jobs. One was a radio announcer; another the secretary to the Aland minister of health, welfare, and the environment; another a physical therapist; one was an opera singer. But the emotional bond among them, forged through the music, remained strong. When she went home to visit, Johanna always rejoined the choir, singing with them, sharing in their petty rivalries, jealousies, and triumphs, both as individuals and as choir members, as if she had never left.

Intermezzo had been a powerful force through much of her life. If only she could recapture that for her students.

CHAPTER SIX

ℒ

"Happy Birthday"

Johanna's own singing style was nothing like the nursery rhymes she had been teaching to the children at P.S. 86. Her voice was a surprise coming out of such a sliver of a girl, deep and growly, more blues belt than Lake Wobegone. Like many Scandinavians, she was raised on gospel. Gospel touched currents just below the surface in Scandinavian culture, primordial feelings of struggle, injustice, tragedy, redemption. Those were themes that Scandinavians embraced in the abstract, wrestled with in private, but that had little to do with the collective code of daily life, the fastidious neatness, law-abiding behavior, and socialist beneficence. Still, bad things happened behind closed doors. Alcoholism and wife beating were rampant in Finland, so much so that government officials had taken to wearing little red ribbons pinned to their lapels to dramatize the problem. Gospel music touched the Scandinavian yearning to break out of the prevailing cultural straitjacket. Inside every Knut Hamsun, there was a Sam Cook or an Elvis yearning to be free.

The brand of gospel that Johanna learned as a child was filtered through the lens of her Lutheran church. Technically proficient, melodic but emotionally repressed, sanitized. Not quite Muzak, perhaps, but close.

When she arrived at Berklee, she immediately tried out for the gospel choir, becoming one of three white students in the group, alongside thirty-nine black students and one Asian. She wanted to sing gospel the way it was supposed to be sung. This was the real thing. The first time she sang in the choir without a sheet of music in front of her she was terrified. Sheet-music had always been her crutch; that was the way people learned music in Scandinavia, by reading the notes. The American gospel tradition was to learn the music by ear.

Berklee's Reverend Gospel Choir was a revelation socially as well as musically. Until then, she had never known a black person and rarely seen one, except on TV and once or twice on the streets of Stockholm. In Scandinavia, especially in a place as homogeneous as Åland, African-Americans represented a glamorous but remote pop cultural ideal; they stood for a kind of musical authenticity that she wanted to emulate, to understand and assimilate for herself. The other singers in the Berklee choir knew every song by heart. Despite her experience with Intermezzo, she lacked their visceral connection to the music. They were playing with extreme musicality and with lots of colorful chords, thick and heavy. It was impressive. Her admiration for them as musicians got mixed in with her feelings about them personally. She had a crush on every boy in the rhythm section. If she was going to sing this music, she needed to feel black, to know what it was to be black, and they could show her. She felt this music was in her blood. She identified. "These are my people," she thought to herself. It was only later, as she became more Americanized, that she realized her enthusiasm could be misunderstood, and felt a twinge of embarrassment. But at the time, she fell in love.

∽

She decided to start the chorus because she was tired of teaching music to 1,000 kids a week in the cafeteria. No matter how hard she tried, the children remained almost faceless, nameless. Some cried for no apparent reason. Others hugged her like there was no tomorrow. Some were African-American. Many were the children of immigrants, from countries as diverse as the Philippines, Guam, Nigeria, Vietnam, or, more recently, Albania. Most of their parents and grandparents were Latin American, from Puerto Rico, the Dominican Republic, El Salvador, Guatemala. For a girl from Finland, who had hardly ever seen a dark face until she was 20, who had grown up on an island in the Baltic Sea, these children were exotic, tantalizing. She couldn't say she understood them. But she wanted to know more about them. Like New York City itself, they had an edge that drew her to them.

In every class a few children sang and danced with more gusto than the rest. They showed a sense of timing or carried the melody in a way that hinted at some natural ability. They cried out for more. "And those are just the ones I can hear," she told Margaret. "I'm sure there are talented kids I don't even know about. Just because they don't sing out loud doesn't mean they're not talented."

When she returned from winter break she sought out Mr. Benardo in the main office. She had to walk past the vestigial time clocks, through the reception area, and around a wooden counter to get there, running the gauntlet of the two secretaries, Maria, the cute one who typed all Benardo's letters, and Carol, the crabby one, until Johanna got to know her and discovered that there was no one better at getting things done. Mr. Benardo's door was usually open. But the only person who could waltz into the principal's office without knocking was Emily Coca, the guidance counselor. Miss Coca seemed to be the only teacher whom Mr. Benardo trusted enough to talk frankly to.

No one was in his office. He waved Johanna in. She took a seat across from his desk. Her heart beat faster. She dreaded asking him for anything. She never knew how he was going to react.

"Mr. Benardo, there are some very talented children in certain classes," she began, tentatively. "I've been thinking that we should have a school choir. The best music I know for this is gospel."

She had belonged to a gospel choir from the time she was not much older than some of these children, she told him, and knew the music well. "I'm sure it will keep the students' attention," she said, "because the music is so catching."

With gospel, she knew she could teach the harmonies by rote, by repetition. There were certain harmonies that were common to most of the songs. So the children wouldn't have to know how to read music.

"Gospel is usually taught by ear," she explained. "We could do it right out of my memory." She wouldn't have to copy the music every time they learned a new song. Copying could be a huge ordeal, and expensive.

"It won't work," Mr. Benardo said. "It's religious music. You can't do that in a public school. It's like the holiday concert. If you do a Christmas song then you have to do a Hanukkah song and a Kwanza song."

"For me it's not only a religious kind of music, it's a style of music," Johanna objected. "It happens to be a Christian message, but a lot of songs don't even have the word 'God' or 'Jesus' in them. It's just like reggae or classical or rock or pop."

Black History Month was coming up in February. The teachers were always talking about how to integrate the arts into the curriculum. Here was their chance. The kids could sing gospel as a backdrop for the curriculum, for learning about slavery or the Civil War or the African-American influence on the Baptist church.

She was revolted by the treacly pop songs—"I Believe I Can Fly"— that so many school choruses sang these days, pandering to tastes shaped by Disney. These were not, in her opinion, destined to be classics. Musically, gospel had so much more to offer. She would teach them syncopation—how to begin the note before the beat—through Siyahamba, a Zulu freedom song. Did it really matter that the lyrics said, "We are walking in the light of God?" When you think of a round, you think of simple, childish stuff, "Row your Boat" and "Frère Jacques." She would show them more sophisticated ways of harmonizing in "Joshua Fought the Battle of Jericho." Rock and roll? "Woke Up This Morning" was a Negro spiritual, but you could sing it with a rock and roll beat, the way she had heard that the civil rights protesters did in the '60s, rallying the troops after a night in jail. There was the oompah of "Down by the Riverside," the slow, heavy hymnal dignity of "Amazing Grace." If it had been good enough for Odetta, then it should be good enough for P.S. 86, or at least better than any concoction ever crooned by Britney Spears.

"Go ahead," Mr. Benardo told her. He was on her side. Start the chorus as a project for Black History Month. If she could pull it off, he didn't see why anyone would object if she kept it up through March, April, or longer. Her heart beat faster, this time for joy.

To be in the chorus, the children would have to show talent. At P.S. 86, good behavior was the coin of the realm. Sit still. Line up in size order. Don't talk unless you raise your hand. Don't annoy the grownups by asking too many questions. This had to be different, more than just another class. The children had to want to be there, to be committed, to feel that they had been chosen to participate in something out of the ordinary.

Even an old-fashioned school like P.S. 86, where children were ruthlessly tracked by ability, had absorbed some of the tenets of progressive education. Competition is anathema to most public schools. Even spelling bees are considered archaic, because they might make the loser feel inferior. An experienced educator would never have auditioned the children.

But Johanna would select the children on merit. There was no point in having a chorus if the members couldn't hold a tune. You wouldn't field a football team with quarterbacks who couldn't throw. The kids would have to audition. Nothing else made sense. But what song did they all know how to sing? Most of the children had never studied music before, not even sung in church. They might know a few words of merengue, a few riffs of rhythm and blues, the top-ten hits on HOT97 FM. (Bup. Bup-bup. Bup. Who let the dogs out? Her littlest students adored that.) But reciting rap wouldn't tell her if they had an ear for gospel.

The school song? If it ever existed, it had been lost in the mists of time. Maybe Mr. Benardo remembered it from his day. But Johanna wasn't going to ask him. She could picture him sneering down at her from under those heavy-lidded eyes and snorting through his mustache. "You think these kids are going to learn the school song? Half of them don't know the first five words to the National Anthem," she imagined him barking. He would bite her head off.

She clutched the smooth iron banister and hoisted herself gingerly up the granite stairs to the attendance office for a quick cup of tea. She sank gratefully into a hard metal chair, her mug of tea steaming before her. Her thoughts turned back to the audition.

"Twinkle, twinkle little star," she muttered under her breath. Nope, they might not know all the words. "A, B, C, D . . . ?" Too babyish. Oh God, what else? "Happy birthday to you, happy birthday to you. Happy *birth*-day . . . happy *birth*-day. . . . " Man, those high notes. Perfect. Or at least—like everything else in this strange new life—it would have to do.

Guitar in hand, she began touring classes, inviting children to audition. The teachers gave her their class lists. She set up two chairs in the hallway outside the class she was visiting and called the students out one by one. She wanted them to be able to sing in private, where they would not feel judged. She wanted them to feel as if they were playing a game.

"Can you sing 'Happy Birthday'?" she would say. "You can sing it to me or to a friend. If you want you can sing it to yourself."

Most of the children were unremarkable. But a few stood out from the first moment.

In fifth grade, she auditioned a slight, impish girl who had trouble standing still. Ashley Alvarez had big dark eyes and a tomboyish build. She had a hoarse, breathy voice, strange for a young girl. But underneath the roughness, Ashley unerringly carried the tune. She seemed eager to please, and yet oddly diffident. This one was definitely in. Johanna discretely put a checkmark on the list next to Ashley's name. "Thank you," she said. Ashley got up and walked back into class. This girl didn't ask whether she had passed the test. She seemed extremely self-possessed for her age, prepared to accept whatever hand fate dealt her, for better or for worse.

Then there was Jamie Flores, with the high, clear soprano of a church choirboy. Unlike the kinetic Ashley, Jamie was slow-moving, deliberate, and thoughtful. He too was small, with thick black hair that fell in straight bangs over his eyes. Although he was only 10, he had the mannerisms of an adult, the way children do when they spend a lot of time in the company of grownups. He seemed to take the audition very seriously, as if his future were riding on the outcome. He was terrific, a true talent, Johanna thought. She had to make sure he did something about it.

But those were the exceptions. Most of the children didn't stand out. At this age, their voices were not well developed yet. You could hardly tell an alto from a soprano. Many of them were shy, or their voices were weak. She had to listen carefully to get past their inhibitions and figure out whether they could just carry a tune.

Vincent Maldonado was one of the maybes. His voice wobbled like a yo-yo on a string. She had a feeling it was changing already and he was having a hard time controlling it. But the way he sang "Happy Birthday," you'd think it was a love song, he put so much heart into it. And he was eager to be chosen. "Can I be in it?" he begged, when his tryout was over.

"I don't know," she said, determined to be fair. "I'll have to think about it." She waited until he had gone back to class, uncertain of what to do. He wanted this so badly. She understood his fierce desire to be recognized; she had been there herself many times. She put a check by his name.

"I think you're born with an ear for music, and you can choose to develop that or not," Johanna told Margaret. "I think there are kids in the choir who were born with that ear."

By the end of two weeks, she had selected eighty-six students. It was only later that she learned that many of them were notorious behavior problems, Vincent most of all.

❧

CHAPTER SEVEN

"Ignore Them"

Where to hold chorus classes was the first challenge. With eighty children in the choir, there were no classrooms big enough to fit everyone. After some thought, Mr. Benardo gave Johanna permission to teach chorus in the auditorium. The stage was crowded with tables and chairs, covered with a film of dust. To Johanna's relief, Mr. Benardo agreed to clear it out. "Good morning staff. Good morning students," she heard his voice during a morning announcement. "We have excess desks and chairs in the auditorium. Any teacher who needs one should come down and take a look. Put your name and room number on anything you want and it will be delivered to you. The rest will be disposed of. This is Mr. Benardo, signing off."

A couple of days later, the stage was empty. Johanna felt as if she had secured Carnegie Hall.

But as she sat alone at the battered black grand piano the first Wednesday morning, a shiver of dread passed through her. She was just that pesky girl with a guitar, who was always bugging the teachers to participate in her music classes. What if they ignored her? What if nobody came?

At the dot of 10, she heard the murmur of children's voices and the bark of a teacher giving orders. She saw the doors swing open stage left, in the back of the auditorium. Like clockwork. Mr. Benardo would be proud. Her heart raced as she watched the children shuffling down the sloping aisle toward her, tittering and elbowing one another. No one appeared to notice Johanna. They had no clue what they were coming down to. She felt an immediate connection with them. This was something they were going to start together. They were going to be friends, buddies.

As the children peeled off like soldiers on parade into the first three or four rows, she stepped down from the stage and stood in front of them.

"I think most of you know me," she said, smiling her high-wattage Broadway smile, bending slightly toward them from the hips, like a mother leaning over her child. "You're here for a very special reason. You have a special talent that you should use and make something of.

"This is the first P.S. 86 chorus we've had in a long time. You shouldn't be expecting hard work, just cooperation. We're going to be a gospel choir, and I want you to try your hardest."

This was not the usual perfunctory greeting. She wanted them to know that this time, they were not in the auditorium to be narcotized by a Disney movie for the convenience of the staff. This was a privilege, which they had earned.

Sorting out attendance over the next couple of weeks, she found that about sixty of the eighty students she had picked were coming to class. Some teachers felt their students couldn't afford to miss academic work and did not let them go. Other students drifted away for no apparent reason.

She also found herself unexpectedly endowed with a co-director, Robert Robertiello.

Mr. Robertiello had been working in the AIMS office. AIMS stood for Attendance Improvement Means Success. (Who came up with these acronyms? Was there an office at 110 Livingston Street devoted to inspirational abbreviations for bureaucratic functions? Was there a slogan to go along with the name? Something like: Your AIMS Are Our Goals. From Your AIMS to the Chancellor's Lips. AIM High for Success. Or, more aptly in this case, AIM for Perfect Attendance.) The four people in the AIMS office—Bob, Bill, Alberto, and Carmen—kept track of attendance, pursued truants, and valued their own privacy. Johanna had come across this fiefdom in her wanderings, and thought of it as a sanctuary. The door was always closed and locked, and there was a coffee machine and a tea maker inside. If she had a few minutes to spare she would knock on the door and call conspiratorially, "Hey, it's me, Johanna." Once inside, she would brew a cup of black tea (ordinarily, she put a big glob of honey in her tea, because it was good for the voice, but they didn't have honey here) and hide out for a while, where she knew no one would look for her. The tea was free.

Bob was known as a nice guy, and free tea was the least of it. But teaching was not necessarily his true calling. He had once wanted to be an opera singer, which was strange because he never sang more than a few scales in front of Johanna or the kids. She suspected that he had perfect pitch.

He was the son of a prominent, flamboyant Manhattan psychoanalyst and sex therapist, Richard C. Robertiello, who had written *Voyage from Lesbos*, a 1959 book about Connie, a "passive homosexual," who renounces her lesbianism at the end of what is termed a successful psychoanalysis. The book later became a cult classic.

Dr. Robertiello had campaigned against the Vietnam War and promised sexual fulfillment through books like *Your Own True Love*, advertised in mod–Carnaby Street typeface in the pages of the *New York Times*. In 1965, he was part of a syndicate that bankrolled Buster Mathis, a 22-year-old, 290-pound heavyweight boxer who was introduced to New York boxing society in a luncheon at the 21-Club.

In 1979, when Bob was in his late 20s, his father published *A Man in the Making: Grandfathers, Fathers, Sons,* a blisteringly candid autobiographical book about the coming of age of himself, his grandfathers, his father, and, of course, his only son, "Bobby." The jacket photo of the author shows a rakish, bearded man with a full head of wiry salt-and-pepper hair. In the chapters about his own development, Richard Robertiello, the son of a tyrannical Italian immigrant physician, described his early upbringing in a townhouse south of the old-moneyed Gramercy Park that looked, in his memory, like the Palace of Versailles, outfitted with marble sculpture and oversized chandeliers. Dr. Robertiello, obviously possessed of a huge and healthy ego, characterized himself as "an analyst, faith healer, African witch doctor, Christian mystic, guru." He freely described his repeated attempts at suicide, beginning with a threat to jump out the window at the age of 12, though, in his account, many of these attempts seemed more histrionic than sincere. He evidently grew more self-satisfied with age, and his suicidal urges diminished. He also bragged, repeatedly, about his sexual conquests and educational credentials, almost in the same breath: Hunter College Elementary School, a New York City public school for children with IQs in the genius range, Townsend Harris High School, also an elite public school, bachelor's from Harvard, medical degree from Columbia.

By the time he reached the very brief chapter entitled "My Son, Bobby," on page 137 of a 185-page book, no son could ever hope to measure up to such a titan of a father. And indeed Bobby did not, his father made no bones about saying. Although the senior Robertiello was, at least in his recollection, an idyllic father in the early years, taking Bobby to zoos, movies, and baseball games, by the time Bobby was 11 his parents had divorced, and father and son had only a perfunctory relationship.

In his book, the elder Robertiello never mentions his son's graduation from the High School of Music and Art, a selective public school for artistically talented students.

He does, however, describe how when the younger Robertiello was in college at the State University of New York at Binghamton (hardly up to his father's standard as an educational institution), he dropped a bombshell. "Bobby decided to become an opera singer, and I passionately hate opera," Dr. Robertiello wrote. "I said to him, 'Why couldn't you become a pimp or a junkie or a bank robber? You really know how to hurt a guy.' But I swear I was kidding, honestly, and Bobby knew it."

But the damage was done. In the preface to the book, he confesses: "Aside from occasional handshakes, I never touch Bobby . . . . I can hardly ever show him affection." He also expresses the wish, at another point, that his son will be "a better father to his sons" than the father and grandfathers were to theirs.

Bob Robertiello did not have any children, choosing a life very different from that of his domineering father. He lived in a modest apartment in Lower Manhattan, part of a Mitchell-Lama complex of affordable, mixed-income housing.

Robertiello had taught musicology at the state university campus at Binghamton and worked as the manager of an executive dining room. He had found his way to P.S. 86 through Mr. Benardo's wife, Carole, a childhood friend. School gossip had it that Bob had had a youthful crush on Carole, and had once wanted to marry her. Whether or not the gossip was true, Bob and Carole were still close, and their friendship only increased Robertiello's allegiance to Benardo.

He was unerringly discreet, and he forgave Benardo's outbursts of temper, even when they were directed at him.

"Bob should be your assistant, don't you think?" Mr. Benardo suggested to Johanna soon after she established the chorus. "He has a master's degree in music, you know. Would you mind?"

She did not mind at all.

Bob was fond of the children, an astute observer and natural psychologist, skills honed through years of exposure to his father's shoptalk. But classroom management was not his forte. He was too gentle for that. So instead of teaching a class, he ended up in the AIMS room, tracking truants, and was available to pinch-hit in other jobs, at one point filling in for an absent security guard.

His operatically punishing father had been a hard act to follow, and through a lifetime of habit, perhaps, Bob Robertiello seemed content to live in the shadow of others. While Johanna chose the songs, played the piano, and coached the children in the chorus, he stood tentatively on the sidelines, shushing them affectionately but ineffectually. It was amazing, Johanna thought, how children had radar for telling when a teacher lacked the fortitude to follow through on discipline. What was it they detected, or failed to detect? A hint of steel in the teacher's voice; a glimmer of ruthlessness in the teacher's eye. Bob didn't have that kind of ferocity in him. He was a warm bath even when he tried to be a cold shower.

His biggest talent was soaking up interesting peccadilloes about the children. Krysten Viruet, he noted, found comfort in food, an observation that would later come in handy. Ashley, he observed, had learned to outsmart her mother, doing what she wanted and going where she wanted while her mother remained blithely unaware. With his psychological acumen, Bob had eerily channeled an intergenerational pattern, for Ashley's angry mother, Ileana, had behaved the same way when she was a teenager toward her strait-laced Cuban immigrant mother, Ana.

After a while, Johanna came to wonder whether Bob was really there to use his considerable observational skills to watch over her, too, in case she did something Mr. Benardo might not approve of. Bob might not be able to keep the children in order, but he kept her on her guard. Benign as he seemed, she knew that everything she did and said would be reported back to Mr. Benardo.

What Johanna really needed was an accompanist. It was hard for her to focus on the singing technique of individual children while she was up on stage playing the piano. "There is no money for an accompanist," Mr. Benardo replied, when she asked him for one. He had heard that one of the gym teachers played piano. "Why don't you ask him?" It turned out the gym teacher was a duffer, and he declined. Johanna returned to Benardo with another proposition. In a school the size of P.S. 86, teachers were sick or absent nearly every day of the week. If Mr. Benardo would hire her friend Kent Emerson as a substitute, then he could earn some money, help out the school, and, on the side, play piano for her during chorus. "I'm starting to think like him," she thought to herself, amused. Evidently so. Benardo approved, and wrote a "Dear Fingerprints" letter to the Board of Education, requesting clearance for Kent to substitute-teach.

Everything was happening so fast. The more she accomplished, the more she felt was possible.

One day, she heard a feature story on the radio about "Save the Music," a campaign supported by VH1, the cable TV music channel, to donate musical instruments to public schools. In return, the schools had to provide a music teacher, at least two music classes a week during school hours, and space after school for children to practice their instruments.

Most of the elements were already in place. They might not win the grant, she told Mr. Benardo, but it was worth a try. "Go ahead," he said, neutrally. In the space that asked what kind of band instruments the school currently had, Johanna wrote "None." That was an easy one. "None, none, none," she thought to herself. She licked the envelope, put it in the outgoing mail, and forgot about it.

♂

There were times when the whole choir was a disaster. "You know this song," Johanna told them, stopping their rendition of "Oh Happy Day" in mid-sentence. "You can't be lazy. You're not listening to the piano. You can't be behind the beat." They tried a second time, but were no better. "Stop! Stop! You need to wake up."

"Some days we get them they're in a coma, practically," Robertiello moaned.

Johanna couldn't blame them. Often they went whole days without recess, fifty-minute period upon fifty-minute period, from 8:30 to 3:00, with just one break for lunch. In Finland, she told Robertiello, the children had forty-five-minute periods of instruction, and after every period, they went outside and ran around for fifteen minutes.

But when the choir was at its best, people gathered in the auditorium doorway to listen.

She taught the children to sing in three-part harmony. Adults would have thought too much about what they were doing, but kids just did it, the way a child will leap off a 10-foot rock into the water below while an adult will stand petrified. When they broke the surface and realized how good they sounded, they were exhilarated. They wanted to do it again.

They sang the tricky syncopated rhythm of "Soon and Very Soon" with breathtaking discipline. "Soon and very soon, we are going to see the king. Soon and very soon, we are going to see the king. Soon and very soon, we are going to see the king. Hallelujah, hallelujah, we are going to see the king." The hard part was to hold back, leaving the right number of silent beats between words. When Johanna wrapped up—twirling her fingers over her head on the word "seeeeee" and pointing down behind her back to punctuate the final "king"—the utter silence that ripped through the air after the last note was as unnerving as a sonic boom.

She taught them to clap out the notes: four beats for a whole note, two for a half note, three for a dotted half. When she wanted them to quiet down, she would clap a rhythm and make them imitate her. Soon, teachers could be heard clapping rhythmically all over the school, as a way of bringing their classes to order.

Johanna's enthusiasm spilled over into the most routine tasks. When she handed out the new schedule of classes, it was written in fountain pen, with calligraphic frills and flourishes.

As word of the chorus got out, Bob Robertiello brought back some disturbing news. Some of the Jewish teachers were grumbling, he said, about the religious content of the songs. This was a public school, duty-bound to uphold the separation between church and state, not a Sunday school.

"What should I do?" Johanna asked Mr. Benardo, half afraid that he would tell her the whole thing had been a mistake.

"Ignore them," he said.

❧

CHAPTER EIGHT

The Dead-End Kid

A bottleneck formed at the auditorium door as the fifth grade attempted to file in for chorus.

"Yo. Move your fat black ass."

Johanna was waiting on stage for them, but she recognized Vincent's voice.

He had a mouth. But she tried not to hear it. He wanted to sing, and that was all that mattered. The other teachers could correct his language, and they did. That job was taken care of. She could concentrate on his breathing, pitch, timing. She would coax him to sing with his stomach instead of his throat, overcoming the fear that his 12-year-old voice, wavering between child and man, would betray him.

"Vincent, you've been singing nasal," she told him.

If there was anyone Vincent would jump off a cliff for it was Johanna. She believed in him when others did not. Within the school, he was perceived as damaged goods. No one would be surprised to see him end up in jail or worse. What had seemed like childish mischief, kind of cute, when he was 5 began to seem pathological by the time he was 10. His options grew narrower with every passing year, his future more clearly preordained.

Flunked fifth grade. Got into fights on the playground, threw food in the lunchroom. But her heart broke when she looked at him. He was small, about 5-foot-1, slightly built, and always wore a baseball cap like a lucky charm. He had a gap-toothed smile, and playful, crinkly eyes. When he sang, he put everything he had into it.

Vincent was in her heart, but he was a brat.

Other teachers didn't understand what she saw in him. "He reminds me of myself," she said. She had been an average student, who excelled at music. Through music, she found her place in the world. Vincent too was a poor student. But in her class, he was among a handful who got A's. Music brought out another part of him. He felt like he was actually good at something, that his low test scores were not going to follow him around for the rest of his life.

☙

When the time came to hand out solos, Johanna called Vincent up to the stage and asked him to sing the solo part to "Oh Happy Day." She had learned it when she was about his age, she told him; she presented it to him as if it were something fragile, precious.

"This was my first solo," she said. "So it's very special to me. Now I'm giving it to you."

Despite the celebratory lyrics, it was a gutsy, mournful song. She encouraged him to put all his pain into it.

"You have to improvise," she told him. "You can't just sing the words straight."

Johanna demonstrated, showing Vincent how to sing the phrase "Oh happy day" over and over again at the end of the song, stretching out the syllables, skittering and scatting like a jazz musician.

Oh happy day.
Oh happy day-y.
When Jesus washed.
Oh when he wa-a-shed.
He washed my sins a-way.

At first Vincent was giggly and embarrassed. But soon he forgot about the other kids watching him and took chances. He looked very far away when he sang, with a furrowed brow and a heart-rending Preslyesque catch in his voice.

To even a casual observer, Vincent's charisma as a singer was obvious. But not to the principal. He had seen too many Vincents to think that this one would be any different. With a certainty and cynicism born of experience, Mr. Benardo knew that the fate of boys like Vincent had been sealed at an early age.

He was a dead-end kid.

☙

One of Vincent's earliest memories is of being cradled in someone's arms—a person of indeterminate gender, maybe male, maybe female—watching fireworks. In this memory as vivid yet elusive as a scene from a movie, the colors leap into the night sky, showers of blue and red sparks, shimmery white jellyfish. A low thundering growl, then a crescendo of cracks like shells exploding in a war zone, the grand finale. Men drink beer and couples dance the merengue, their limbs loose and fluid. His uncle, the salsa singer, croons Tito Nieves' "Sonámbulo":

Sonámbulo, dicen que soy sonámbulo
Porque te quiero a ti
Eres la mujer más bella,
la mujer que yo adoro

eres la más preferida,
por eso te canto este coro

His mother, Ruth, is young and happy. She tosses her long black hair, shakes her round bare shoulders. The gold crucifix glints at her throat and her black eyes shine. A hand caresses her arm. Slowly, he realizes that it is his hand. His fingers graze the skin inside her elbow, warm and soft, like a favorite sheet worn thin and velvety with washing. Was he dreaming? No. He is sure this really happened. He was there. He knows. It was a party for him. "I guess we were on the roof," he says. "It was my birthday."

But just as likely it was not his birthday, not exactly. Vincent Maldonado was born on the Fifth of July, not the Fourth, no Yankee Doodle Dandy he. That was the story of his life, a near miss. He wanted to be somebody, he itched to stand out, and he often did, in the worst possible way. If a chance to act out came his way, he did not hesitate to grab it. His mother wrung her hands over his bad behavior, but she didn't know how to stop it. She pleaded and sometimes she cried. But she did not want to scold him too much. She was afraid of losing him. She had been abandoned by too many other men.

Vincent was born in a shelter for battered women, where his mother had fled to escape the father who would continue to drop in and out of his life, holding out the promise of something better just beyond the horizon. Ruth had been depressed and barely functional most of her adult life. She took sleeping pills and tranquilizers and supported the family through "PA," public assistance, and occasional handouts from boyfriends.

Ruth's father had tried to rape her when she was 11, she said, but had been interrupted by her mother. It took her 20 years to summon the courage to confront him. "You remember what you did to me when I was 11?" she screamed into the telephone. They hadn't spoken since.

Ruth spent her childhood in Cabo Rojo, her mother's hometown, near Mayaguez, Puerto Rico, a town that had not offered much in the way of opportunity but, at least to Ruth, had felt secure. Her mother took in laundry and ironing. Her father had migrated to New Jersey, where he drove a delivery truck. The family dreaded his visits, but at least they did not come too often. Ruth, the second of six siblings, was raised by her grandfather, Tomas. She called him "Papi," and he called her Tatita. He doted on her. She served him coffee and bread.

Papi had named her by opening the Bible and finding "Ruth" where the pages fell apart. Her sisters had fancy city names, Lucy, Maribel, Jeanette. Hers was the old-fashioned one. To Ruth, their two-bedroom wood and cement house felt as big as a mansion. She played with the chickens, the dogs, the ducks, and the pigs in the yard as if they were pets, although they were kept for slaughter. The little chicks followed her to school, but she didn't go there very often. She preferred being at home, cooking and cleaning. She was spoiled.

Only the visits from her father, José, cast a shadow over their lives. One day, when Ruth was about 8, José asked her to make him coffee. But she was playing jump rope in the scrubby yard with her sisters and some neighborhood girls, and she forgot. He beat her with a wire.

Another night the children heard a stick thudding against flesh and their mother, Luz Maria, crying. They cowered under a bed in the next room while Lucy, the oldest, prodded Ruth to go out and see what was happening. "He'll kill her if you don't go," Lucy said. When Ruth refused, all five children—Alberto had not been born—ventured out together. Their father hesitated at the sight of them, and in that momentary reprieve, their mother fled. Mother and children hid together in a crawl space under the wooden house. After a while, they smelled smoke and heard a fire crackling. José had stuffed newspapers and garbage under the house and touched a match to the debris. Luz Maria and the children scrambled out and raced across a field to a neighbor. Their house burned to the ground, and Ruth's father fled to New Jersey.

When Ruth was 11, her mother took the children to find José. They arrived at Newark Airport on a snowy day in 1971. Ruth had never seen snow before, and everything looked white and magical. Her uncle picked them up, and what he had to tell them spoiled the magic. Her father was living with another woman, and had two children by her. The family could not live with him. Luz Maria and her six children found temporary lodging in a Manhattan hotel. They skipped Ruth's birthday celebration because, her mother said, they could not afford a party.

After four months they found an apartment in the South Bronx, but Ruth had trouble adjusting. Her English was rudimentary and she did not do well in school. Eight years after she arrived in New York, she learned that her beloved grandfather had died. Five months later, her mother died too. Her mother had been her only anchor in New York. They looked so much alike that people sometimes asked if they were sisters.

Ruth was now 19, a shy, motherless, overaged tenth-grader at Taft High School. She was sent to live in her aunt's apartment in the Bronx and, overcome by grief, developed a bad case of anorexia nervosa, dropping to 90 pounds from 130. She dropped out of Taft, quit her job as a cashier in a grocery store, and was hospitalized. She spent a week connected to an IV. She did not recover fully for a year. "I lost my mind," she said. "I remember one time, I was walking in the street, I felt my body flying in the air. Then I don't remember nothing."

When Rafael, the boy downstairs, came courting, she thought she had found someone strong enough to save her. He was two years younger, only 17, but he looked older, thick-necked and powerfully built. He had his own car, a 1972 Mercury Capri, and was earning $275 a week as a second-year apprentice carpenter. Everyone called him Ralph.

Ralph knew his way around the city like the back of his hand. Ruth, on the other hand, could hardly speak English eight years after arriving. She had been put in a bilingual education program at school, where she was able to function in Spanish. She picked up what little English she had from the black girls on Tinton Avenue. It was safer to associate with them than with the Puerto Rican girls, who were always getting into gang fights—waged with garbage cans, bats, and bottles—with the white girls in the neighborhood. Twenty years later, Ruth still speaks broken English.

They had their first child, Cathy, in 1982. Ruth quit her job in a hardware store to take care of the baby. She had become an unmarried, barely literate wife and babymaker, totally dependent on a man who was still a teenager, himself a high school dropout with a vain and reckless streak. It would have taken a stronger and more resourceful woman than Ruth to avoid ending up as a single mother on welfare.

Ruth makes no attempt to hide these stories, or her version of what happened next, from Vincent. Her life as she remembers it is as lurid as the most outrageous supermarket tabloid story or Spanish novella, and she tells it all in unexpurgated detail as her children sit nearby, watching TV, sipping Coke. Her children can only sympathize and vow to help her when they are old enough. "Sometimes I ask her about my childhood," Vincent says. "She says she doesn't remember." He understands that her mind is fragile and forgives her.

Unable to afford an apartment of their own, the young couple moved in with Ralph's mother. She lived in Kingsbridge, not very far from P.S. 86. A second daughter, Christy, was born in 1985. Then, Ruth recalls, things started falling apart. Ralph was out of work; he began drinking too much, snorting cocaine, and smoking crack. Ruth was six months pregnant with a third child when Ralph came home one night and found no food in the house and no dinner on the table. She had nothing to cook, she told him.

She remembers that he flew into a rage, beating her so badly that she called 911. The police came and threatened to arrest Ralph. His mother begged for mercy and promised to straighten him out. An ambulance took Ruth to the hospital, where an attendant took pictures of her injuries and sent her home again. The next day, Ruth went out for groceries and felt a gush of blood against her leg. She sat on the sidewalk and told Cathy: "You go upstairs to your grandmother and your father, tell them I'm sick." After the miscarriage, Ralph visited her in the hospital bearing a bouquet of roses and a card that said, "I'm sorry." He wooed her back.

Shortly after, she became pregnant with Vincent. "Oh my God, again, again. He'll kill me this time," she thought. Packing up the two girls, she fled to the shelter for homeless women and children. Vincent, a 6-pound baby, skinnier and weaker than her first two, was born on July 5, 1988. They stayed in the shelter for eight months, until she could qualify for Section 8 rent subsidies and find her own apartment.

Ralph was crazy in those days, Ruth says. He once killed their Chihuahua because it had broken its leg and was in pain, barking too much.

Ruth and Ralph Maldonado remember two starkly different lives together, and it is hard for an outsider, who wasn't there to witness events as they unfolded, to reconcile the two sides or determine which is true. Perhaps both versions are equally true, by omission. Perhaps events that are important to one person seemed insignificant to the other, and vice versa.

About the only thing they both agree on is that the relationship fell apart.

Ralph doesn't remember Ruth having a miscarriage, and he doesn't believe that she entered the homeless shelter out of fear. She went there so she could qualify for Section 8 housing assistance, he says. If you were a woman without a man in the Bronx, that's what you did, you worked the system.

And Ralph admits that he was not there for her. He was ashamed of that now. He had done drugs; everybody did in those days. But he had quit cold turkey, after the drugs had brought him to the brink of suicide. Even when Ralph was at his worst, his father always had been good to Ruth, sending her and the children money for food and clothing.

☙

Musical talent skipped over Ralph, but it runs in the family. Ralph's father, Victor, is a guitarist, and performed in a mambo band that opened for Tito Puente. Ralph Mercado, the great Latin music producer, was a family friend. Ralph himself used to hang out with Marc Anthony, the Latin heart-throb, at a club on Westchester Avenue, before Marc Anthony made it big. There aren't many degrees of separation between celebrities and ordinary working-class stiffs in el barrio. Ralph is pleased that the musical gene appears to have resurfaced in Vincent. If you put your mind to it, he tells his son, if this is what you want, you can do it.

Ralph has aged well. Pushing 40, he is slimmer than he was in the photograph he keeps in his wallet, which shows him in his youth, astride his Harley. He looks sharp these days in his mustache and pencil-thin goatee. Vincent is looking more and more like him, with the same wide, expressive mouth and soulful eyes. When they are together, Vincent seems awestruck by his father's magnetism and self-assurance, much as his mother once was.

After a motorcycle accident, Ralph moved to Allentown, Pennsylvania, and began working as a security guard. He is fixing up a five-bedroom Victorian house there, next door to a house owned by his father. It's a good neighborhood to raise children in, and once he has settled down, he plans to bring Vincent to Allentown. A boy needs his father. If he can make a good man out of his son, maybe his own past will be forgiven; that will be his way of redeeming himself.

But one school year passes, and then another, and Vincent continues to live with Ruth. It is unclear who is at fault. Has Ralph reneged on his promise? Is Ruth unwilling to let Vincent go, even though she talks about it? Is Vincent reluctant? Or do they exist in a kind of chronic stalemate, in which passivity is the norm, and no one is able to take the initiative to make a change?

"Vincent is going to live with his father," Ruth will say brightly. It is her standard riposte to bad news. She says it after Vincent has failed another class, after the school has called to complain about his lateness, as if living with his father will be his salvation. But she admits that she would hate to see him go. Vincent is her only son. Every mother knows that daughters grow up and leave you. The sons are the ones who stay loyal, no matter where they are. The world is harder on boys. Ruth tries to protect Vincent, even if that means pampering him sometimes. She does not want him to turn against her.

Ralph insists that he is faithful, in his fashion, to the woman he calls Ruthie. He has told her that she is the only woman who will bear his kids. Ruth interprets this as a veiled rebuke, for she, on the other hand, has had a fourth child, Caila, born in 1995. The father, José, a refrigerator repairman, does not live with them. José puts lemon and salt on Vincent's skinned knees and helps make ends meet when the welfare runs out. Vincent says that José is a nice man. "He never really raises his hand to me."

Vincent is accident prone. His front teeth are mysteriously chipped. Another time, a flaming red welt of a burn stretches diagonally across his cheek, beginning at the inner corner of his right eye.

Ruth often gets calls from school, asking her to come to the office please, for a conference about Vincent. Sometimes she goes, but more often she does not. What is the point of submitting to another round of hectoring? They make her feel as if she is to blame when he misbehaves, as if she is a bad mother. She has done her best. Mr. Benardo handles these incidents well, she says. "He has a good heart." He has tried to be understanding with Vincent, from the first time he got into trouble when he was very little and had taken a small knife to school. "Mr. Benardo said Vincent and another boy had been playing with the knife and this was not allowed," Ruth recalled. "He said he could make a report. But he hoped it would not happen again, so he didn't do it."

There have been a couple of times when Vincent punched his older sister, and when his older sister punched him. Children quarrel, but Ruth doesn't like it. She tells Vincent: "All this what you are doing is wrong. If you want me to be your mother, you can't do this. You're my son and I love you but I can't accept this. You're hurting my family. This is your sister's life."

In 1999, Ruth and her kids moved from Kingsbridge to a poorer section of the Bronx, on the Grand Concourse near 181st Street. Most evidence of grandeur had deserted this section of the Grand Concourse, though the name remained behind like a bad joke. The family lived in a six-story red brick building shrouded with scaffolding. The scaffolding has collected trash the way the bottom of a lake gathers boots and tires. Tacky storefronts litter both sides of the avenue—fast divorce, Getty gas, a beauty salon, bodega, Popeyes, travel agency, insurance broker.

Inside the apartment, the picture moldings hint at a more elegant past. Ruth has painted the apartment herself, a bit clumsily, in cheap landlord paint, white walls with lemon chiffon moldings. She has hung a faded black-and-white studio portrait of her mother, who looks like her twin. The photographer has retouched the portrait to highlight Luz Maria's seductive carmine lips and rouged cheeks. Ruth scavenged the rest of the art from sidewalk trash heaps: a large oil painting, executed in a queasy yellow and gray, of a generic city skyline, a gauzy Manet poster of women in frilly dresses.

Public assistance provides the family with $457 a month in food stamps and $150 in cash every 15 days. Sometimes Ralph sends child support. Section 8 covers all but $57 of the $1,071 in rent for their three-bedroom apartment.

For pocket money, she makes party favors for weddings and baby-showers. She made 150 of them for export to the Dominican Republic, little glass vases decorated with gold ribbons and netting. Vincent was proud of her.

The doctor has told her to look for work outside the home. "Otherwise you stay in your house thinking, thinking, thinking," she remembers the doctor saying to her. She does brood, she can't help it. And sometimes her back hurts so badly she can't get out of bed.

If she could get out of this crummy neighborhood, things would be better. "We're moving to a private house," she often says, as if such a move might happen tomorrow. She has the Section 8 voucher, and she is going to go house-hunting. Since they are about to move, there is no point in unpacking the cardboard boxes stacked floor to ceiling against one wall of the bedroom that Vincent shares with his uncle Alberto, a handyman. But the months keep passing, and the family is still there.

In the room he shares with Alberto, Vincent's bed is neatly made, the blue-flowered sheets turned at the top, while his uncle's bed is rumpled and strewn with discarded clothing. Maybe Vincent's compulsive neatness is his way of keeping some measure of control over an uncertain household.

So far, Vincent's misadventures have been petty, childish stuff. He threw a tray of spaghetti and meatballs in the cafeteria. He exploded a popper during a test. He is only 12. Unlike many of the adults around him, he has not given up on himself.

He has been told that he inherited his father's temper. "I think there are good people and bad people," Vincent says. "I think good things happen to bad people and bad things happen to good people. I'm probably a bad person. But a good bad person."

When he joined the chorus he was repeating fifth grade. His first time in fifth grade had been a disaster. The class went through three teachers. It would have taken a stronger student than Vincent to overcome that handicap.

Vincent hadn't thought about becoming a singer before. But when Johanna walked into his class with her guitar, he could feel the excitement of the other kids, and he wanted to be part of it.

CHAPTER NINE

✑

"Vem Kan Segla"

For the first time, Johanna began to see the children as individuals. She came to school with a renewed sense of mission, as her priorities began, almost without her realizing it, to shift from her own singing career to the chorus. She hoped to give direction to at least a few lives, and she took two of the most talented boys in her chorus, Vincent and Jamie, under her wing.

The two boys could hardly be more different—Vincent the budding delinquent, Jamie the altar boy and math whiz.

What was it about certain songs that made particular children come alive? For Jamie it was "Vem Kan Segla," or "Who Can Sail," the folk-song that was almost a national anthem in the Aland Islands.

Vem kan segla forutan vind?
Vem kan ro utan aror?
Vem kan skiljas fran vannen sin
Utan att falla tarar?

Jag kan segla forutan vind.
Jag kan ro utan aror.
Men ej skiljas fran vannen min
Utan att falla tarar.

(Who can sail without the wind?
Who can row without oars?
Who can be separated from a friend
Without shedding a tear?

I can sail without the wind.
I can row without oars.
But I cannot be separated from my friend
Without shedding a tear.)

"This song is in my heart," Johanna told the chorus. "It's from my hometown. You can't mess it up." She told them that the music mimicked the rising and falling of a boat on the waves. "It comes up, builds, and comes down. Every piece of music is built upon stress and release. That's called dynamics. If you sing every piece of music the same way, never loud, never soft, they're going to fall asleep on you."

Singing the rueful, haunting poetry of "Vem Kan Segla," it was the melodramatic Jamie, mourning the latest bruise in his life, who was transformed into someone magical. His voice filled with yearning and loss, summoned from who knew where, since on the surface Jamie could boast one of the more stable existences at P.S. 86.

Jamie Flores had been surrounded by music at home. When he was little, he had asked his mother, Marie, to write down all the words to Walt Disney musicals: *The Lion King, Anastasia, Little Mermaid.* He learned them all. He had sung in his church choir. His stepfather, Mike Muñoz, was a senior computer technology engineer for a car service fleet, and Marie was the fleet coordinator. But Mike had engineered recordings for his own father, Tisziji Muñoz, an avant-garde jazz guitarist. Jamie's parents had been good friends at Brooklyn Tech, one of New York City's three most selective public high schools, to which students are admitted based on their rank on a citywide entrance examination. Mike and Marie went their separate ways after high school, but rekindled the relationship later, when Marie was on the rebound from her first marriage.

Jamie was in the top-tracked class at P.S. 86, and certificates for perfect attendance decorated the walls of his bedroom. His parents didn't want to push him too hard, but they hoped to get him into the Salk School of Science, a competitive middle school, in a middle-class neighborhood of Lower Manhattan, distant both in miles and in expectations from Kingsbridge. Anything to save him from Junior High School 143, the neighborhood school, where fewer than 10 percent of the students passed standardized tests in mathematics.

The first time Johanna heard Jamie sing, in his ethereally high falsetto, she sent a note home telling his parents that he had talent, and should learn to play an instrument. He still had the voice of a child, and was singing in the same range as a girl. He sang all the songs in falsetto. Every child should be able to do that, but many of the kids didn't know how. The boys especially didn't understand how to get up high. But somehow, Jamie did. He had a beautiful voice, very secure, and good technique.

Despite his stable home life, Jamie had a melodramatic side, which he seemed able to turn on and off like a faucet. Johanna would find him mourning the father he never knew as if he were a fatherless child, not a boy well looked after by a stepfather who loved him and his mother and was a good provider. Another day, she saw tears running down his cheeks and Jamie confided that his aunt had died. "Do you need a hug?" she asked. "Yes," Jamie said, throwing his arms around her. Did his aunt really die? Johanna could never be sure.

❦

Johanna barely noticed Pierre, the wallflower: dedicated, quiet, nearly invisible. He must have made an impression on her during his audition, or she would not have admitted him to the chorus in the first place. That was one of the great frustrations of teaching, how easy it was to ignore the quiet children, the ones who were not demanding. It was unfair, she knew, and she could not pretend that she was innocent. Pierre's mother, Candida, was a force in the school, an active member of the Parents' Association, dedicated to her nine children while her husband, Pierre Sr., worked as a doorman in a posh building on the Upper East Side of Manhattan. Candi and her children were like the duck family in *Make Way for Ducklings*. Everyone stood aside to let them pass. Candi, a strong-willed, petite woman, about 5-3, who sometimes wore white gloves to cover eczema, seemed to go everywhere with six boys and three girls trailing behind her, one smaller than the next, yet looking very much identical like nested dolls. Johanna imagined that Pierre's understated temperament came from being the oldest of nine, expected to set an example of maturity and responsibility.

But there was one song that made Pierre glitter.

Joshua fought the battle of Jericho, Jericho, Jericho. Joshua fought the battle of Jericho, and the walls came tumblin' down. You can talk about your king of Gid-e-on. You can talk a-about your man of Saul. But there's none like good old Josh-u-a. At the battle of Jericho.

Johanna would smile as, from the corner of one eye, she caught a glimpse of Pierre side-stepping, the way she had taught the children, snapping his fingers and rolling his thin shoulders like a lounge singer. He could have strutted right out of the Frank Sinatra–Sammy Davis ratpack. Mr. Cool. Then Vincent would punch Keshauna in the arm. "Vincent! Pay attention," she would scold, her attention diverted, and Pierre would fade into the background once again.

૭૦

Erica Davies was another forgotten child. Well, no, that wasn't fair to say. Johanna had given willowy, almond-eyed Erica a solo, the female part opposite Jamie in "Vem Kan Segla." No one could say she had ignored Erica's high, clear voice, her poise and sweetness. Whatever role tonsils might play in shaping a voice, it was uncanny how much the tone and character of the children's voices reflected their personalities. But like Pierre, Erica's most prominent quality was her good behavior. "She was always the girl that I could rely on," Johanna recalled. "If I needed something done, I would go to her." Erica was very hard on herself, and the pressure sometimes showed in a tiny tic, a tourette-like shiver. She seemed desperate to get out of the Bronx, the way Johanna had been desperate to get away from Aland. Her ticket out would be her grades.

She was a straight-A student, selected to participate in Prep for Prep, an intensive summer and weekend enrichment program designed to place bright, disadvantaged minority children in top-ranked private schools. She was named for her father, Eric Davies, an actuary who had been a teacher in Nigeria. Though her parents were divorced, he lived nearby and kept in touch. Her mother, Nila Cadornigara, a Filipino immigrant, was a preschool teacher who had nurtured Erica's love of learning by reading to her. In their spotless apartment, sparsely furnished with an overstuffed plaid couch and gauzy pleated white curtains, Erica's mother had filled a blond wood storage cabinet with a collection of Dr. Seuss, Childcraft encyclopedias, and Thomas the Tank Engine books. Erica aspired to be a lawyer or a pediatrician, so she could help people and "right wrongs." She drank in *Law and Order,* as if memorizing scenes from the TV show could help her pass the LSAT. Her friends thought of her as a leader, level-headed, sympathetic. She practiced medicine on them. Stomachache? "Take some Pepto Bismol," she would advise. Or, "Drink a cup of chamomile tea and call me in the morning." Itch? "Try Lanacane."

Her own distress was harder to soothe than a stomachache. By fifth grade, Erica was ostracized for being different, for wanting more out of life than Kingsbridge had to offer. Children accused her of being snooty for getting good grades and going to Prep for Prep, and taunted her for wearing dowdy brand-X clothes instead of GAP and Old Navy. Erica had the impression that her fifth-grade teacher, far from discouraging such behavior, egged on her tormentors. "When those girls started bothering me, she sort of blamed me," Erica said. The teacher picked Wednesdays, the one weekday when Erica had to go to Prep for Prep, to assign extra homework. It was deliberate, Erica was sure. The final blow came when Erica made the chorus and her best friend did not. Her friend deserted her. "She thought I was rubbing it in," Erica said, morosely. "I was just excited. I thought she was my friend."

She consoled herself by thinking that if she could just get through sixth grade, one more year, "Then I'll be leaving here and they won't bother me anymore."

✐

There was something elusive about Ashley. She was like one of those 3-D images that changes when you tilt it, a pretty girl from one angle, an old crone, wrinkled and cunning, from another. Her family recognized her ancient side, and teased her about it. "La viejita," they called her, "the little old woman." Some children were born wise beyond their years, and Ashley was one of those.

A born blues singer, with her preternaturally deep, hoarse Janis Joplin voice, Ashley gravitated toward songs that exuded earthiness and danger. Someday, she would know how to sing bawdy and bring the house down. You could picture her in strapless satin and belting, "Oh Lord, won't you buy me, a Mercedes Benz . . . . Dialing for dollars is trying to find me . . . . Worked hard all my lifetime, no help from my frie-ends." Someday. Despite her incorrigible side, she was Benardo's favorite, the one he trusted to be poised, circumspect, and calculatingly bland when educational dignitaries visited the school. When visitors wanted to talk to a student, Benardo tapped Ashley. He could trust her with adults. She had the cynic's ability, honed by ample experience with white lies, disappointment, and betrayal, to psych out hidden motives and dissimulation, and the consummate con artist's knack for revealing no more than was required. Johanna and Benardo responded to different signals. Unlike some of the other children, proud Ashley had not been raised to feel or behave like an underdog, so she did not trigger Johanna's protective instincts. For now, no song seemed to fit "la viejita," this cronelike pixie, so Ashley had not been assigned her own song. She remained, incongruously, unfairly perhaps, a member of the chorus, no more and no less prominent than anyone else.

℘

CHAPTER TEN

A Boy from the Neighborhood

Margaret thought highly enough of Johanna's talent to hope that she would not squander it in the anonymous isolation of a neglected public school in the Bronx. At the same time, she feared losing this lucky find of a teacher to more illustrious pursuits and wanted to give her a reason to stay. Trying to be helpful, Margaret invited Johanna and her roommates, a guitar player and a bass player, to perform at her house in Scarsdale. The soiree would be like a coming out ball for a debutante. Maybe, Margaret thought, some of her well-to-do friends would offer Johanna an engagement or two, a wedding, a party, a chance to make some extra income. In Scarsdale, even a wedding could lead to better things. You never knew who might be there, just a face in the crowd: an agent, an impresario, a studio head.

It had been a long time since Margaret had heard music in the house. The old piano that had faithfully traveled across the country with the Bartelme family had been relegated to the laundry room. In its hulking frame, the upright preserved the spectral sound memories of the past. Joe had played a newsman's rendition of "Sentimental Journey," looking to Margaret's fond eyes like a cross between Hoagy Carmichel and Edward R. Murrow. Her son, Tony, preferred guitar and harmonica and Peter, team sports. Margaret played easy Bach and Chopin preludes, though not in public. Nicki was the one who took piano lessons, and Margaret missed her, the youngest and last to go. Having Johanna and her friends over gave Margaret the warm feeling of having Nicki and her friends back home again, laughing and filling the house with their easy, youthful physical presence. What a hard fate, being a mother.

"I spoke to Nicki yesterday," Margaret's best friend, Dorothy Pack, would announce lightly, off-handedly. As a nascent adult, Nicki was more likely to pour her heart out to Dorothy, her surrogate mother, than to Margaret, her real one. So Margaret looked forward to the late-night telephone conversations with Johanna, fretting over the latest boyfriend's refusal to commit. It was a pretty safe bet that Margaret knew more about Johanna's romantic attachments than Lillemor did. Just as Dorothy knew more about Nicki than Margaret. That was simply the way things worked; she accepted it.

Johanna agreed to the gig because she was fond of Margaret. She rarely sang for free. There were times when she did it by default, like the nights she performed at the Cornelia Street Café for the cover and gave the paltry earnings to the band, keeping none for herself. If she didn't take her singing seriously, who would? The truth was, though, that she made most of her money selling her CD's at festivals and concerts.

About fifty people came to the party, friends and the 30-something children of friends, the Scarsdale crowd, artists, importers, teachers, investment bankers, an architect, a doctor. They gathered on cozy couches in Margaret's castle-like living room, under the arched stained glass windows, dark wood-beamed ceilings and Moorish tile accents.

Johanna wore her cap-sleeved black velvet, her favorite wrinkle-free fabric. Margaret wore a black sweater that exposed a strip of midriff. A man she knew, an artist, sidled up to her and said archly: "Risque, Margaret. Naughty, but nice." For a woman in her 60s, Margaret had a very presentable midriff, flat as a washboard. If she couldn't show some skin in her own house, where could she?

Johanna sang Gershwin, Rodgers and Hart, happy, romantic music, while the guests ate comfort food, lasagna, butterscotch brownies, organic salads. A fire glowed in the fireplace, and votives and candlesticks flickered on the coffee tables. The black velvet night pressed through the picture windows against the black velvet of Johanna's dress.

No further gigs in the homes of wealthy suburbanites materialized out of that night for Johanna, but she did capture the imagination of a couple in the crowd: Howard and Dorothy Pack. By some cosmic coincidence, Howard, who was about to turn 80, had attended P.S. 86 in what seemed, even to him, like an eternity ago. He knew that his wife's friend Margaret worked there, but his own connection to the school had seemed irretrievably far in the past. Now this young jazz singer had nudged his childhood back to life.

Making her debut at Margaret's soiree, Johanna had barely noticed Howard Pack. He had been another dignified face in the crowd. But he was to become one of her most powerful allies. Not that Howard Pack would ever take credit for anything that happened to Johanna. He preferred operating behind the scenes, on his own terms. He had the disinterest in personal aggrandizement that came from being a self-made former shipping magnate, comfortably if not extravagantly rich, confident in his own skin and too scarred by personal tragedy to care much what others thought of him.

It was Margaret who took the next step to bring him in, to make him part of the dense web of personal connections that shaped the culture of P.S. 86 and the education of its students.

Like Margaret, the Packs lived in Scarsdale, on a winding cul de sac. Pack had commissioned Marcel Breuer, the Bauhaus-trained modernist architect, to build his low-slung, coolly geometric white brick and glass house, which stood out on a street of conventional colonials. Inside, the walls were hung with modern art, and little ancient artifacts from Mesopotamia, including a dancing nude Aphrodite holding a wreath, adorned a wall of recessed nooks and crannies.

Margaret and Dorothy Pack had become close friends through their participation in charitable and civic affairs. In an affluent suburb like Scarsdale, many wives didn't need to work, but she and Dorothy were not knitters, or cooking buffs, or ladies who lunch, either. (Dorothy liked to tease that she was good at "assembling" meals from the local gourmet grocery, artfully arranging medallions of salmon, roasted sweet potato chips, and beets with the stems left on like little green tentacles, after the hard labor of peeling, cutting, and cooking had been disposed of, no doubt, by those Mexican immigrants who worked in every restaurant kitchen these days.) The women's movement had not passed them by, but it hadn't exactly swept them up into its militant embrace. They were neither Stepford wives nor soldiers in Betty Friedan's army, but well-educated, ambitious, underemployed suburban housewives looking for a way to pass the time and feel useful. So to curb their restlessness, Dorothy and Margaret turned to good works.

They met while volunteering at the Hudson River Museum, in Yonkers in the mid–1970s. Then they went on to host a public-access cable television program, for the benefit of the Scarsdale adult school, in which they interviewed interesting local people—"to prove to our husbands that we can do it," Margaret said, half-jokingly. Dorothy— pretty, poised, athletically slender, with a mischievous glint in her eye— was the consummate hostess, and not just on the TV set. Conversation, good humor, curiosity, all the social graces seemed to come naturally to her, though, like most people who have a facility for keeping their guests amused and flattered, she secretly worked on her technique. She read the *Times* and *The New Yorker* from cover to cover and was always prepared to discuss wars in distant lands or what Safire and Dowd had written lately. She was not shy about expressing her opinion and gently extracted enough personal details about the people she was with ("And just what do you do?" "Where did you go to college?" "Where do you live?") to enable her to shape the conversation around their interests. She was never pushy, interjecting herself only when conversation lagged. Her languid self-confidence and buoyant energy seemed ill-matched to Margaret's more brittle, cautious exterior. But they clicked. Dorothy knew how to crack Margaret's stiff social armor and make her giggle like a schoolgirl. Margaret had a coy, gossipy side that Dorothy enjoyed. And both women admired Howard, who had once been a boy from the northwest Bronx.

Howard M. Pack, born in 1918, had been in the first group of children to attend P.S. 86 when it opened, transferring over from Public School 33, just a short distance away at Fordham Road and Jerome Avenue. P.S. 33 was right under the elevated subway line, its windows rattling every time the trains went by. Young Howard was grateful to flee to a beautiful, clean, quiet new school. The neighborhood in those days was mainly Jewish and Irish, with a few Italian immigrant families moving in. There were no blacks, no Puerto Ricans, "no people of color," Pack recalled. It was a modest neighborhood, with good solid housing, and the Jewish children were mainly first-generation Americans. "The second generation, the Kuhns, Loebs, Schiffs, were already on Wall Street," Pack said. His father, Benjamin, the first generation of a Russian émigré family, ran a loft with a partner in Manhattan's garment district, at 27th Street and Seventh Avenue, manufacturing Persian lamb coats for women and selling them wholesale. His ancestral name wasn't Pack, but Howard Pack doesn't remember, or perhaps doesn't choose to remember, what it originally was. "Pack is the name I was born under," he said dismissively. Although the Packs were probably better off than many families at P.S. 86 in the 1990s—after all,

Benjamin Pack owned the business—Howard Pack didn't feel that way. "We were lower middle class," he insisted. "It was a very hard-scrabble business."

Pack, the oldest of three siblings, was, by his own account, a boy in a hurry. He was embroiled in a perpetual competition with a cousin, also named Howard, two years his senior, who had been accepted to Columbia at the age of 14. Perhaps because the example of his cousin's precocity had been drilled into him, Pack never felt satisfied with his situation. "P.S. 86 was an average school," he said, wistfully. "It wasn't anything like those fancy schools, like Horace Mann. But it was a good school. We had a lot of Irish teachers. The principal, Mr. Klein, was a legend. He was German; a martinet; very strict."

By sixth grade, he was so far advanced in his studies that his teacher didn't see much point in keeping him in class all day. Young Howard spent most of his time in the principal's office, running errands, and was also assigned to tutor another student. He didn't mind too much because the teacher, Mrs. Callahan, had a son, Parnell, who swam for Columbia. Howard hoped that, by association, he might end up at Columbia too.

Pack did end up skipping a grade and going to Columbia, though at a more normal age than his cousin. He assumes that many of his classmates did well, but not famously so. "Nobody became president of the United States" is how he puts it. His own good fortune was not handed to him on a silver platter. He graduated from Columbia in 1939 with a degree in economics, after spending a large part of his senior year playing the horses. "I was a gambler," he said. "That makes you an entrepreneur."

After Pearl Harbor he spent the war doing cryptanalysis for the Navy, then found himself back in the needle trade with his father. In the garment district, he became close to another disgruntled scion of a furrier, Joseph Kahn. Kahn's uncle, Ben, was the furrier to Jackie Kennedy, making a leopard-skin coat that became a trendsetter and was chronicled in the fashion press. Pack's father never achieved quite the same high profile. But still driven to keep up with the Kahns many decades later, Pack does drolly recall that the family business sold a Persian coat to the wife of Andrei Vishinsky, a state prosecutor during the Stalinist purge trials and Russia's chief delegate to the United Nations after World War II.

Pack and Kahn used to meet for lunch at the Fur Club, the furriers' answer to the Harvard Club, in the Statler Hotel, opposite Penn Station. There, over whatever was on the menu that day, they would scheme about how to get out of the family business. So it happened that in 1950, they hatched the idea of capitalizing on the reconstruction of postwar Europe.

Two years later, with about twenty investors, including as many relatives as they could muster, they scraped up enough money to buy two World War II Liberty ships at a bargain basement price, on good credit terms. Greeks dominated the shipping business, and they found a Greek-American to manage their ships. "Those were the years when Europe was starving," Pack said. "We carried wheat for England; France needed coal. From that we started to buy tankers." The Korean War brought them their first windfall, as they chartered their ships to carry military cargo, a practice they continued through the Vietnam War. Though they were formally known as Transeastern Associates, everyone in the industry called them Pack and Kahn, and the PK logo marked the stack of every ship.

In the beginning, they kept one foot in the fur business, spending about 40 percent of their time in shipping. They couldn't get a complete divorce from the detested needle trade as long as the Greek supervisor rebuffed their efforts to become more engaged in the day-to-day management of their ships, telling them that everyone he worked with spoke Greek and they wouldn't be able to communicate. "There were no Jewish people in the shipping business," Dorothy explained. "There was one," Howard Pack interjected, "and he let us have a desk." About a decade after purchasing its first two Liberty ships, Transeastern Associates had expanded to ownership of thirty-six bulk cargo carriers and had leased about fifteen more. In 1965, Pack and Kahn purchased Seatrain Lines, a struggling coast transporter of cargo and railroad cars. By the time Kahn died in December 1979, the company employed 3,000 people and had revenues of $250 million a year.

Along the way, they took some attention-grabbing risks. One coup was buying the *Manhattan*, the largest commercial cargo carrier to fly the U.S. flag, from Stavros Niarchos, the Greek tanker operator, soon after its debut in 1962. Because of her size, the *Manhattan* was an object of fascination in the shipping industry, though shipping experts speculated from the beginning that she was a white elephant. But this didn't seem to matter much to Pack and Kahn.

They chartered the boat to Esso, which used her as an icebreaker to plow a route through the fabled northwest passage to Alaska, as an alternative to building an oil pipeline. Ultimately, the pipeline won out.

In the winter of 1969, Pack and Kahn decided to invest $6 million in leasing part of the moribund Brooklyn Navy Yard to build commercial ships. The deal was spectacular enough to rate a White House press conference, where it was announced by Vice President Spiro Agnew and New York City's Mayor John V. Lindsay. The company committed to providing jobs for hard-core unemployed New York City residents, and said it would have a payroll of as much as $10 million in its first year of operation. Seatrain built four ships with government financing, but the reopening of the Suez Canal gutted the oil super-tanker business. "When the ships were finished the market was finished," Pack said.

He had always run his business as something of a gamble, and gamblers expect to lose, and sometimes to lose their shirts. "We think of ourselves in a way as portfolio managers, in the sense that we make decisions among the various opportunities open in the shipping industry for the best investment of our cash and management capabilities and energies," Pack told *BusinessWeek* in 1969, when his company was at its peak.

In February 1981, Seatrain, which had already cut operations, declared Chapter 11 bankruptcy.

"I hung around for the reorganization period," Pack said, and then he retreated to his home in Scarsdale, to his golf game, and to a new form of venture capitalism, the biotech industry.

As the children at P.S. 86 might say, having studied fables as part of their curriculum, wealth does not necessarily bring happiness.

The years after Pack and Kahn declared bankruptcy brought their share of personal pain. In December 1991, Pack's son, Daniel, a neurologist who lived in nearby Armonk, New York, was killed in a baseball-card deal gone bad. Daniel Pack, a collector, had paid a dealer, Joseph Gordon, $70,000 for baseball cards that he later discovered were worth about $5,400, according to testimony at the murder trial. When Pack confronted Gordon, the dealer shot him in the head.

William M. Kunstler, the radical civil rights attorney, defended Gordon, who was black. Gordon's 17-year-old son, Chad, was the main witness against his father. In what one account described as a Perry Mason–like turn of events, Kunstler turned on Chad as he sat in the witness stand, accusing him rather than his father of committing the crime, after a sexual encounter with Daniel Pack. Kunstler claimed that the father had only helped dispose of the body, to cover up for his son. The scenario seemed to come out of thin air, unsupported by the evidence. Chad Pack called the unexpected accusation "an outrage." The prosecutor denounced it as "pure fantasy." A jury agreed, convicting the elder Gordon of murder in 1993.

The murder cast a shadow over the Packs, but was not talked about to outsiders. It had, perhaps, drawn Dorothy and Howard closer to Margaret, who had supported them through the ordeal.

ↁ

As Howard's 80th birthday approached in the fall of 1998, Margaret tried to think of something special to do for him. He had enough material things. Margaret asked Miss Small's third-grade class at P.S. 86 to make birthday cards for her friend Howard Pack, a distinguished gentleman who had attended their school the very first year it opened. If she had any ulterior motives for the project, they remained unconscious.

On the morning of Howard's birthday, September 21, the Packs were at their country home in the Catskills. Dorothy pulled out the cards. Howard read each one two or three times, turning it over and studying it like something precious. The children wished him a happy life. They hoped he would make a lot of money. The messages were childish and touching. But one card stood out for its harshly abstract art and absence of sentiment, and Pack was particularly struck by it. "He was the outcast," he said later of the boy who had made this card. "You could tell he was a disturbed kid." Pack wanted to send sweets to the school, but Margaret suggested giving books instead.

So he bought thirty paperbacks, one for each child, most of them historical biographies. He inscribed each book to a particular child, thanking him or her for the birthday wishes, and tucked a crisp dollar bill inside the cover. Then he made his first visit to P.S. 86 in nearly seventy years. The building looked just as he remembered it, with the granite-clad walls and the two-story entrance, flanked by up and down staircases. Dorothy came with him, and they made a striking pair. Howard is tall, about 6-foot-1, thin, with a full head of white hair, a knowing yet abstracted expression, and a tart sense of humor. Dorothy is completely gray-haired, yet still youthful and sylph-like. Although she is his second wife—they married in 1961, after his first wife died— they are so close that she finishes his thoughts and seems to have heard every story before, no matter how far in the past.

As he presented the books to the children, he told them a little about each of the subjects, Amelia Earhart, Abe Lincoln, Jackie Robinson. The children were impressed by his erudition, but Pack recalled, "You should have heard them when they found the dollar bills."

Dorothy remembered that as she and Howard left the school later, the children were at recess and threw themselves against the playground fence to say good-bye. "Oh, I was touched by the whole thing," Pack said. "I never felt so important in my whole life. Well, it piqued my interest in the school, put it that way."

Pack wanted to do something more for his old school, and as Margaret may have covertly hoped, he soon figured out a way to recover the connection.

After retiring from the shipping business, he had tried his hand at a more contemporary form of venture capitalism, investing in the pharmaceutical industry. He had always been interested in medical experimentation. In exchange for some Seatrain stock, Rockefeller University had let him "fool around feeding rats," as he put it, investigating the causes of obesity. From there he went on to start a tiny biotech company with a psychologist as a partner, which very soon morphed into Emisphere Technologies, after the board hired an MD-MBA from Wall Street to take over the management. Emisphere burgeoned into a sizable biotech company listed on the NASDAQ. The company drew "a tremendous amount of speculative interest," as Pack put it, and became part of the biotech bubble. Sensing an opportunity, he bought shares in another company for $3 and sold them for as high as $200. He sold 5,000 shares at inflated prices and turned them into the nucleus of the Pack Foundation. As he cast about for a mission for his foundation, along came the children of P.S. 86.

The alternatives would have been Columbia University, his alma mater, or George Washington High School, the school in Washington Heights that he had graduated from. Neither appealed to him. George Washington High School had become a failing ghetto school where there would be, he imagined, little accountability for donations. At Columbia, "I'm a tiny fish in a big pond." But at P.S. 86, "I'm the biggest fish, the only fish. And I knew Margaret. I was giving it to Margaret as much as to the school." By channeling the money through

Margaret, Pack would maintain some control. He stipulated that his grant would go to support the arts.

The first installment, Pack promised, would come through in October 2000.

Benardo, who had once contemplated diverting arts money into test-prep, was swept up in the excitement. Who could have predicted that P.S. 86 would have its own homegrown tycoon, who would appear out of nowhere to become a generous benefactor? Margaret Bartelme might not be Caroline Kennedy, who later lent her cachet to raising money for New York City schools by networking among the rich and famous; Howard Pack was no Bill Gates, despite their similar wiry builds and relatively modest antecedents. But for the Bronx, they would more than do. Shelly Benardo had no complaints. To show his gratitude, he dug Pack's old report card out of the archives and presented it to him. Pack had been a straight-A student.

CHAPTER ELEVEN

❧

The Sublimated Love Affair

On Sundays, she worked as a paid member of the choir for an Episcopal church in Hoboken, and that's how she met James.

He saw her first. His New Year's resolution for the year 2000 had been to start going to church a little bit more. He had been brought up Episcopalian in Ohio, where faith and sports—James Staffan played them all—were part of the fabric of life. It had been pounded into his head that the value of money should not be underestimated, that he had to be able to make an honest living, that he couldn't depend on anyone else to see him through. So at the age of 21, he was well on the road to financial stability, studying for a master's degree in technology management at Stevens Institute of Technology, and holding down a technology consulting job with Arthur Anderson, the accounting firm. But something was missing. Going to church, he thought, might satisfy some yearning for spiritual connection, for a god beyond work and money. That's when he noticed Johanna, blond and sizzling, singing in the choir.

He began looking for excuses to meet her and found an opening through his fraternity faculty advisor, who also sang in the choir. "If you ever go out to brunch with her, invite me along," James told his advisor. One Sunday, the advisor did, and James managed to sit next to Johanna. She told him she was from Finland.

"What part?" he asked.

"You won't know it," she said.

"I know my geography really well," James insisted. "Try me."

"Aland," Johanna said.

"In the Baltic Sea, right above Gotland," he shot back. "The A in Aland has a little circle over it."

"How did you know that?"

"I had a really hard geography teacher in high school," he said, laughing.

He joined the choir to get to know her better, and at first she stubbornly ignored his advances. He was attractive, 6-feet-6-inches tall, sandy-haired, vaguely Scandinavian looking. He was extroverted and energetic, always upbeat. But he was six years younger than she was, so why waste time? After so many boyfriends, she had grown cynical about men. What was it that Cheryl Hemenway, her student-teaching supervisor at Berklee, had called her all those years ago? "Sadie, Sadie, married lady." Well, Cheryl had spoken too soon. Nobody wanted to commit these days, let alone a 21-year-old like James. He was not the kind of guy she was looking for. From February to April, she hardly gave him a second glance. But that didn't stop him from trying.

He persuaded his fraternity brothers at Delta Tau Delta to hire Johanna and a quartet to perform during the cocktail hour for the fraternity formal, just so he would have a chance to see her outside of church. But it was his faculty advisor who paved the way for the romance, again. One night, the advisor invited everyone in the choir to his house for dinner after an evening concert, and Johanna went along.

She was the only woman there. James sat next to her and they talked only to each other. Then he drove her home to Manhattan. He was a good listener, and she found herself telling him about her illness. It didn't seem to bother him. It was a warm night in the middle of April. He kissed her good-bye.

She had always dated musicians. They had no money; they never slept; they were never there when she needed them. They always cared more about their instruments than about her. Even though she understood the love of an instrument, she still put her relationships first, her music second.

James was different. He was a gentleman: gallant, chivalrous, a little bit macho, but in the nicest way—a true Midwesterner. He had always followed his head, he told her. He was practical and good at math. Now he wanted to follow his heart. He had a musical side. He had played Frank Butler in "Annie Get Your Gun" at Washington High School. He had played saxophone in his high school jazz band. He loved the fact that she was doing something she really wanted to do. He admired her for being so devoted to the kids at P.S. 86.

He wanted to marry her. He would move to Stockholm if that was what she wanted.

"Come on, I don't believe you," Johanna would say. "You're too young." But in the end she couldn't fight him anymore. He was convinced they were going to be a couple. He was going to take care of her. He didn't care if she ended up in a wheelchair. Love was hard to find. He would take it in a wheelchair if that was the way it had to be.

He started learning Swedish and sending her emails in Swedish, not caring that his grammar was topsy-turvy. Before she knew it, she had fallen head over heels in love. It seemed she could never do anything halfway.

☙

She didn't go to the doctor very often. But when it came to her voice, she could not afford to take any chances. She had lost her voice and suspected she might have nodes on her vocal chords, a nightmare for a singer. She was teaching her classes at P.S. 86 through sign language, and by clapping out rhythms for the children to follow. This couldn't go on much longer. After a few days, she decided to see a throat specialist. He told her that her vocal chords were swollen but would recover. She just needed to rest them. The doctor was reputed to have Madonna as a patient, and Johanna was impressed. He must know other good doctors, she thought.

So she asked him to recommend a neurologist. She had lived with muscle spasms for as long as she could remember, and she had known for seven years that the weakness in her legs was probably related to muscular dystrophy. Her older sister, Cocki, had been diagnosed with muscular dystrophy when Johanna was 20, and the disease was genetic. But Johanna had never received an official diagnosis. The Finnish doctors had told Cocki that there was little she could do to arrest the progress of the disease. Maybe, Johanna thought, a New York doctor could offer more encouraging advice. Everyone knew that New York doctors were the best.

A few days later, she found herself in Betty Mintz's midtown office. Johanna might as well have picked a doctor out of the Yellow Pages. She was looking for emotional support, but found herself treated briskly, professionally, and briefly. The appointment lasted no more than fifteen minutes. Dr. Mintz asked her to sit on the floor and then return to a standing position.

"It's obvious you have muscular dystrophy," the doctor said. "It's common for siblings to get it." Johanna could have a biopsy or muscular reaction test for further confirmation, but Dr. Mintz added, "I wouldn't even bother."

"Is there anything I can do about it?" Johanna asked.

"No—sorry," Dr. Mintz replied. "I can write you a note giving you permission to get a handicapped parking sticker."

Dr. Mintz tore a piece of paper from the pad on her desk, dated it March 27, 2000, and scribbled: "To Whom It May Concern: Ms. Johanna Grussner suffers from a muscle disease and should have a handicapped parking sticker."

Johanna didn't know what else to say. The parking permit meant little to her. She didn't own a car. In a daze, she accepted the note, wrote a check for $395, the cost of the examination, and left. She was terribly disappointed. At that moment, the businesslike neurologist seemed like the coldest person she had ever met.

Maybe the relationship with James had made her overconfident, giddy, careless. Maybe she had let her guard down. But when she least expected it, things at school came to a boil.

Elsa Coriano, a fourth-grade teacher at P.S. 86, asked Johanna if she would be willing to give lessons to her 14-year-old daughter, Carlina. Johanna felt she could hardly refuse a request from a colleague, and she liked Elsa, a single mother who was raising two children while pursuing her teaching career. Carlina turned out to be a timid girl whose untrained voice had potential, but with a long way to go. Johanna gave her lessons in Elsa's classroom once a week after school, while Elsa graded papers. Elsa was hoping that the lessons would help Carlina, then in eighth grade at a nearby middle school, pass the audition for an arts-oriented high school, like LaGuardia.

As Johanna began planning her end-of-the-year concert, she asked Carlina whether she would like to sing a solo, while Elsa's fourth-grade class sang backup. Carlina had graduated from P.S. 86. "You went to this school," Johanna urged. "You'll be a role model for the younger kids." Although hesitant at first, Carlina agreed. Johanna chose one of her favorite songs, Simon and Garfunkel's relaxed, upbeat "59th Street Bridge Song."

On the night of the concert, a standing room–only crowd filled the auditorium: mothers, fathers, brothers, sisters, uncles, aunts, cousins, and grandparents. Baby carriages occupied every nook and cranny. In Kingsbridge Heights, the operative adjective when it came to families was not "nuclear" but "extended." Johanna's musician friends made up the band. Carlina's solo was a novelty and a big hit with the audience. During the final bows, Rob Pape presented Johanna with a bouquet of flowers and made a little speech about how much she had meant to the school, and how they were all looking forward to having her back in the fall.

Everyone left in a good mood, humming the words to Carlina's solo: "Slow down, you move too fast, You got to let the morning last, just kicking down the cobblestones, Looking for fun and feelin' groovy. . . . "

As Johanna prepared to go out for dinner with Rob Pape, Margaret, and two other teachers, she was called to Mr. Benardo's office. It was hot, and the building was not air-conditioned. Johanna's colleagues said they would wait outside, hoping for a night breeze.

"Sit down," Mr. Benardo said.

He wanted to talk to her about Carlina and Elsa, he said. He didn't understand the point of giving a former student a starring role in a P.S. 86 concert. How did Johanna think that made the other children feel? Carlina had taken a solo that might have gone to another, more deserving child. Johanna was here to teach the students of P.S. 86, not the children of teachers. How did she think the parents felt sitting in the audience, knowing their own children had been passed over for the child of a teacher? The whole thing smacked of favoritism, of nepotism. It was bad for the school, and bad for Johanna. Why would she do something so misguided? There must be something he didn't know. What was in it for her? Had she been giving lessons to Carlina? Had Elsa paid for those lessons?

Johanna tried to explain, but he was too angry to listen. All she could do was cry.

After yelling at her for what seemed like an hour, he snapped: "Go to the bathroom and wash your face." That was her cue to leave. As she turned on the tap, she looked in the mirror and saw that her mascara had run down her cheeks in black gashes.

The sun was setting by the time she got downstairs and her friends were hungry, impatient, and worried. Rob Pape took one look at her swollen eyes and said, "Honey, you don't look like you want to go to a party." Johanna nodded. She had lost her appetite and went to bed with an empty stomach.

She was still in agony. Everything had gone so well. The concert was perfect. Carlina, an innocent 14-year-old girl, was in heaven. Why did Mr. Benardo have to ruin everything?

After yelling at Johanna, Mr. Benardo chewed out Elsa. Elsa had allowed her daughter to skip the last period at her school so she could be in the concert. It was irresponsible of her as a mother and a teacher, Benardo said, to take her child out of school. Elsa didn't even try to explain that the only class Carlina had missed was gym. She had learned from past experience that with Mr. Benardo, the only proper response was, "Yes, sir. Yes, sir. Yes, sir."

Elsa didn't cry. But she was seething inside. She locked herself in a bathroom stall and silently screamed until she could recover her composure.

The next day, she went looking for Johanna.

"I'm sorry," she said.

"I'm sorry, too," Johanna replied, hugging her.

Neither of them had known that the lessons were against the rules. If they had, they told each other, they would never have gotten themselves into this mess.

"I'd take you out for a bottle of wine," Elsa said. "But I have a liver condition. Keep doing what you're doing. You're good at it. And don't worry about him. He has a Napoleon complex. The only reason he got mad is because he didn't know about it. He had to rebel because he wasn't asked. He always has to have the upper hand."

For his part, Benardo had no doubt that Johanna had tried to conceal the relationship. He accused her of lying about it. "Johanna was running a business, making money," he said. He considered that unethical on school property.

Margaret tried to defend her protégé. Johanna should not have taken money from Elsa, but she did not knowingly break any rules. Mr. Benardo was being too hard on her. But Benardo couldn't see it that way.

"He felt she was not innocent," Margaret said, shaking her head at the ferocity of the principal's anger. "After that, he gave her all kinds of trouble." Margaret never completely understood Benardo's reaction. "He had a strong sense of right and wrong—I guess," she said, with the faintest trace of irony in her voice.

Johanna was glad to go back to Aland that summer. She tried to put the incident with Carlina behind her. James didn't let Johanna forget him. He sent her email messages every day for seventy-seven days, from June to August. He was so crazy about her that he began running for hours at a time, just to get his mind off her. He ran so much that he lost 45 pounds, dropping to 210 from 255.

Partly because of James, she was acutely aware of the tension between her two lives that summer. She wanted to find a way to bridge those two worlds, the New York world and the Aland world, the world of her childhood and the world of her adulthood. Without that, she thought, she would never feel whole. She thought about living in Stockholm with James. And she fantasized about taking the kids in her chorus out of the Bronx, about showing them a different world from the one they were used to. She wanted to show them that life didn't have to be hemmed in by mean-spirited rules and regulations, whistles and megaphones, taking tests and sitting in the auditorium. If only she could show them her world, where there was no bad weather, only bad clothes.

Wouldn't it be great, she mused, if she could bring the children to Aland, as a kind of childhood exchange project? They had given her so much of their childhood; maybe she could give part of her childhood back to them. It was only a fantasy, but a nice one.

∽

She returned to school in September to find the lobby stacked with boxes. "Hey—Danny," she said, throwing her arms around her favorite security guard in a bear hug.

"Johanna. How was your summer?" Danny replied, cheerful as always. "You have a delivery."

Johanna looked again at the boxes in the lobby. They were for her, she realized. "*Herregud*," she whispered. "Mr. Benardo is going to kill me." She clutched her forehead, as if the gesture could pull out the memory of what she had signed. She wouldn't have placed such a big order for anything. This must be a mistake.

"Take it easy," Danny urged. "Here's the invoice. I'm sure it's OK."

Johanna let out a whoop. The VH1 grant. She had won it! The invoice listed sixty-six instruments, more than enough for a band, and music books. Prying open the cardboard boxes, she found flutes, oboes, a bassoon, bass clarinets, alto, tenor, and baritone saxophones, trumpets, horns, trombones, tubas, and a drum set.

A condition of the grant was to provide instrument lessons and set up a music room where children could practice after school. Christof Knoche volunteered to teach wind instruments, and Jamie was among the first to sign up, choosing saxophone. What a brainy, daring choice. Johanna was tickled. Not a trumpet or a flute, but a saxophone.

Mr. Benardo had been reluctant to give her a music room until now; the school was overcrowded. But he couldn't hold back any longer. He gave her a classroom on the fourth floor. She would have to share it with special-education classes. Johanna didn't mind. She worried more about the other kids being distracted than about her music students. But when she asked to have an upright piano moved from the mini-school to her new music room, Benardo balked. Custodians did not move pianos, and there was no way he could justify paying for a piano mover. If she could do it herself, Benardo said, shrugging, he would not stand in her way.

She was ashamed to admit it, but sometimes in this life the only thing a girl had to fall back on was feminine wiles. Whatever worked. She sweet-talked an assistant principal, two security guards, Bob Robertiello, and James into dragging the piano from the minischool into the main building. They rode up five floors in the elevator (the elevator stopped only on odd-numbered floors), then carried the piano down a flight of stairs to the music room. The piano weighed 1,000 pounds, the wheels fell off, and Johanna was afraid that someone would get hurt. But it—and the movers—arrived safely. To show her gratitude, she treated the men to a chocolate cheesecake from the Greek diner. Out of politeness, she invited Mr. Benardo to have some. He declined. "Give me the receipt," he said. "I can pay you back for that."

❧

That fall, James took her home to Washington Courthouse, Ohio, to meet his parents. They owned two roller-skating rinks, one run by his mother, the other by his father, and Johanna went skating for the first time in years. Holding hands with James, she forgot that anything was wrong with her legs and skated as if she were a child again.

For a couple of months, she managed to stay clear of Mr. Benardo and out of trouble. When he finally called her into his office, she felt a pang. Was he going to bring up Elsa and Carlina again? His scolding still hurt. But he greeted her as if nothing bad had ever happened. He was in a buoyant mood, practically floating. And what he had to say surprised her even more.

Something good had happened, he said gleefully, something that involved Johanna and Margaret. P.S. 86 had received a big donation, and it was earmarked for the arts.

"If you had one wish," Mr. Benardo asked, his pale-blue eyes widening behind his thick glasses, "what would you do with the money?"

Johanna didn't have to think about it. "I wish I could take my gospel choir to Aland and show them where I come from," she said.

Mr. Benardo laughed. But he did not say no.

The first installment of the Pack money had come through in October. All money was fungible once it was in the school budget. It seemed to Johanna that Howard Pack's money liberated Mr. Benardo, giving him the confidence to take chances, to be creative, to think about doing things he might not have done otherwise. Like Howard Pack, Shelly Benardo was a gambler at heart. Now he had a few more chips to work with.

Over the next few weeks, Mr. Benardo brought up Johanna's wish nearly every time he saw her. He seemed to be mulling it over. Sometimes he was dismissive, saying that he didn't see how they could possibly take a trip like that. Other times, he asked her for details: Where would they stay? What would they do? The idea began to take shape, and one day, he made her an offer, though it sounded more like an ultimatum.

"Do you still want to take the kids to Finland?"

"Yes. Why?"

"If this is ever going to happen, you have to do what I tell you to do and get everything I need. I'll tell you what to do, and you'll do it."

"Just tell me what you need," she said. But she hardly dared believe it was going to happen.

ഈ

At Christmas, it was Johanna's turn to take James home to meet her parents. You never knew what to expect in Aland in December. Sometimes, there was only cold and slush. This time, everything was picture-perfect. A heavy blanket of snow covered the ground, glistening in the sun. The highlight of the trip was New Year's Eve. They had been invited to Johanna's cousin's house to celebrate. Johanna and James rode there with Bodi and Martin on the same old kick-sleighs—sparkkalke—that the girls had used to go to school on snowy days when they were little. The women sat in the chairs on the front of the sleds, the men stood on the runners in back, kicking the sleds forward. James, who had trained for the marathon, loved it, but kick-sledding was not enough.

Overall, the trip was disastrous. James was accustomed to keeping busy with friends, school, work. Sledding wasn't enough to occupy him for two long weeks. There was nothing much for him to do except being there and taking long walks. Aland was very dead in the winter, and he was unprepared for it. There were only two channels on TV, one in Swedish, the other in what sounded to him like Finnish with Swedish subtitles. He had brought only one book with him. Johanna was busy planning concerts, and all the others were busy with their lives. James was alone for much of the time. He freaked out. He couldn't stand the isolation, the constant darkness, the culture shock. He was furious when Johanna and her family unconsciously switched to Swedish around the dinner table, not bothering to translate for him. He missed familiar rituals: The Grussners ate ham for Christmas dinner; his family always had turkey. They didn't count down to the New Year.

He actually went to Stockholm to interview for jobs, in an earnest effort to make good on his promise to move there with Johanna. A Swedish technology consulting firm even made him an offer.

But on the plane ride back, he knew that something had changed between him and Johanna. During a layover in Brussels, Johanna asked him how he had liked the trip.

"It was OK," James said.

"Just OK?" Johanna said, disappointed.

"Yeah, just OK," he said.

"Why wasn't it great?" she demanded. "What was wrong with it? Was there something the matter with my country?"

"No," he said. "I missed my friends. I missed my family."

Johanna was hurt and angry. James believed in true love, but he felt her love was not unconditional. To love her, he had to embrace the life she had envisioned, and at the age of 22, he wasn't sure he could do that. They didn't speak during the seven-hour plane ride back to New York.

When they got into the airport limousine, James told the driver there would be two stops instead of one. He carried Johanna's bags upstairs for her. He could never let her carry her own bags. Then he said good-bye. This time, there was no kiss.

That month, AT&T offered James a position managing technology projects for a $70,000 salary plus a signing bonus. He owed Johanna $8,000 that she had advanced him for his college tuition, but he was so bitter that he stopped returning her telephone calls, and didn't start paying her back until much later.

Johanna sublimated the breakup by planning the trip to Finland. She didn't believe she was ever going to meet anybody again. She told herself she was going to devote her life to music and to the kids.

Mr. Benardo wanted a clear plan of action. What airline would they take? Where would they stay? Where would they eat? What would the kids do all day long? What kind of transportation would they have while they were there? She would come home from gigs at 3 A.M. and send emails to Finland, as people there were going to work. She would wake the next morning to find their answers. Amazingly, it all came together. Johanna was the hometown girl who went to America and made good, and everyone was eager to help.

The Aland telephone company donated phone cards for the kids. The post office offered postcards and stamps. Gun Carlson, the cultural minister, arranged a guided tour at Kastelholm, the medieval castle. The *Albanus*, a replica of a historic sailing ship, agreed to take the children on a Baltic cruise, sponsored by the hometown newspaper. Chips Apb, the potato chip factory that was one of the archipelago's main industries, offered a tour. Nils-Erik Eklund, president of Viking Line Cruises, said he would treat the children to breakfast on the *Rosella,* followed by a guided tour of the ship.

Peter ("Peppe") Lindback, the governor of Aland, reacted as if the children were visiting dignitaries and promised to meet the chorus for lunch at the Grussner family's café. There would be horseback riding and minigolf. The kids would have a chance to pet the animals at the agricultural college. Johanna's hometown parish agreed to cover lodging, meals, and insurance, except on the first and last nights when the children would stay with host families, most of them friends from her old church choir, Intermezzo. The kids exchanged email and letters with the kids in Johanna's childhood school.

Benardo even left it up to her to find the best airfare and bus transportation. Johanna sparked a bidding war between Finnair and SAS. Finnair won the competition, by throwing in a free ticket.

"It seems like in the states, time is money," Johanna said. "People would rather give you a check for $5,000 because it doesn't take a lot of time to write a check. Over there, they don't have that kind of economy, but they love to help out in any other way that they can."

The chorus would leave Kennedy Airport on Finnair Flight 006, departing at 5:55 P.M. on May 11 and arriving in Helsinki at 8:50 A.M. the next morning. After a quick tour of the city, they would make a connecting flight to Mariehamn, the Aland capital, and arrive there in late afternoon. They would have seven full days in Aland, before returning to New York again on May 19.

For the last night in Aland, she planned to invite the entire town of Mariehamn to a joint concert starring the P.S. 86 chorus and her childhood group, Intermezzo.

Getting the Board of Education, normally more concerned with test scores and political patronage, to approve the trip took a huge organizing effort on Johanna's part and the willingness of Mr. Benardo to think strategically and pull strings. When the central board was moving too slow and Finnair was threatening to cancel its bookings, Mr. Benardo pulled the Rudy Crew card out of his sleeve.

With a Zelig-like knack for being in the right place at the right time, Mr. Benardo had met Rudy Crew during the Christmas break in 1999, at a pivotal moment in the history of the New York City school system. Crew, after being chancellor for four years, had just been ousted by Mayor Giuliani's allies on the Board of Education, after a bitter feud over vouchers and other educational policy matters.

Benardo, something of a restaurant buff, was eating at Cello, a three-star French fish restaurant tucked in a cozy Upper East Side townhouse. Cello had a $62 prix fixe menu and a wine list deep into champagnes. Benardo looked over at another table, and there was Crew, sitting with someone Benardo didn't recognize. Benardo introduced himself, and told Crew how sorry he was about what had happened. Project Arts, he told Crew, was one of the best things that had ever happened to his school. At this point, the former chancellor introduced his dinner companion, who turned out to be Schuyler Chapin, the city's arts commissioner.

Based on that encounter, Benardo later asked Chapin to serve as a ceremonial principal for a day, and Chapin did, further cementing his bond to P.S. 86.

So when the Board of Education balked at the trip to Finland, Benardo called Chapin. Chapin called a deputy chancellor. Within half an hour, the trip had been approved.

But nobody expected the Board of Education to pay for the trip, not directly anyway, and the chorus still had to scrounge up $18,000 in airfare. Rob Pape, Mr. Pop Culture, suggested writing to Oprah and Rosie O'Donnell, two of his favorite TV personalities, for help. Johanna did. Silence. Neither replied. Mr. Benardo stepped in, calling a politically connected teacher he knew at another school. This teacher was able to land a $5,000 grant from the local councilman, Adolfo Carrión, Jr. Carrión gave $5,000 in discretionary city money. The Rent Stabilization Association heard about the trip from two landlord members with P.S. 86 children in their buildings. It gave another $5,000. For the last $8,000, Mr. Benardo, who had a certain amount of discretion over his nonteaching positions, used money that would otherwise have gone to pay for a school secretary, a position he left unfilled.

In New York, the children prepared their passports and bought new clothes for the concert they were scheduled to deliver on their eighth and final night in Aland. Many of the children had passports already, because they regularly shuttled to the Dominican Republic to visit family. One needed the last-minute intervention of a congressman. Despite the passport, though, that child dropped out, her mother either too disorganized or too anxious to allow her to go, and Johanna made a last-minute substitution.

In Aland, Uffe Grussner was itching to drive the tour bus and Lillemor fretted over what to cook for a chorus dinner at the Grussner house: rice or potatoes?

There were too many children in the chorus. They couldn't all go to Finland. It would be a financial and logistical nightmare. Mr. Benardo decided on twenty-four children as a manageable number, and Johanna had to hold another audition. Ashley was extremely anxious about this. Her preternaturally calm behavior during the first audition may have stemmed, Johanna now realized, from not understanding what the chorus was about. Now it was part of her reality. Ashley had often been kept out of chorus by her teacher, and she knew that her position was already shaky. She complained constantly to Johanna that it was unfair to even think of excluding some children from such a special opportunity. Ashley desperately wanted to go. Johanna refused to promise anything, but secretly worried about how she would handle Ashley if she didn't make the cut. She tried to stay neutral, to think about the children only in the present moment, as she kept records of their performance in class. She wanted the process to be completely above-board, so she held the final audition in front of the entire chorus.

One by one, the children walked up to the stage, took the microphone, and sang a song in front of their schoolmates. She could sense the tension in the auditorium. Some of the children thrived on the public exposure, and put everything they had into it; others cringed.

In the end, the decision turned out to be easier than she had anticipated. Going down the list of names, she had penciled A's and A-minuses next to some of them; those were the children who made the cut. Ashley was one of them, along with Vincent, Jamie, and Erica. To Johanna's relief, none of the children disputed her choices.

CHAPTER TWELVE

Ͽ

A Fifth Avenue Address

Ashley Alvarez was not the type of child a visitor would expect to find at a school like P.S. 86. She held herself aloof from everyone around her. She was exceptionally poised, with the arched spine, open shoulders, and graceful, light-footed walk of a natural athlete, a gymnast, or a ballerina, although she was none of these. She seemed a keen, unabashed observer, fixing people around her with her direct gaze, daring them to challenge her. At other times, she wore a blank, expressionless stare like a "Do Not Disturb" sign. If she had been a character in a Victorian novel, you might guess that she was the one whom the author had chosen to rise out of the slums and become, by virtue of her wit, charm, and beauty, a fixture in high society, her low-born past now a carefully guarded secret. Little Dorrit, maybe. Or you might look at her and think *Pygmalion*, with Ashley cast as the lowly flower girl clever enough to fool a Hungarian count into pronouncing her "Of Royal Blood." You could see her, at a slightly older age, as a delicate but audacious Audrey Hepburn lookalike, magnetic enough to seduce a rich Svengali, who would whisk her away to a jet-setter life in the capitals of Europe. Her old schoolmates would marvel at the transformation, while recalling that she had always seemed to float a level above her station in life.

All these fantasies might cross your mind on first impression, without knowing too much about Ashley, and the funny thing is, you would be on the right track. For Ashley had looks, talent, intelligence, and—most crucially of all—contact with a world outside the stifling ghetto streets on which most of the children at P.S. 86 were growing up and taking their own measure. Although she was an indifferent student, she had the enterprising spirit and will to succeed that sometimes matters more than good grades in school. And she had seen enough of the world outside the Bronx to be capable of envisioning a more promising future for herself than a menial job and an apartment five blocks from the one where she grew up. That simple ability to think beyond the confines of her environment set her apart from many of the other children.

Then again, you might be overstating the case. Ashley was a strange mercurial creature, outgoing one day, alienated the next, the product of an unstable family life that flitted in and out of the middle class, and even flirted with membership in New York's insular high society. Her maternal grandmother, Ana, was a Cuban immigrant who slaved as a nurse to put her only and late-born daughter, Ileana, Ashley's mother, through one of Manhattan's upper-crust private high schools, where she associated with rich girls from the Upper East and Upper West sides and acquired her debutante airs. Photographs of her in her 20s show a strikingly self-possessed young woman, her chin-length brown hair set in glossy waves and combed smoothly around her head like a helmet. She holds her chin high. Her gaze is serene and knowing. She looks as if she belongs in a yearbook from Brearley, the all-girls school where Ivy League graduates teach the children of high society for low pay, grooming girls like Gwyneth Paltrow to take the world by storm.

Ileana's lifelong weakness had been that she was still caught up in the immigrant experience. Her hard-working and methodical mother had put her on a path to upward mobility. Her private school education and experience seemed to hold out the promise, with some luck, of vaulting over an entire economic stratum from lower middle class to upper middle class in one generation. But in her teens, a huge gulf separated her from her private school classmates. She was burdened by her background as the child of a Spanish-speaking mother, newly arrived from an impoverished Caribbean country, working in a relatively low-status job. She resented her mother's long hours at the hospital and rebelled against her admonitions to study hard and think about college. In her carefree youth, she lived for today and took for granted the advantages her mother had given her. She didn't know that she was perilously close to falling off the precipice of middle-class life into poverty and second-class citizenship.

When Ashley, by then a third-grader, arrived at P.S. 86 in 1998, Ileana was in her early 30s, and had the glib tongue and self-assurance of a suburban soccer mom. But her aura of middle-class competence was undercut by the bizarre exterior of a performance artist or punk rocker, the kind of style you might expect to see on Astor Place, in the East Village, but not on Reservoir Avenue. Small hoops adorned her pierced lip and eyebrow, and when she spoke, a gold stud glittered in her tongue. She did not seem to care too much what others thought of her. The teachers at P.S. 86 were accustomed to parents who were deferential toward authority and overprotective of their children, who kept their criticism, if they had any, to themselves. They were accustomed to parents who had learned that the best way to cope with the school system was not to be demanding, for demands only invited rebuffs and even reprisals. Parents who made demands were written off as nuisances. Parents who were helpful, and waited for the principal or the teachers to give them orders as to what to do, were rewarded. Parents at P.S. 86 had been trained not to take too much initiative.

The teachers didn't quite know what to make of Ashley's mother. She addressed them as equals, and even sounded like one of them, articulate, discerning, reasonably well educated. She seemed to give Ashley much more liberty than other parents gave their children. Was she some kind of post-hippie, one teacher wondered. She would have blended in nicely among the countercultural playground mothers of a progressive school in the East Village. But in the northwest Bronx, her unconventional appearance led teachers to think, mistakenly, that she was a bit addle-headed, a space cadet. It was almost as if she had wandered into Kingsbridge by accident. In fact, Ileana was much more calculating than the teachers suspected. But it was true that this was not necessarily the life she envisioned for her daughter. She seemed to think of herself as Alice, having fallen down the rabbit hole. She was as startled as everybody else to find herself in the realm of the Queen of Hearts, and expected to find her way out soon enough. She was only passing through, and never meant to stay.

From the age of 9, Ashley's mother, Ileana, grew up in a grand brick and limestone apartment building on Fifth Avenue, an address that she was astute enough to brag about in a city where real estate announces your pedigree more certainly than a Cartier watch or a Vuitton handbag. In New York City, every store clerk and bill collector draws an instant impression of wealth and social status from the address on your telephone bill or your credit card application. Fifth Avenue has presumptive cachet, just as surely as the Grand Concourse will cut you down a few notches.

"My mother's Fifth Avenue apartment" rolled easily off Ileana's tongue. Without knowing the cross-street, no one would guess that this portentous address was actually as counterfeit as the Cartier watches and Vuitton handbags that Sudanese street peddlers sell to gullible tourists on Seventh Avenue. She didn't have to mention the cross-street—102nd Street—that exposed her as living at the northern extreme of Fifth Avenue, where in those days she was more likely to rub elbows with the junkies, bodegas, and botanicas of Spanish Harlem and the struggling tenants of nearby housing projects than with the psychiatrists, financiers, and celebrities who lived farther south. Still, her mother's building was not unimpressive, even twenty years before the late-'90s real estate boom. It overlooked Central Park (though Ileana's apartment did not). And it had all the accouterments of middle-class respectability: a uniformed doorman, neatly clipped hedges along the front walk, and a well-appointed lobby.

But its location, on the borderline between the Gold Coast and El Barrio, reflected the tension that shot through almost every aspect of Ileana's existence, and she passed that sense of dislocation down to her daughter Ashley.

Ashley's grandmother, Ana, had grown up in postwar Havana, Cuba, the daughter of a butcher and a seamstress from rural Spain. Like many petit bourgeois, the family were anti-Castro. One after another, Ana's relatives fled to Miami. Urged on by an aunt, Ana, too, longed to flee Cuba, and with that goal in mind, she began taking English lessons after school when she was 16. At 17, she married her English teacher, who was ten years older and struck her as the height of sophistication. They had a son, Saul, together, and both of them became nurses—she, by passing the exams for a prestigious program at Calixto Garcia Hospital and the University of Havana.

By the time Saul was 4 or 5 years old, they had divorced, and Ana, immersed in nursing school, lost custody of the boy to his father. She had Ileana by a second husband before that marriage, too, fell apart. Ana was ambitious and wanted to be a nurse-anesthesiologist. But because her desire to emigrate was on the record, and she was not a member of the Communist Party, she found it difficult to find work or advance in her career. Her ex-husband and their son, Saul, fled to Miami first. Despite the divorce, the extended family then helped Ana and Ileana, who was then 4, to find a place on one of the last "freedom flights" out of Cuba in 1971.

After three days in a refugee camp, they settled with a friend of the family in a small apartment on Gerard Avenue, near Yankee Stadium, in the Bronx. Ana's nursing skills were in demand, and she immediately found work in a nursing home. Four years later, she found a permanent job at Mt. Sinai Medical Center, at Fifth Avenue and 100th Street, in Manhattan, the beginning of a more stable life for her and her child.

But tragedy struck at about the same time. When Ileana was 8, her 19-year-old half-brother, Saul, who had been living with his father in Miami, came to live with them in the Bronx. Ileana idolized Saul, a tall, muscular, handsome young man with golden curls, which he had inherited from his mother, who was often told that she looked like Ingrid Bergman. Ileana didn't know that Saul had come north because he was suffering from psychological problems, and that the family hoped a change of scenery might help him.

As she was about to leave for work one morning, Ana heard a shot in the stairwell one floor up. She ran upstairs and found her son, Saul, lying dead in a pool of blood. He had shot himself with a rifle his mother didn't know he had. It was July 8, 1975, the day after Ana's birthday.

Ileana was visiting relatives in Florida when the suicide occurred, and she never really understood that her brother was dead. His disappearance remained a mystery until she was 13, when an aunt told her that Saul had committed suicide while strung out on heroin. Yet even before she learned the truth, Ileana wondered what had happened to her adored older brother, and felt that her mother was withholding something from her. In hindsight, Ileana traces much of her later rebellion and hostility toward her mother to that early sense of betrayal.

Ana, for her part, wasn't ready to deal with the sorrow and pain of Saul's death, and never realized that Ileana would uncover enough information on her own to fill in the blanks. Instead, Ana drowned her sorrow in working, and working hard became her therapy. She joined the intravenous nursing team, and was the one always called on for the hard cases, to insert needles when no one else could find a vein.

Sometimes, Ileana complained that her mother spent all her time working, leaving Ileana to do the cooking, cleaning, and ironing—leaving her without enough mother-love. There were only two shifts in life, Ana used to tell her daughter, one to spend on living, one to spend on working. You either lived on welfare, where the mothers were with their children all the time, or you worked, and Ana didn't see how taking welfare could be a good influence for her child. So she worked.

Unwilling to stay in the building where Saul had died, Ana moved to Washington Heights, but felt unsafe there. As a Cuban, she held herself aloof from the Dominicans and Puerto Ricans who made up much of the population in the Heights, and the Dominicans and Puerto Ricans made no secret of their resentment of Cubans. Within six months, she had charmed a building superintendent into arranging for her to rent the one-bedroom apartment at 102nd Street and Fifth Avenue, two blocks from her work. She moved with the help of her future husband, a German Jew who had fled Hitler to Argentina, then moved to New York City where he worked as a carpenter.

The move from Washington Heights to the Upper East Side was a 4-mile trip down the Harlem River Drive, less than half an hour by car. But psychologically, it was second in momentousness only to the leap Ana had made in going from Cuba to Miami. She and her daughter were moving to Manhattan, the center of the universe, the place that people in the other boroughs called "the city," as if Manhattan below 96th Street were the sun and the outer boroughs were mere planets orbiting around its brilliance.

Ileana remembers that day—January 20, 1977—as if it were yesterday. They ordered Chinese food and, surrounded by stacks of moving boxes, ate it with plastic forks straight out of the takeout cartons, while watching Jimmy Carter's inauguration on TV. It was a new beginning for the country, and for Ana and Ileana.

To mark their rise in the world, Ana took Ileana out of public school and put her in sixth grade at St. Francis de Sales, a nearby Catholic School. Ileana was smart but unruly. She was about 10 when the nuns called Ana one day to tell her that her daughter had gone out for lunch and not returned. Ana was dying her hair. She threw a handkerchief over her half-dyed hair and began searching the neighborhood. She found Ileana at a bodega playing arcade games. Exasperated, she put Ileana in Julia Richman High School, a public school, but once again, there were problems. Ileana was identified as white, and the other girls thought of her as white, and she became scapegoated by the black and Hispanic girls who dominated the school. In ninth grade, Ana moved her to the Baldwin School, a small private school on the Upper West Side of Manhattan, respectable but a social rung below white-glove schools like Chapin and Spence. Private school, Ana thought, would give her daughter the education and social finishing she needed to rise up in the world. But Ana never anticipated the sordid underside of the private school experience: the dabbling in drugs and drink, the ferocious jockeying for social position that would stigmatize her daughter for having a Hispanic surname and for being the child of a striving immigrant. This was a world in which it was not enough to be respectably middle class; to be popular, Ileana came to think, it was better to be filthy rich and pretentious, or, as Ileana put it, "a snob."

Ileana cut classes. Her biology report card showed thirty absences—an automatic fail. Her Spanish teacher wrote: "Ileana's 'I don't care' attitude is not welcome," adding that Ileana had been asked to leave the class five times for inappropriate behavior, such as polishing her nails.

Ileana tried to forge a $25 check signed by her mother into a $225 check, and was caught by the bank teller. Ana has saved that check all these years, as a bitter souvenir of what she went through with her only daughter.

Mother and daughter felt stung by the perhaps innocent judgments of Ileana's classmates and teachers. While visiting their apartment, one classmate asked why they didn't have a maid. Another time, the school director called to say that Ileana had been found carrying a knife in her pocketbook. Maybe Ileana needed a knife to protect herself in the neighborhood where she lived, the director said, but she didn't need one in school. Ana was livid. "I'm going to give you my address so you can see where I live," she retorted. "I don't need a knife where I live." Because Ileana's last name was Alvarez, she fumed, the director assumed they lived in the projects.

Ileana felt alien, but blamed her mother. Ana was raising her as if they were stuck in the 1950s, as if she were a vintage 1955 Chevy that had been preserved in mint-condition by the Cuban sun. But this was the 1980s. Ana sent Ileana to school wearing pretty Florence Eisman–type dresses, purchased at thrift shops, while other girls wore torn jeans and T-shirts. On her first day of school, Ileana showed up in a long khaki skirt, flat-heeled saddle shoes, and a blouse buttoned up to the throat. People asked her if she was a teacher. For her first school dance, her mother crimped her hair into ringlets. When Ileana got to school, she was mortified that she didn't fit in at all, went to the cafeteria, and ran cold water over her head to wash out the curls.

Ileana found refuge in drama, working as a stage manager and lighting director for school shows. But that, too, had its downside. Her drama teacher, whom Ileana idolized, liked to take her favorite students to a nearby restaurant and allow them to order Scotch, just to see how they would handle it.

"That was the school where I learned about pills," Ileana recalled. "There were twelfth-graders falling down flights of stairs at 12:30 in the afternoon."

One of her classmates was Jennifer Dawn Levin, whose sordid 1986 murder made the Baldwin School notorious and may have contributed to its bankruptcy and closing just two years later. In August

1986, a bicyclist found Levin, 18, strangled in Central Park, her partly nude and badly bruised body sprawled under a tree behind the Metropolitan Museum of Art. She had graduated from the Baldwin School that spring. A friend, Robert E. Chambers Jr., who had not attended the same school, pleaded guilty to manslaughter in her death, saying it occurred during rough sex.

Ileana and Levin became friendly in the ninth and tenth grades, in part through drama class, and Ileana recalls going with Levin to her father's Soho loft. Through Levin and other classmates, she participated vicariously in what the *New York Times*, while covering the murder, called a culture of "private schools, fancy apartments, foreign vacations, and underage drinking." But she remained on the margins of that world. Her classmates could dabble in uppers, downers, alcohol, and promiscuity and still count on the safety net of family money and connections to keep them afloat. Not so, Ileana. In tenth grade, Ileana turned her back on private school and Fifth Avenue and everything they stood for and ran away from home.

At 16, she moved to a shabby brownstone turned cheap hotel near Penn Station, where she paid $40 a week rent for a tiny furnished room with a sink in the room and a communal bathroom in the hallway. She shared the building with, among other tenants, an AIDS-infected heroin addict, an illiterate super with a cocaine-addicted wife, and an elderly Greek immigrant who seemed the sanest person in the building but, in her teenaged opinion, was hopelessly old-fashioned because he wore his pants pulled over his bellybutton. But at least she could talk to him.

She got a job scooping ice cream and survived on bologna sandwiches, milk, and strawberry ice cream, which she stored on the ledge outside her window because she had no refrigerator.

When Ana came looking for her, Ileana pretended that she was not home.

Ileana became pregnant almost immediately and, over the next decade, went on to have four different children by four different men: Javira in 1985; Steven in 1987; Ashley in 1990; and the last, Zoey, in 1995. Recognizing that she couldn't raise her first child in her roach- and mouse-infested apartment, she gave the baby to her mother, who raised Javira until she was 9. Ileana turned to men as substitutes for mother-care, and some were more dependable than others. Steven's father was a lifeguard. She met Ashley's father playing paddleball. She would take Steven in his stroller to the park and play paddleball all after-noon, mesmerized by the rhythmic pock-thwock of the rubber ball against the racquet, and soothed by the endorphin high. Sometimes, the whole group of paddleball players would jump into a van at sunset and drive to a court near Yankee Stadium, where they could continue playing under klieg lights until after midnight.

After Ashley was born, Ileana qualified for federal housing assistance. She reclaimed her oldest daughter, Javira, and took the three children to live in a two-family house in Castle Hill, in the north Bronx, near the border with Westchester County. Ana was distraught at losing Javira, but there was nothing she could do.

Ileana enjoyed what she called her gypsy life. Sometimes, she put the children in a van with blankets, some food and drink, and a bucket for a toilet, and went clubbing with her girlfriends. Or she would take the kids to City Island to watch the seagulls. While pregnant with Ashley, she almost graduated from nursing school, but lost her appetite for nursing during a phlebotomy course, when she had to take blood from a little boy. Her mother's specialty had been taking blood. Ileana could not do it.

She calmed down after meeting Zohair, a Moroccan immigrant known as Zoey, who became the father of her fourth child, also named Zohair. They shared an interest in pets and opened a pet shop on Fordham Road, with two partners. With Section 8 paying all but $400 of her $1,050 a month rent, Ileana moved to a three-bedroom apartment in Kingsbridge, near P.S. 86. Ashley was in third grade.

By the next year, Ashley had drawn the attention of guidance counselors. In the fall of fourth grade, a substitute teacher was covering Ashley's class, and the girl asked to go to the bathroom. The teacher refused. Ashley threw herself on the floor in the back of the classroom and began writing in her notebook. The teacher told her to get up, and Ashley became hysterical. Ileana was called to school and found Ashley in a guidance counselor's office. The counselor showed Ileana what Ashley had written in her notebook: "I want to die. I don't want to live anymore." Ileana had to get help for her child, the counselor said. This girl could be suicidal. She would not be allowed back in class until Ileana presented some evidence that her daughter had been evaluated.

Ileana took Ashley to the psychiatric emergency ward of Montefiore Hospital, where mother and daughter were asked a series of questions and sent home with a paper promising that she would be given follow-up care. With the help of the hospital and P.S. 86, Ashley was assigned a psychiatric counselor. Ileana also talked to Ashley, telling her that she was not crazy, but that it would be easy for strangers to think so if she had another hysterical outburst. "What you do is what people see," she told her daughter. "If you want to act like you're possessed, they're going to put you in a straitjacket." Yet Ileana was pleasantly surprised by Ashley's counselor. The woman turned out to be warm and sympathetic, and the whole family became attached to her and looked forward to her visits.

After the conflict with the substitute teacher, Ashley had one other crisis, in November or December. She was going through a phase in which she only picked at her food, eating and drinking very little. Ileana put meat, rice, beans, and potatoes in front of her, but Ashley was interested only in lettuce and cucumbers. Ileana didn't worry too much at first because Ashley had always been petite. But then Ashley started complaining of abdominal pain. At 4 A.M. one night, she woke up screaming. Her mother rushed her to the hospital where she was diagnosed as severely constipated and dehydrated and given intravenous fluids.

That February, Johanna chose Ashley to be in her chorus. Ileana noticed a difference in her daughter right away. Ashley smiled more. She sang at home the songs she was learning, and she demanded that her mother attend the chorus concerts. Ileana had never been involved in school activities before, but the concerts meant so much to Ashley that she had to go. The chorus, Ileana thought, gave Ashley a badly needed outlet for her emotions. She had discovered something she could do well, an activity that brought her recognition and praise.

Ileana reconciled, though uneasily, with her mother, and the children were frequent visitors to Ana's home on Fifth Avenue. Ana cooked plantains and paella for them, bought clothes for the children, took them to the movies, to Disney World, and to see the Christmas window displays at Saks and Macy's and Lord & Taylor. Ileana's latest boyfriend, Zoey, provided the domesticity that Ileana lacked. He was content to keep Ileana company if she wanted to go out, but he was more of a homebody by nature. He took over the cooking and baked bread. Because of his work in the pet shop, the house was always full of animals: Domino, their watchdog, a staffordshire terrier, and Hershey, a chocolate dachshund.

On weekends, the family drove down to the Poconos and spent the day catching turtles and newts to sell to pet shops in New York City, as a way of picking up spending money. On a good day, after just three hours bending over puddles of muddy water, they could clear $120— at $1 per newt. Ileana bought Ashley a one-person rubber raft at Walmart, so she could drift in the lake, scooping up baby turtles with a net when they stretched their heads out of the water.

Zoey caught pumpkinseed, talipia, pickle fish, and sunfish. Ileana joked that if they ever went broke, they could survive in the Poconos by living on fish and wild turkey. Ileana bought computers for the children. Javira liked to read romance novels and papered over her walls with magazine pictures of movie stars. Steven decorated his room with photographs of cars. Ashley liked to listen to her mother's old Jackson Five and Tina Turner albums. Ileana watched *20–20* and *Dateline* and saw the messes very rich people had made of their lives, and she did not feel so bad. You could have money to blow and live in a mansion and still be unhappy.

Ileana felt her family was on the right track, especially Ashley. Ashley had enormous promise. Everybody said so. She had absorbed the residue of sophistication and drive that Ileana had retained from her two intense years at the Baldwin School. She was not the type of child you would expect to find trapped in a ghetto school. She seemed like a girl you might meet ten or fifteen years later at a café in Paris, a bit wistful, but ambitious. Growing up the third of four children by four different fathers, to a mother who was as restless as a gypsy, had not been easy. But maybe the fragility of her position in life, fluttering between being middle class and poor, was what had given her the determination to shine.

CHAPTER THIRTEEN

ভ্ল

"Please Trust Us"

On March 19, 2001, Mr. Benardo sent a letter to the homes of the twenty-four kids Johanna had chosen. Erica Davies got one of them. "Your child has been selected to participate in a trip to Finland . . . ," the letter began. When her mother showed her the letter, Erica got butterflies in her stomach. She didn't dare believe this was happening to her. Things like that didn't happen to kids at P.S. 86, Erica thought. It was probably some project they had cooked up to get the kids' hopes up, to make them feel good, a motivational tool that would come to nothing in the end. She had been disappointed before by adults who made promises and didn't keep them. This letter was like those envelopes filled with prize coupons for homes and cars and vacations that come in the mail crowing, "You're a winner," then you find out there are all kinds of strings attached. It might not be definite, just sort of an idea.

But it was definite.

❧

Well in advance of the trip, Mr. Benardo circulated a Question and Answer sheet, on his official stationery, headed "The Kingsbridge Heights School." As in other schools throughout New York City, the numbered shorthand is the designation most often used by parents, teachers, and students at a school in ordinary conversation. But on official letterhead, which calls for more gravitas, the ceremonial name traditionally comes first. The Kingsbridge Heights School is one of the more humble names in a city of schools commemorating heroes from the Wright Brothers to Martin Luther King Jr. Some communities have even opted to change the names of their schools, replacing heroes they consider outdated with more relevant ones. P.S. 86 has been content to remain a school named after a neighborhood. But in its austerity, the name conveys a certain dignity. No one will ever accuse the Kingsbridge Heights School of falling victim to trendiness and fads.

The Q&A, one page, double-sided, covered all the nuts and bolts questions. Who will participate? When will they go? Where will they go? Will a child ever be left alone? The informational sheet assures parents that there would be no co-ed slumber parties. No hanky panky. Sleeping quarters would be separated by sex and closely supervised by staff.

To those who might question the educational value of a trip abroad, Mr. Benardo promised that the children would be required to keep journals of their daily activities and thoughts, and noted that they would be visiting a local elementary school. What could be more educational than visiting a school? It was a section that seemed calculated to satisfy the most knee-jerk of bureaucrats at the nether levels of the Board of Education. As always, Mr. Benardo treated his largely invisible bosses the way a parish priest accommodates the power of the Cardinal who exercises ultimate control over his livelihood, but has only the most glancing knowledge of its everyday exigencies—with a kind of pained resignation.

Along the same lines, Mr. Benardo assured anyone who might care that standardized tests would not be overlooked, that they'd be administered before departure. They would learn the results after they returned. Sacrifice the system's high standards in the name of fun and games? Johanna thought sarcastically. Banish the thought.

To the children at P.S. 86, the standardized tests were no laughing matter. They mattered a great deal.

Someone like Ashley, who was literate, quick-witted, but inconsistent—capable of earning good marks one day and failing the next—would rise or fall on the basis of her standardized test scores. If her math and reading scores were good, they would compensate for poor grades and allow her to be promoted to the next grade. If they were bad, she was sentenced to be left behind.

Tests had become more important than ever during the years that Johanna was at P.S. 86. While Mayor Giuliani was touting his commitment to the arts, far away in Albany, Richard P. Mills, the state's education commissioner, was ushering in a new era of judging schools by their scores on standardized tests.

Mills was as understated and wooden as chancellor Crew was charismatic and impetuous. (In a gesture that mixed modesty, self-confidence, and skepticism toward his chosen profession, Mills disdained being addressed as "Dr.," saying his master's degree in business had been more demanding than his Ph.D. in education.) Appointed at about the same time as Crew, Mills set his sights on fixing failing schools and upholding high standards for teachers and students. His most controversial initiative, mirroring standards movements in other states like Texas, Massachusetts, and Florida, was to require more rigorous testing of students in fourth and eighth grades and to raise the standards for high school graduation.

New York City and State had always had a test-driven system, in which high school students had to pass either a Regents examination, for an honors diploma, or a Regents Competency Test, for a basic diploma, in order to graduate. But it was widely acknowledged that the competency tests were pitched at no more than an eighth-grade standard, if that, and some critics argued that they gave teachers an excuse to let students slide through school without the skills they needed to make it in the job market. Mills and the state Board of Regents, who appointed him, argued that New York, with its long tradition of testing, should stick to the basic scheme of graduation tests, but make the tests harder and more meaningful. To pass them, children would have to begin preparing as early as elementary school.

Mills introduced the new reading and mathematics tests in fourth and eighth grades. These tests were designed to be the building blocks on the way to the examinations for high school graduation. The old tests had asked students to choose from multiple-choice answers or fill-in blanks. Like all multiple-choice tests, they encouraged students to guess at answers and did not reveal individual students' strengths or weaknesses in any way that could then be used by teachers to adjust their lessons. The new tests required students to read fairly long passages from literature, history, or scientific publications. They then had to outline important points and write short answers to a series of questions, culminating with longer essays that demonstrated mastery of concepts like the main idea, supporting details, and the creation of a narrative with a beginning, middle, and end. The English test lasted three days and even included a day when the teacher read a passage out loud and students had to take notes and answer questions about what they heard. Similarly, the new math tests gave points not just for right answers but for clear explanations of how the students arrived at the answers.

The tests had an immediate effect on curriculum, forcing teachers to think about genres of literature—like fables and nonfiction—and to focus on writing skills as they never had before. Because the test results were published in daily newspapers statewide, they also sparked implicit rivalry among schools, school districts, and communities to show who had the best scores. Real estate brokers have long understood the relationship between school reputation and home prices. Now the state Education Department would take that a step further and use test scores to determine which schools were doing their job and which were not. Those found to be lacking would be put on academic probation, alarming parents and humiliating principals and teachers.

Benardo felt the testing pressure no less than others. One time, when test scores showed a decline, he hectored the entire school—explicitly addressing teachers as well as students—over the loudspeaker. Benardo told everyone that trips and other fun events would be canceled until the teachers buckled down and helped their students do better on the tests. Many of the teachers felt humiliated by this public dressing down.

Johanna dared to hope that her music lessons might help the children score higher on the tests. She had heard Project Arts contractors argue that music developed literacy and math skills like classification, sequence, pattern identification. She wanted to believe that.

⁄𝒪

The families were told that the mid-May weather in Aland would be in the 50s during the day, low 40s during the evening. They should pack appropriate clothing, including some kind of rain protection. But at an assembly before the trip, Mr. Benardo admonished the parents that this did not mean they had to go out and buy new clothes.

"If anybody here has a problem with clothes, don't keep quiet about it. I can get it," Mr. Benardo said.

Although he didn't realize it until later, when the children unpacked their bags in Finland, many of the families proceeded to ignore his advice, spending hundreds of dollars on practically new wardrobes.

The children would be representing the Bronx and their families in a new land, and they should make the best impression possible, their parents reasoned. By the time the day of the trip arrived, the children had stocked up on not just clean underwear, nighties, and pajama shirts and trousers fresh out of the plastic wrappers, to maintain their modesty, but enough designer labels to establish their status as respectable citizens: Gap, DKNY, Old Navy were well represented.

Despite the high-minded vow to make the children write journals, Mr. Benardo had his own ideas about how to make the trip an enriching experience. For one thing, if the children saw a McDonald's in Finland, he warned them in his sternest voice, they would not be permitted to eat there. They were not going to learn anything about other cultures by going to a foreign country and reverting to American junk food.

Johanna briefed them on the kind of food they could expect to eat in a Finnish household. When they woke up the morning after their arrival, she said, they shouldn't expect dry cereal, only Muesli, boiled eggs, and rye bread. "In Finland and Sweden it's salt that counts," she said. "You'll have meat for breakfast. Bread with butter. Ham, pepperoni, and cheese. Maybe tomatoes and cucumbers. The word 'smorgasbord' is a Swedish word."

She urged them to bring a gift for their hosts, just a trinket, preferably a souvenir of New York. Then she launched into a lecture on the proper way to make their beds, half a reminder that they should be thoughtful enough to do so, half a warning that the bed-covers would be different from what they were used to. In Finland, people didn't put a top-sheet on their beds, she said. They slept under down blankets, covered in a big cloth envelope. "You turn the cover inside out first," she explained, gesturing with her hands since there was no bed in the school auditorium. "Then you pull it over the quilt like a sausage skin." Once you've laid the completed quilt on the bed, she continued, you don't just let the edges hang down. You fold them under, so they look neat. She sounded like an IKEA catalogue, which probably would have been useful in illustrating her instructions. As it was, the children listened politely but looked baffled.

This wealth of practical information left some of the parents dissatisfied. Several sought out Mr. Benardo for personal reassurances that their children would be well taken care of. One was Keshauna Sanders' mother, Janet. "I'll only send her if you can guarantee her safety," she said, wringing her hands. "Nothing better happen to her."

But what could she be afraid of? Mr. Benardo wanted to know. That the plane would crash?

No, it wasn't that, Janet said. What was bothering her was that Keshauna was 13, a sweet young girl who had never been very far from home. Janet wouldn't even send her to a playdate without checking on the other family first, and here she was sending her an ocean away, to stay in the home of a family she had never met—"especially with a man in it." Men had started to notice Keshauna when she walked down the street. How could Janet be sure this man was not a child molester? How could she be sure she could trust him?

Mr. Benardo thought this over. "Well," he finally said, looking faintly amused. "The only thing I can't do is a police background check." Janet laughed in spite of herself.

There was another thing, she persisted. The dark-skinned children from the Bronx would stand out in fair-skinned Finland. What if the Finns were prejudiced?

Mr. Benardo promised to check on Keshauna personally, and to give the parents the telephone numbers where their children would be.

Some of the Finns expressed similar doubts. Their image of the Bronx had been formed by *Fort Apache, the Bronx*, and by dimly remembered footage of Jimmy Carter strolling along Charlotte Street and turning the South Bronx into an international shorthand for urban abandonment. It didn't matter that P.S. 86 was in the northwest Bronx, or that suburban-style tract housing had risen from the ashes of Charlotte Street. Certain names—the Bronx, Detroit, Cleveland—connoted wild, violent, filthy places. Aland was just the opposite: orderly, secure, clean, comfortable, prosperous. For children unfortunate enough to be growing up in the Bronx, ignorance might be the best antidote. Why give them a taste of champagne and strawberries, when you would be sending them back to subsist on water and dry toast? "Do you really think it's such a good idea to bring Bronx kids over here to see the way we live?" one friend asked Johanna. "They might be jealous."

Johanna knew this was an exaggeration, but she did worry that there was a kernel of truth in this notion, that the Bronx children would feel inferior when they saw the high standard of living in Aland: the neatly clipped lawns, litter-free streets, freshly painted houses. Then she thought about how she felt every time she went home. Home is always going to be home, and your parents are always going to be your parents that you love more than anybody. It doesn't matter where you come from. You always long for home, whether home is in the middle of the Bronx or an island in Scandinavia.

Everybody was on their best behavior. Only the spirited Ashley could not contain herself.

As her class lined up to go down to the lunchroom one day, Ashley noticed that the teacher, Miss Bonfiglio, had left her purse behind on the desk. When the class reached the stairs, Ashley slipped out of the line, turned back and crept into the empty classroom. She rummaged in the teacher's purse for her wallet, took out $7, and stuffed the bills in her jeans. She was careful to leave some money behind, to throw off suspicion. Seven dollars was so little. Miss Bonfiglio would never notice. Then she dashed downstairs and caught up with the other kids in the cafeteria.

While they were eating, Miss Bonfiglio must have remembered her purse, and she sent Lauren upstairs to find it. Then the kids went to the auditorium for the numbing ritual of waiting for lunch period to be over. As the other kids read, talked, and slept, Ashley noticed Miss Bonfiglio come in and call Lauren aside. When Lauren sat down again, she was crying.

"What happened?" Ashley asked. Miss Bonfiglio had accused Lauren of stealing the $7. Ashley felt bad. Lauren was her friend. She didn't like to see her cry.

She wanted to help Lauren, but if she confessed that she had taken the money, she wouldn't get to go to Finland. So she decided to write an anonymous note, promising to give back the $7. She sneaked into the office and shoved the note into Miss Bonfiglio's mail slot.

A couple of days later, Miss Bonfiglio asked Ashley to write down the words that had been in the note. The handwriting matched. "Please don't tell Mr. Benardo," Ashley begged. Miss Bonfiglio said she would wait until after the trip to say anything, but only if Ashley returned the money. This was a problem. Ashley had split the $7 with a friend, and they had already spent it. She had to borrow $7 from another girl. The girl told her mother, who told Benardo, who confronted Ashley.

"Tell me the truth," Mr. Benardo said. No matter what had happened, if she told the truth about it, she could go to Finland. "I didn't do it," Ashley said, staring straight at him, her eyes glazed with tears. She was lying. But Mr. Benardo believed her, or acted as if he did. "All the teachers think you should go," he said gently. "So I'm letting you go."

One day just before the trip, as the chorus rehearsed, Jamie began sobbing during his solo and had to stop. By now Johanna was used to this, not only from Jamie. At nearly every concert, one of the boys in the chorus—it was always a boy—broke down. Johanna had stopped being alarmed by it. She had come to expect it. These children had so much stored up inside them, and they were not allowed to show their feelings, especially the boys. When they sang, the music touched something inside them, and they started to cry.

It was as if Jamie intuitively understood the foreign words. In Finland, Johanna predicted, it would be the audience that would start to cry when Jamie, in his chillingly high, unearthly voice, began to sing: "I can sail without wind; I can sail without oars. But I cannot part from my friend without tears."

⟳

"The kids are going to be singing in a church, right?" Sonia Goyco demanded, accosting Johanna after school one day. Sonia's daughter, Lissette Alvarez, was in the chorus.

"What are they going to wear?"

"Well," Johanna replied, caught off-guard. "P.S. 86 T-shirts, I guess."

Sonia didn't like the idea. The kids couldn't perform in a foreign country wearing the ratty old T-shirts, washed and faded, that they had worn on a million ordinary everyday field trips. It was embarrassing.

"They need gowns," Sonia said. "Choir gowns."

She had a friend who was a seamstress. This woman could make them.

"That would be nice," Johanna said, hesitantly. "But I have to ask Mr. Benardo."

Absolutely not, Mr. Benardo said. There was nothing wrong with T-shirts. They showed school spirit. This was not a professional chorus, and they would not pretend to be one. Besides, he wasn't going to authorize spending scarce school funds on gowns.

Sonia was disappointed. It wasn't right, she said. All the mothers wanted their children to have gowns. Don't worry about the money, she told Johanna. Her friend didn't need to be paid; she would sew them for free.

"OK," Johanna told Sonia. "Just don't say anything to Mr. Benardo for now. I'm sure he will change his mind."

What harm could it do? The gowns would make the kids feel good, and their mothers would be happy. These mothers could be like guerilla warriors when it came to defending their children. Johanna knew better than to cross them.

As D-Day, Friday, May 11, approached, Mr. Benardo began feeling uneasy about the bus he had hired to take the children to the airport. They had managed to raise $18,174 in airfare, and yet could not cough up the last $500 for the bus fare. Each student needed to bring in $22 to pay for the bus—not too bad, he thought, for out-of-pocket expenses. But a week before the trip, they were dragging their heels; only one student had obliged.

"There is no money coming in from parents, so I guess the bus trip is canceled," he announced at an after-school meeting with the children and their families. "It's terminal 8. I'm telling you this because I can't tell you enough times, and I don't want any confusion. The trip is eight hours. You've got to sleep on the plane. If you're taking the train to the airport, you should leave at 1:30. If you're going by car, 2:30. My biggest concern is that we'll get there and you'll be tired and start crying and say you want to go home to America. That's why we picked you."

Jeremy piped up that he did not have to sleep on the plane, because he could stay up all day and all night.

"You'll be exhausted," Mr. Benardo assured him. "You'll be sleeping and snoring with your mouth open on the plane."

He felt guilty about canceling the bus, which is why he had hinted that he might change his mind if the parents forked over the bus fare. The parents at P.S. 86 were accustomed to hardship, to being told things were impossible to accomplish. Rather than rallying and coming up with the money, they reacted with passive resignation. He imagined parents stuck in traffic jams or taking a wrong turn on the way to the airport and missing the flight. Some of them did not even own cars. Car fare to Kennedy cost more than $22, so the bus was a pretty good deal. He imagined half of the kids being left behind. What a nightmarish turn of events that would be after they had gotten so far. Three days before the trip, he had to concede that the parents had called his bluff. It was time to run up the white flag. Maybe $22 was a bigger obstacle than he had realized; he couldn't let $500 spoil the whole trip. He would pay for the bus out of school funds.

A note went home to parents (not guardians, Mr. Benardo was not the type to be distracted by politically correct jargon; either you had parents or you didn't and if you didn't, you still knew what he meant), apprising them of the latest developments.

Dear Parents:

After giving the issue considerable thought and after hearing from you I have decided to provide free bus transportation from P.S. 86 to the Finnair terminal at JFK Airport. The bus *will not* wait at JFK Airport and will not transport you back to P.S. 86. Any parent who sent $22.00 for bus transportation will have that money returned. Remember, though, you will have to return to the Bronx from JFK Airport on your own. The bus will leave P.S. 86 promptly at 1:45 p.m. The bus will not wait for any latecomer.

If you have any questions or concerns please contact me.

Respectfully,
Sheldon Benardo
Principal

Shortly after, a second, more emphatic note went home, this time signed by Johanna. It was strategically studded with capital letters and exclamation points, a classic of its kind, a bureaucratic parody straight out of *Up the Down Staircase*. Sometimes you couldn't overstate the obvious.

"IMPORTANT MESSAGE TO ALL PARENTS OF CHILDREN GOING TO FINLAND!"

"There is a bus that leaves P.S. 86 on Friday at 2:00 PM. It is free, and there is plenty of room for luggage. There will also be room for ONE adult per student, but the bus is NOT going back to P.S. 86. The parent has to return at own cost.

Therefore, WE STRONGLY URGE you to say good-bye to your child at P.S. 86!!! We will do our farewells at 1:30 PM. There are many reasons why it is best to have the WHOLE group on the bus.

1. If you get stuck in traffic with your own car, the plane will NOT wait for you!

2. If the BUS gets stuck in traffic, the plane will wait for us.

3. Airports are chaotic. There will be no time to spend with your child there.

PLEASE TRUST US.

Wednesday night, Mr. Benardo called Johanna at her apartment, the first time in three and a half years that he had ever done so. He was going to be absent the next day, he said, because he needed to spend some time with his wife before the trip. "Let me know if you need anything," he said brusquely. Johanna was touched by his concern. She was happy to get that phone call. He was reaching out. Even though he addressed her in his gruff Mr. Benardo way, it still warmed her.

On Friday, nearly all the parents gathered at the school to say good-bye to their children. There were hugs, kisses, and a few tears, and Mr. Benardo watched with satisfaction as every last child boarded the bus. Many of the parents boarded with them. As the bus driver gunned his engine, the rest of the parents jumped into their cars. The bus headed off to Kennedy International Airport with a caravan of private cars in pursuit, like the members of a wedding or a funeral.

CHAPTER FOURTEEN

✍

On the Road

With the bus full to the gills and Johanna in charge, Mr. Benardo was only too glad to drive to the airport in the tranquillity of his own car. There was a limit to how much self-sacrifice could be demanded of any commander-in-chief. He did not ask for luxury, just a little peace of mind away from the chaos of twenty-four overexcited fifth- and sixth-graders who were no doubt at this moment climbing the seats of the bus while Johanna tried to harness their nervous energy by leading them in a chorus of "Siyahamba."

He, on the other hand, could concentrate on meeting them at the Finnair terminal. He eased his well-worn green Buick out of the parking space reserved for him by a crudely hand-lettered sign saying PRiNCiPAL ONLy, wired to the chain-link fence and backed onto Reservoir Avenue. The spring weather had been unseasonably hot; he could tell an August heat wave was in the cards, just when his summer break would come due. It was only mid-May but it felt like mid-

July already. The flower beds in front of the school had started looking droopy by 11 A.M. these last few days. Ted Pannullo was probably paying overtime to keep his precious impatiens watered, on top of the usual chores like mopping the cafeteria. In the front seat next to Mr. Benardo was Emily Coca, Mr. Benardo's spiky-haired, no-nonsense guidance counselor. There weren't many people he trusted enough to let down his guard around, but Emily was one, maybe the only one. She didn't put on any airs. She could keep a confidence. She had been a hairdresser once, and had the hairdresser's knack of sharing intimacies, helping you feel good about yourself. "I've got a Gund dog here," Emily said, grinning, as she pulled a little caramel stuffed animal out of the carry-on bag at her feet. "And I've got a bunch of beanie babies, in case any of the kids get homesick on the flight." She had thrown in a bottle of Advil to soothe her own headaches. She pulled out a cellphone. "I just need to leave a message for my daughter before we go," she said, dialing her home number.

The air conditioning on the Buick was busted, so they rolled down the side windows, which wasn't much of an improvement. The heat radiating off the asphalt streets poured in the windows as if they had opened the door of an oven. "Remind me never to go to Finland at 2 o'clock on a Friday afternoon," Shelly cracked as they crawled across the pot-holed Major Deegan surrounded by cars like a crust of bread by a swarm of minnows. "I hope the transmission is going to hold up."

They talked shop for a few minutes, in the desultory, abbreviated code of a husband and wife, two people who know each other so well they can finish each other's sentences, fretting over their wayward children.

"Vincent's older sister is beating him up again," Shelly muttered.

"I guess you can't get his mother to come in, huh?" Emily commiserated.

Shelly had no children of his own, and he followed the ups and downs, the neuroses and accomplishments, of his students and staff as closely as if they were his own family. He was not always easy to get along with, but he was a shrewd observer of others, and had the mental energy to devote to the task that a family man might not.

The test scores at Public School 86 might not be the best, but no one could question Shelly's dedication. He hadn't been away from P.S. 86 for more than two days in a row in his ten years as principal. Handing the keys over to the five assistant principals left in charge during his absence (he had named one of them to be the temporary No. 1 among equals, the secretary of state) made him feel a little emotional, a mix of anticipation and gut-churning anxiety. Like a homeowner leaving his precious house in the care of a neighbor for a few days, he imagined coming back to find it robbed and ransacked.

Maybe he appreciated Emily Coca's earthiness because he felt no need to show off himself. He rarely wore a tie at school, though he usually wore a sports jacket. He had dressed for the flight more or less the way he had told the kids to dress during one of the pre-trip assemblies in the school auditorium: "sweatshirt, comfortable shoes, long-sleeved shirt, jacket."

He had on faded jeans, sneakers, and a baseball cap. But instead of a sweatshirt, he wore a slithery black satin bomber jacket with the legend "Only Natural Highs" embroidered in soaring script across the back. He felt like the Fonz, or maybe Al D'Amato pretending to be cool. Except the jacket was a private joke. He wouldn't normally go out and buy a bomber jacket. With Shelly, a certain deadpan humor, a sardonic twist, was always preferable to straightforward self-expression, even in fashion. The jacket was a souvenir from one of those anti-drug campaigns the public schools had been forced to endure, to little evident effect. But it had not originally belonged to Shelly. A teacher had come to him in search of a better assignment. "What will you give me for it?" Mr. Benardo had asked. The teacher got the assignment, Shelly walked away with the jacket. That pretty much summed up Shelly Benardo; he was an operator.

Frankly, he had underestimated Johanna when she first arrived. He had seen a lot of eager young teachers come and go. There was no reason to think she would be different. What was it that James Mason, the washed-up impresario, had seen in the unknown Judy Garland in *A Star Is Born*? "That little something extra." Maybe Johanna had it.

Still, this trip was a big responsibility, and he wondered if he had made the right decision, had been too easily caught up in the excitement of planning it. As he thought ahead now, driving to the airport, he was feeling—oppressed would be too strong a word—but worried. They had eight days ahead of them. It's not that he expected a catastrophe. But the most mundane occurrences could trip them up. Somebody, a child or a teacher, could suffer a sprained ankle or a broken leg. A kid might not be able to sleep at night, or might not like the food. He had had to speak to many of the parents—Janet Sanders was by no means unique—to convince them that he could take their kids 4,100 miles away and bring them back in one piece. He was concerned that the staff would burn out. They had just been through a stressful period of preparing for and administering standardized tests. That was why he had favored young, single teachers in deciding who would go on the trip. "I tried to pick people with vitality," he said. "Everybody had an understanding of what was expected of them on this trip."

As he had anticipated, the presence of doting parents added to the chaos at the airport, as they snapped pictures and cluttered up the aisles, unwilling to leave until their children had been ushered out of sight. What was really just an ordinary school field trip, only a little longer and farther afield than normal, had been turned into some kind of cataclysmic event, as if the children were being sent away indefinitely. Mr. Benardo stood silently on the sidelines, squinting through half-closed eyes in a posture of pantherlike readiness, as Johanna, her face already creased with stress and fatigue, gathered passports and consulted with a Finnair representative. Watching the scene, he was struck not only by the tearful parting scenes with the families but by the quantity of luggage Johanna had brought along for herself: seven big suitcases. She parceled them out among the children to avoid over-weight penalties on the flight. They were packed, she told the children, with her books and winter clothing.

Strange, Mr. Benardo pondered. Wouldn't she be needing winter clothing in New York? He filed this thought in the back of his mind. There was no point in confronting her amid the chaos of the trip; the fall semester was still months away. The other adults stood by, letting Johanna handle the arrangements. Margaret Bartelme waited next to Dorothy Pack, who looked serenely out of place, dressed for much finer company than they in Jackie-O sunglasses and Cole-Haan clogs. Mr. Benardo privately resented Dorothy's presence ever so slightly. She wasn't part of the team and added to the pressure of the trip, making him feel judged by an outsider. But it would have been churlish, let alone polit-ically risky, to say no to the wife of the school's wealthy benefactor.

Johanna herded the children to the gate for Finnair Flight 006 to Helsinki, their red backpacks bobbing behind them, while Vincent's mother cried inconsolably, as if she might never see him again.

The Finnair agent took up the rear and cackled at his favorite joke: "We are sending you to HEL."

PART TWO

❧

Aland, Finland

CHAPTER FIFTEEN

℘

Homecoming

"My hair is turning blond," Eralis Ventura, a somber 11-year-old, said over and over to anyone who would listen, her new sneakers squeaking on the gray cobble stones worn smooth by the centuries. "See?" She lifted the long, wavy strands of her jet-black hair to show the coppery tinges at the ends. Then in consternation, she pondered the chocolate brown backs of her thin small hands. "I'm dark now," she said apologetically, "because I just got back from DR," the Dominican Republic.

Of all the kids, Eralis was most defensive about her dark skin when the students arrived in Helsinki. They had an eight-hour layover in the capital city before taking off in a prop-plane for Johanna's home base of Aland. But Eralis was not the only one to feel as if she had arrived in an alien land. The children realized immediately that they had crossed a global racial dividing line. People stared at them; some smiled kindly, realizing that they were a school group. In New York, there were enough dark faces on the street for them to feel part of the crowd. Here, on the streets of Helsinki, the only dark faces they saw as they strolled through the old city were the Andean men in traditional fedoras playing folk music on wooden pipes in the street bazaar, a scene that could have been lifted right out of Times Square. Everyone else was blond, or red-headed. Especially red-headed—stunning shades of strawberry blonde, coppery red, and even blood orange, which would have looked exotic back home but seemed to be completely within the realm of normality here.

They were less impressed with the buildings, which, though painted in austere Scandinavian ochres, browns, reds, and oranges, to the eyes of the children were just big and old. Buildings in New York were big and old, too; there was nothing special about that. Johanna and four children in her care wandered into Stockmann's, the big department store, filled with glittering American-style displays of housewares and electronics, for an orange juice. Johanna taught the children their first Swedish words: "Tack," for thank you, "Tack-tack!," if they were very grateful; "hej," for hello, "hej da," for good-bye. That should come in handy.

Eralis nestled playfully into Johanna's lap as they sipped their drinks in a small juice bar. She wondered what her host family would look like. She predicted—correctly, it later turned out—that they would have blue eyes and blond hair, "and be white."

"Do you know, when I was a kid I always wished I had brown eyes and brown hair," Johanna said.

But her attempt at solidarity was lost on Eralis, who suggested that if Johanna sincerely wanted to be dark, that shouldn't be so hard to accomplish. "You could paint your skin brown, color your hair, and put on contacts," she advised.

Was Eralis's malaise a bad omen for the trip? Johanna wondered. Although some of the kids had traveled before, they had always gone to a familiar place, in the company of family. During this trip, the kids would be spending the first night in Aland on their own with the Finnish host families, who were total strangers. There would be no familiar adults there to help them adjust. Johanna and Margaret would be staying at the Grussner home, the rest of the faculty in a hotel. Then for the next five nights, everyone but Johanna would transfer to the Lutheran campground; that should be easier. Finally, the kids would return to the host families and the faculty to the hotel for the seventh and last night in Aland.

Then there were the expectations. They had all come with such high expectations—perhaps no one more so than Johanna. What would her hometown think of these kids she had cajoled them into embracing? Would they measure up? Would she? Would her friends and family like them? She couldn't bear to think of the kids disappointing anyone—or being disappointed.

∾

At 6:14 P.M. Saturday, the two-propeller plane touched down in Mariehamn, the Aland capital, after a half-hour flight, and the children wiped the sleep from their eyes. Johanna strode across the tarmac into the boxy, small-town terminal and, with a flourish, announced to the chorus, straggling behind her: "This is my land." She stopped in front of a taciturn man with a full head of straight white hair, a Viking fringe of beard, and rectangular steel-rimmed bifocals. A rust-colored, fringed suede jacket covered his shoulders.

"This is my father," she said, breaking into a little-girl grin that momentarily washed away all the strain of the last sixteen hours.

"This is my daughter," Ulf Grussner responded drolly, a slight smile flickering across his face as he stepped out of the crowd of curious onlookers—small businessmen, bemused, weather-beaten farmers, the crow's-feet deeply etched around their eyes, the local dentist, Mikael Lagstrom, a cheerful fellow in a short-sleeved button-down shirt, who informed anyone who would listen that the chorus had come to the right place because everyone in Aland loved to sing. He himself, he said, belonged to a sea chantey group. Standing shyly in the background were the long-awaited host families, a bevy of Lutheran church members, younger on average than the rest of the bystanders, and, indeed, strikingly blond, blue-eyed, and pale-skinned.

In a reprise of the motley caravan that had accompanied their departure in the Bronx, the chorus took off in a red bus belonging to Johanna's father, with him at the wheel, while the host families took up the pursuit in their cars. "Should we count?" Johanna asked Mr. Benardo, her teacher-reflexes kicking in. "I think we should," he replied. Twenty-four. "We're golden," the principal said.

Johanna stood in the front of the bus, facing back toward the passengers, like the tour guide she had once been, and began a running patter on the sights. They had arrived during the spring thaw, and the embankments bloomed with tiny blue and white windflowers that were Johanna's father's favorites. "I can't get him to visit New York in the springtime," Johanna told the children, speaking languidly through a hand-held mike from her position in front of the bus, "because he says he can't leave the flowers even for one day." The roads looked pinkish, the pavement tinged with Aland's native red granite. Tall forests of pine and spruce stretched out all around them. The landscape was nothing like Helsinki—or New York. There were no tall buildings.

The tallest towers were the steeples, topped with black iron crosses, of the massive medieval churches. The formidable churches, built of rustic stone blocks, dotted the landscape, and seemed designed as fortresses against infidels and monuments to withstand the centuries. The houses were more modest. Most were small cottages made of wood, often painted either yellow or red, with blue doors. Yellow was the color of the aristocracy, because yellow paint had been more expensive in the old days; so yellow traditionally designated the house of a sea captain or perhaps a minister. Red was the cheaper, workingman's color, marking a farmer's house. Though these days you could no longer tell the occupants by the color of their house, the traditional colors had been maintained. The blue doors were reputed to ward off trolls, evil spirits, and—more prosaic but just as much of a nuisance—flies.

The lifestyle, though it looked affluent enough, seemed remarkably simple and rural. The fields had been plowed, but nothing was coming up yet from the furrows. Nearly every backyard boasted a wooden birdhouse, the varying dimensions and off-kilter angles suggesting they were often homemade. Paved bicycle paths criss-crossed Mariehamn and meandered far into the countryside, and Alanders appeared to ride their bikes as naturally as Americans drive cars. A gaggle of three-speed bikes had been parked, all blithely unlocked, outside Sparhallen, the town supermarket, their wire baskets empty as if waiting to be stuffed with the Spartan but wholesome necessities of Scandinavian life: tins of "Fisherman's Friend" lozenges, medicinally flavored with tangy anise, tubes of salty pink cod-roe paste, rock-hard rye crackers, boxes of raspberries and cartons of sterilized milk, which could be stored without refrigeration. There were few people out and about as the bus turned on Nygatan.

"This is one of the main streets, but there aren't many people out now because it's 6 in the afternoon. At 2 o'clock in the morning, there will be a lot of people out here," Johanna said, still narrating the impromptu tour. After midnight, the bars would be packed. "I've got to warn you that it's going to be pretty much bright all night, so you better cover your windows with the curtains. You're going to wake up early otherwise."

Looking around at the quaint streets of Mariehamn, which appeared to have changed little in 100 years, Mr. Benardo realized he had worried in vain that the children would be tempted by McDonald's. Helsinki was one thing, but since arriving in Aland, they had not seen a single fast-food outlet. This was small-town stuff.

❧

When Alanders say their home is a special place, they are not just being chauvinist. Aland, an archipelago of 6,500 rocks and islets (the largest being Fasta Aland, the Main Island), has just 25,000 inhabitants but a strategic location between Sweden and Finland that has made it one of the more unusual and coddled ethnic minority enclaves in the world. From the thirteenth century until 1809, Finland, including the Aland Islands, was part of Sweden. But after several wars against Russia, Sweden had to give up Finland, and Aland became part of the Russian Grand Duchy of Finland. As the Russian empire disintegrated, Finland became an independent republic.

In 1921, the League of Nations, eager to bolster the young Finnish nation, ignored the protests of Aland and granted the islands to Finland rather than Sweden, their historic motherland. But in a concession to the Swedish-speaking population, the League of Nations decreed that Alanders would have greater autonomy than other Finns.

As a result, Aland has held a privileged position within the Finnish state. Aland flies its own flag, which looks much like Sweden's blue and yellow flag, but with a red cross superimposed. The islands retain the Swedish language, culture and customs, and most Alanders, Johanna among them, speak and write Finnish with substantially less fluency than Swedish. Aland controls its own education, social services, and health care, while Helsinki is responsible for trade and foreign policy. Aland is a neutral, demilitarized zone.

Shipping and tourism are the archipelago's main industries. Finland negotiated a tax-free status for Aland when it joined the European Union, which turned Mariehamn into a hub for Baltic Sea ferries selling duty-free beer, liquor, cigarettes, candy, and toys. In Sweden, teetotalling laws have made a pint of beer nearly as expensive as a hospital visit in the socialized medical system. So Swedes often take the ferries just for a brief drinking vacation. As the Bronx kids were already sensing as they rode Uffe's bus, Aland is affluent, even by Finland's high standards; unemployment is low and poverty virtually unknown. (Perhaps reflecting that affluence, studies have shown that Aland's inhabitants are healthier than those of the mainland, suffering from a lower incidence of diabetes, heart disease, and mental illness.)

All these indicators, from prosperity to good health, put Aland firmly on the opposite end of the socioeconomic spectrum from the Bronx. So from the moment they touched down in Mariehamn, the children had crossed an invisible divide.

Yet as a chorus, the Bronx kids had come to the right place. Music is an obsession peculiar to much of Aland. So many Alanders like to sing that in 1996, they gathered together to set a world record, recognized by the *Guinness Book of World Records*, for the longest singing chain ever. To achieve this distinction 4,000 Alanders (including Johanna's uncle) formed a one-kilometer singing chain along Esplanade Avenue in Mariehamn, and sang (exactly what, was not recorded) under the direction of Kaj-Gustav Sandholm, the music director of Mariehamn Church, and twelve conductors linked by earphones.

The first stop after the children arrived was a small welcoming ceremony at the white-steepled parish hall in downtown Mariehamn. The "forsamling," or parish, was an overwhelming spiritual presence in the town, a center of community and a repository of shared values. Out of Mariehamn's 10,000 residents, 9,400 belonged to the four Lutheran churches.

The host families had already arrived and stood in the circular driveway waiting. They were young people in their 20s and 30s, many with babies in their arms and toddlers at their sides, who had grown up with Johanna in her Finnish gospel choir, Intermezzo. A table had been spread with a vase of daffodils, a bowl of fruit, frilly sliced cucumbers and sliced tomatoes, open-faced ham and cheese sandwiches, and, to drink, hot tea. When someone remarked on the hospitality, not just here but for the five days that the children would stay at the Lutheran campground, the vicar, Jan-Erik Karlstrom, a rail-thin, bearded, 40-ish man in tortoise-shell glasses, said dryly, "I think children need food," as if to point out that in this way, children everywhere were exactly the same and that not to have fed them would have violated a basic law of nature, let alone decency.

Mr. Benardo engaged the vicar, a fellow keeper of souls, in a conversation about the managerial demands of his parish. Vicar Karlstrom, the principal learned, had been promoted from parish pastor in a county of 600 people, where all 600 belonged to the congregation, to the spiritual leader of a town of 10,000, a scale commensurate with the size of the task Mr. Benardo faced at P.S. 86. Mr. Benardo sympathized. "Everyone you see everyday has come to you possibly in a crisis," he reflected, marveling at the responsibility his Finnish counterpart faced. Vicar Karlstrom lamented the difficulty of keeping his flock focused on values like raising moral children and being loyal to their community, rather than on more material concerns like making a high salary. Despite the relative affluence, opportunity was limited in Aland, he said, and many of the younger people emigrated. "It's an island. You have always to think how do we survive."

The reception was unstintingly generous, but not without a touch of chauvinism. Like Johanna, the vicar had an almost mystical belief in the transformative power of this small, rocky archipelago, which, unlike big cities, had accommodated rather than conquered nature. "This is the best month in Aland, because of the flowers and the birds and the seabirds, when the trees are not naked and nature is coming up for a new life," Vicar Karlstrom said in his awkward but eloquent English. "Here it's free. It's near nature. Their life is different. I have never been in the Bronx, or in New York. I shouldn't say this. But it's what I believe."

Or perhaps he intuited that having come this far on a trip that had at first seemed preposterous, the children were about to embark on an inner voyage that was much more profound than the number of miles

they had covered. They had been granted seven days of possibilities—
possibilities for doing good in the world, social possibilities and personal possibilities—that were greater than any they had dreamed of at
home in the Bronx. "I think if the children are going to speak with the
children here, they will find something," the vicar mused. "But I think
they can't understand it until many, many years later."

༚

CHAPTER SIXTEEN

The Law of Jante

The children split up in twos, threes, and fours for that first night with their host families. The original plan had been to organize twelve pairs of families for twelve pairs of children. But even in Aland, the supply of altruism was not unlimited. People had their own lives to live. "The excuses were many," Siv Hallback, who was in charge of enlisting families, later recalled. "They had so much to do. They had their own families to do stuff with. They were going to their summer cottages for the weekend. They had to clean the house." Some people apologized that their houses were too small to offer separate bedrooms for the guests, although Siv tried to reassure them that was not necessary, even a mattress on the floor would do. She had heard, she told them, that one of the boys, Pierre, was one of nine siblings, so surely he for one would not be too picky about having his own room.

Was it really the call of the country house, the dust bunnies under the bed, that held the Finnish families back? Or was it something more subtle, maybe not quite conscious, the discomfiture of having strange children from a far-off land invade the sanctity of their homes and families? Not that they expected the Bronx kids to steal their jewelry or bully their children, not exactly. They didn't really know what to expect, and that was the problem. They knew only that these children didn't look like their children, probably didn't eat or dress or live like their children. They wouldn't know what to do with them, even though it was just for one night.

Ultimately, Siv recruited nine host families, counting her own, representing a range of middle-class professions in Aland.

Tomas Lundberg, a 38-year-old bachelor, the department secretary for the Aland Department of Social Affairs, Health, and the Environment, loaded four of the boys—Jamie, Vincent, Rickey Colbourne, and Matthew LeBron—into his little red Ford Fiesta and drove them to the house that he shared with his widowed mother, but which was big enough to fit four boys comfortably. The airy, one-story wood and white-brick house, nestled into a landscape of stones and trees, had been designed by Tomas's father, Klas-Erik, a lung doctor. Dr. Lundberg had chosen the architecture, a spare, functional style reminiscent of Frank Lloyd Wright, to show off his collection of paintings by Juhani Linnovaara, the Finnish artist. When the boys arrived, Tomas's mother, Inga, was in the kitchen whisking cream and setting out rice crepes and dried-fruit soup, a traditional Aland appetizer served on festive occasions. Tomas instructed the boys to leave their shoes at the door, showed them the shower where they could wash up, and led them to their rooms, where the beds were made with colorfully printed duvets, tucked under at the sides, just as Johanna had described. "This is my father," he told Matthew, showing him a black-and-white photograph of a stern-visaged man, as if it would have been disrespectful not to introduce the patriarch of the family, even if the old man could not manage to be there in the flesh.

It did not take long for the small-town nature of Aland life to assert itself, the almost incestuous web of connections that Johanna had simultaneously fled from and found herself constantly drawn back to. As the boys made their way to the kitchen, they found Helena Lundberg, with her 14-year-old daughter, Karin, waiting for them. She had come not only as Tomas's elder sister but as an emissary from Johanna's mother, her closest friend. She lived outside of town, "only a kilometer from Johanna's mother," she told them. Helena was so much a part of Johanna's family that she might as well be a fourth sister. In acknowledgment, Johanna's mother had bestowed a nursery nickname on her, Nena.

As Nena introduced her daughter the boys stared frankly at Karin's sunset-red hair. By now, the travelers had come to think of the spectrum from umber to carmine as the ubiquitous national hair-color, an enviably attractive symbol of genetic insularity and, perhaps, superiority. Helena noticed the glances. "It's not natural, of course," she revealed, with a slight stutter. Red hair was the latest Nordic fad, available at the nearest pharmacy. Surely, the Americans had noticed that flaming locks were far less common among Finnish men than Finnish women, an imbalance that defied genetic probability. In one stroke, Nena, a biologist by training, with the empirical mind of a scientist, established her forthright character and slammed shut the hair-color gap between Finns and Americans.

"Your mother called, just half an hour ago," Helena told Vincent. Vincent glowered for a second, then banished the thought of returning the call as reflexively as he would swat a fly landing on his nose. The boys wandered from room to room, silently absorbing their comfortable, uncluttered harmony, the blond pine and oak floors, serene abstract paintings, and picture windows that flooded the house with a soft white light, even though it was after 8 P.M. Vincent's mother, perhaps still sitting by the phone, seemed very far away in her cramped sixth-floor apartment. In Vincent's house the art on the walls had been salvaged from sidewalk trash heaps, the light from the Grand Concourse cast a harsh glare, and a cacophony of car alarms, police sirens, and boom boxes intruded from the streets outside. An unpainted, riveted steel skin sheathed the lobby door, the antithesis of a welcome mat, like an obscene gesture aimed at every person who entered the building or passed by. No wonder, given the general aura of unkemptness, no one thought twice about littering the sidewalks of Vincent's neighborhood with fast-food wrappers, empty beer cans, crack vials, even used Pampers. The ugliness was so deep, so rampant, that it seemed to stem from an incurable infection of the soul of the people living there. Yet it seemed equally possible that it had originated in a conspiracy of indifference and perhaps even contempt among the landlords, merchants, police, city planners, and city fathers who had allowed the once-grand Grand Concourse to deteriorate into a ghetto where standard rules of behavior, esthetics, and civility—rigorously enforced in affluent enclaves on Fifth Avenue, Park Avenue, and Central Park West—did not apply. It would not be surprising if someone like Vincent had been so spiritually impoverished by his upbringing that he was incapable of appreciating the difference between Woolworth's and Tiffany's, the ghetto and a home on Fifth Avenue, his apartment and the Lundberg home.

But he could. "It's beautiful," Vincent said softly, as he stood in the bedroom where he would be sleeping that night, and he meant it.

Nena, more interested in nature than in interior decorating, introduced the boys to the slender trees framing the house, their branches blistering with buds. These trees—*Sorbus intermedia,* she said—belonged to the apple family, and in a short while the buds would open into white flowers "that smell like cat." Pretty to look at, but you had to hold your nose as you came in and out of the house. After that, though, the flowers would turn into berries, which, in a botanical version of the fairytale about the ugly duckling, turned out to be deliciously edible. Nena looked around to see if the boys had appreciated her little botanical parable.

Jamie gave her a thoughtful look, then went inside to join Matthew at the piano, where they noodled out "Vem Kan Segla" like a serenade to their hosts. The house seemed to be waiting for an occasion like this, when it would be filled with children. Tomas was well-known as the good-looking man about town, the former competitive swimmer gone slightly to seed, who showed little inclination to trade travel, night-life, and independence for domestic obligation.

The children—"my boys," as Tomas was already referring to them in conversation—were happy and relaxed; their host had done his paternal duty. Tomas extricated himself as quickly as possible and sank into an easy chair in front of the TV. Soccer beckoned. As the hubbub of the game filled the room, Vincent and Jamie drifted in to watch with him. It was the World Cup semi-final, the U.S. against Finland. Perfect timing.

That was Tomas's house. Similar scenes unfolded in eight other households as Johanna, Mr. Benardo—keeping his promise to Janet Sanders and the other parents—and Uffe Grussner, still at the helm of his bus, made the rounds of every host family to tuck the children in. Priscilla Mercedes and Erica had caught a little fish in a creek behind the house where they were staying. They wanted to eat it, but their hosts said it was too small to cook, so they let it go. Eralis, who had been so melancholy when they first arrived, contemplating her brown hands, perked up as she cradled her host family's 6-month-old baby. "My aunt has, like, twenty-five kids to babysit," she said contentedly. As Eralis played with the baby, Kimberly Lopez, forgetting that she was no longer a little girl, sat in the baby's swing and promptly landed on her bottom in the dirt as the rope broke under her weight. Everyone looked panic-stricken for a moment, then burst out laughing.

It took Jeremy and Pierre a little while to adjust to what seemed an overly cavalier attitude on the part of their hosts, the Nyholms, toward the likelihood of kidnapping and theft. Like all of the children the boys had overpacked, bringing much bigger suitcases than they really needed for a week's stay. Their luggage took up the space in the family car where the Nyholm children would otherwise sit. So Tracy instructed her sons, who were 7 and 9, to wait for them in a small playground across the street from the parish house. Their father would be back for them in twenty minutes. As the car pulled away, Jeremy and Pierre stared anxiously out the rear window at the children who had been left behind, as if they feared never seeing them again. To get to the Nyholm apartment, they had to climb up three flights of stairs. Tracy's husband went ahead, carrying Jamie's bag. Tracy, who was pregnant, did not want to do any heavy lifting and told Pierre to go upstairs and leave his bag outside until her husband could come back down and get it. Pierre refused to budge, standing sentry next to his suitcase.

As a foreigner herself, Tracy understood cultural dislocation. She had first come to Aland as an Australian au pair, and later married the older son of the family—Karl-Johan—who had been away in college. The uninhibited Scandinavian attitude toward nudity had been particularly vexing until she got used to it. So before the boys from the Bronx arrived, she warned her husband and two sons to keep their clothes on in front of the visitors.

That night and the next morning, the children gave out the gifts they had brought from New York, more precious for having been carried such a long way. Eralis offered jagged little black and gray stones that she had gathered from the park near her house; Jennifer Padilla had lugged three bags of bagels.

Several of the host mothers were touched to see the children take visibly new clothes out of their suitcases. Among the comfortably middle-class Aland families, it was popular, almost chic, to buy clothes from Emmaus, a consignment store connected with a local peace organization, which dedicated the profits to charity for poor Baltic states like Latvia and Lithuania.

But the Bronx kids didn't have the luxury of wearing inexpensive second-hand clothes, especially so far from home. They might be middle class in their own minds, but it was too easy for them to be perceived otherwise. Brand-name clothing conferred instant middle-class credibility.

Tomas Lundberg was struck by one thing above all about Vincent—how unfailingly polite he was. He never stopped saying thank you. Tomas had been the same way when he had gone to a swimming contest in Sweden as a youth. Before he left home, his mother told him to mind his manners, and he did, as conscientiously as he could. He guessed that Vincent's mother had done the same. He had no way of knowing about Vincent's reputation as a troublemaker. He had never met Vincent's emotionally fragile mother, who seemed tethered to the real world by a very thin thread. Here in Aland, Vincent could start over with a clean slate, as a gracious, well-behaved young man, much as Johanna had started a new life, unencumbered by her past, when she had arrived in Boston nine years before. It was up to Vincent to decide what to make of the chance.

Johanna and her father arrived exhausted at the Grussner house at 2 A.M. Johanna's mother, Lillemor, opened the door and Johanna fell into her arms, sobbing, overcome by the exhaustion and the pressure of being in charge. At the same time, she was exhilarated. They had done it, really done it. They had come all this way, the children were safely settled down, having a wonderful time. Lillemor took her into the kitchen for a glass of red wine, then sent her up to bed. "I'll send the cat up after you," she called.

Johanna climbed the broad flight of wooden stairs to the second floor, the place where she had watched cartoons on TV and argued with her sisters when she was little. In the center was a spacious loft space with a wood-beamed ceiling. This was the family room, defined by a large orange shag rug and three couches in a horseshoe arrangement facing the television set. Uffe could often be found, in his blue and green plaid bathrobe, lying on one couch watching the nightly news, sometimes in the company of his son-in-law, Martin, who lived with Bodi and their cat, Blue, in the tile-roofed carriage house (now equipped with the requisite sauna) next door. On the right, Johanna passed her parents' room. On her left she passed the large spare room, outfitted with a heated waterbed and floor-to-ceiling shelves of her mother's books, mainly novels, from classics to potboilers, in English and Swedish. Johanna crossed behind the couches and turned left into a small ante-chamber, used for ironing. There, she ducked her head to enter a low doorway leading to a narrow flight of shallow stairs. This was the way to the tiny attic room under the slanted eaves, hardly bigger than a sailboat berth, that had been her childhood bedroom. She found the pink-flowered wallpaper, wide plank floors, and two parallel single beds covered in nautical-patterned quilts exactly as she had left them. Tacked on the walls were photographs of a young Johanna wreathed in flowers, some newspaper clippings, and a poster from the Isabella Stewart Gardiner Museum in Boston, these mementos suggesting that the occupant of the room was a girl of about 18. Her room had been frozen in time, halfway between childhood and adulthood, still unresolved. This had never bothered her before, but now she cringed.

A swirl of anxiety disturbed the glassy surface of her euphoria with the sudden impact of a pebble dropping into a pond. Who had she become while her past waited patiently under glass for her to reclaim it? The music teacher? The jazz singer? American? Scandinavian? A vibrant young woman with her whole life ahead of her, or a future cripple, damaged physically the way some of her students had been damaged psychologically? She had never told any of them about her illness. But maybe that was what had drawn her to them, had made her reach out to them, her sense that despite the gulf that separated them, they were all damaged goods, and that together they might be stronger than they were alone.

She willed these thoughts to go away, as she undressed for bed. Every-thing had gone so well. They had so much ahead of them. Tomorrow would be even better.

While Johanna had severed her ties to Aland as a teenager, her sisters had matured and set down roots. Cocki, now 33, with long straight blond hair and a reserved smile, had married a local boy, a construction inspector eight years older than she, whose son from a previous rela-tionship was about to turn 16. They had three children of their own. Of the three daughters, Cocki had followed most closely in Lillemor's footsteps, becoming first a schoolteacher and then the administrator of government-funded literary projects, like poetry festivals, writing sem-inars, stand-up comedy shows, and a debate.

Johanna's younger sister, Bodi, and her fiancé, Martin Cromwell-Morgan, were the intuitive ones, the free spirits. They liked to tell how they had fallen in love at first sight when their eyes locked across a crowded nightclub, and planned to distill their own Schnapps for their wedding. Bodi was also the most flirtatious of the three sisters, as youngest children often are, the one who batted her eyelashes and knew how to seduce with a sidelong glance or a conspiratorial wink. They seemed a perfect match, although Bodi was 23, and Martin was four-teen years older. But the sunburned crow's-feet around his eyes and his rakish red beard seemed to convey soft edges, kindness, and mild amusement more than age. Martin, who was British on his father's side, Finnish on his mother's, had spent his early childhood in London. He had roamed the world before settling in the family compound with Bodi. On Sundays, Martin would put on his double-breasted black chalk-stripe suit, gray shirt, and gray tie and drive his motorbike to a village church, where he took his post as the caretaker, lighting candles and standing at the right moments during the service so the congregation would know when to stand. He found the job through serendipity, a method that suited him. The minister had advertised the position, but nobody had answered the ad. "Do you want it?" the minister asked Martin. Martin liked the hours, so he took it.

Paradoxically, physical distance increased Johanna's loyalty to her family. She wanted to strike out on her own, to distinguish herself from them, and yet she mourned the part of herself that she had left behind. Bodi felt connected to Aland as a place and to its folk traditions, which she tried to capture in her musical compositions. But Johanna's connection was personal; she missed her family more than her homeland. She wished she could be content with life at home. But for an ambitious person, the archipelago could feel very small and confining. Everybody knew everyone. You could not reinvent yourself; you were an accretion of every moment of your life. Leaving was almost a necessity.

To Lillemor, her daughter's discomfort was a symptom of the Law of Jante, first articulated by Danish-born Norwegian writer Aksel Sandemose, a psychoanalytically inclined novelist, in his 1933 book *A Fugitive Crosses His Tracks*, an attack on provincialism, envy, the competitive dynamic, and the social forces of repression. Jante was a village that, like Aland, laid down a code of behavior, and didn't suffer deviation. The Law of Jante had become famous throughout Scandinavia, where even those who had never read the book knew its ten commandments as well as the biblical ones:

> *Thou shalt not believe thou art somebody.*
> *Thou shalt not imagine thyself any better than we.*
> *Thou shalt not believe thou canst teach us anything.* . . .

and so forth.

Alanders were proud of people who succeeded abroad. But if someone elected to remain in Aland, she was expected to be what the Swedes called "lagom," a model of moderation, no excesses in either direction, demanding neither too much nor too little. But where did this magical average reside? When was it good to be written about in the newspaper, and when was it not? Once Alanders had lived outside, it was often difficult for them to calibrate these fine differences when they returned home again. The Swedish concept of "lagom" was almost untranslatable. The ultimate in "lagom" was to blend in completely, to disappear, to have no profile at all. This Johanna couldn't do.

Sometimes, she thought she had encountered the Law of Jante at P.S. 86 in as virulent a form as she had ever experienced it in her homeland. P.S. 86 was a village among the 1,200 New York City schools. It operated as a closed society, with its own distinct and insular culture. When Johanna tried to assert herself, Mr. Benardo, the keeper of the school culture, felt compelled to cut her down to size. She could not think she was somebody. She could not think she was better than them. She could not think that she could teach them anything. She had, by some ironic twist of fate, found her way in life from a real small town to a metaphorical small town, a home as confoundingly bewitching, nurturing, and repressive as the one she had fled. The denizens of P.S. 86 shared the villagers' disdain for the outside world—in this case, symbolized by the bureaucracy at 110 Livingston Street, the New York City school system's headquarters. Mr. Benardo and the teachers lived by their own wits, their own code of behavior, and tried to fly under the bureaucratic radar whenever possible. They had a sense of "them and us." Idiosyncrasy and talent could flourish, but only so long as it did not disturb the collective sense of well-being, and the principal's ironclad leadership.

As in Jante, the survival of the community was more important than any individual. Yet, as Sandemose wrote, "By means of the Law of Jante people stamp out each other's chances in life." At P.S. 86 as in Aland, one incited envy at one's own risk.

⁂

Downstairs, Margaret, who was staying at the Grussner house that night, lingered in the kitchen under the milk-glass chandelier with Lillemor, polishing off the bottle of red wine. They sat face to face, surrogate mother to real one, across the rough-hewn antique table. Margaret sat on the eighteenth-century high-backed wooden pew, covered with homemade pillows flattened by time; Lillemor took her customary place to Uffe's right, if he had been there. Each one knew, without having to say it, how it felt for the other to play the role of the wife and mother—pushing, supporting, picking up the pieces—and to be taken for granted. Each one could forgive any unwitting ingratitude, no matter how hurtful. Lillemor and Margaret had never communicated or set eyes on each other before, but they felt an instant bond. For three and a half years, while Johanna had been away from home, Margaret had been the one she turned to. Johanna had gone home to Harlem and called Margaret in Scarsdale. They had had long conversations late into the night. "I knew all her relationships with the people she knew in New York City. I would meet all her boyfriends, and there were a lot of them," Margaret said. "I liked Nick. James I thought was too young for her. I think she really needed someone from Scandinavia. Americans are too American."

What was Johanna's life like at P.S. 86, Lillemor wanted to know. Johanna was very talented, Margaret said carefully, and she risked sacrificing some of that talent to her teaching. "I really think she should move on after three or four years," Margaret said. "I kind of understand what she wants to do, I think, and where her objectives are, and she does want to be successful professionally. She's different from other music teachers; she has a professional aura. She handles the public well. But if you don't take advantage of that when you're young you lose, you lose out. I really want her to take advantage of her youth and her talent. Teaching will always be there. I just don't want her to get bogged down in school and miss opportunities."

Margaret had tried to encourage Johanna's music outside of P.S. 86.

She had gone to her shows and had invited Johanna and her friends to perform in that musical soiree at her house in Scarsdale.

But Johanna was also headstrong, which had sometimes put her on a collision course with Mr. Benardo. She had tried to set her own agenda, which did not go over well. If there was one principle that Mr. Benardo adhered to, Margaret mused, it was that he and only he set the agenda. Margaret regretted that he had been so hard on Johanna, scolding her over the private music lessons, for instance. Then there was the time Johanna had invited Frank, the pony-tailed young security guard, to sing during a concert. Mr. Benardo had reprimanded her for that, too—Margaret never understood why.

Lillemor was a good listener, a careful interrogator, the kind of person who withheld judgment, revealing her thoughts only implicitly in the questions she asked. It was hard for her to be objective about Mr. Benardo's treatment of her daughter. She felt pained that Johanna had cried and that she, her real mother, had not been there to comfort her. She missed Johanna, and often wished for her to come home. But she also knew that her daughter stayed at P.S. 86 because she loved what she did, because she hoped that she would be able to make a difference in these children's lives. Yet like Margaret, Lillemor had doubts. She worried that her daughter would be disappointed, that she had invested too much of her ambition in the chorus, that her expectations were too high.

"What do you think will happen to these kids after the trip?" Lillemor asked.

"I think going back to New York will be a shock," Margaret replied.

"But where will they be in ten years?" Lillemor persisted.

Margaret hadn't anticipated that. The idea that this trip might alter the course of the children's lives, maybe ten years into the future, had never occurred to her. The trip had always seemed like a lovely idea, but supremely impractical. She was still amazed that they had even pulled it off. At the moment, she was more focused on the immediate responsibility of shepherding twenty-four children through a week in a foreign country and getting them home in one piece than on anything that might come after. To think that giving a concert in Finland, more than everything the children had gone through in all their years at P.S. 86, could have a lasting impact on their destinies seemed, well, misguided. Johanna was not the only teacher these children had ever had and, however talented in her field, probably not the best, either.

She couldn't look Lillemor in the eye and say those things. There was no point in diminishing Johanna's accomplishments. After a few seconds of uncertainty, she looked straight out between the curtains of her brown hair and answered as diplomatically as she could.

"I guess that's a question for psychiatrists."

CHAPTER SEVENTEEN

❧

A Society of Women

Among her friends, Lillemor Grussner was known as a nurturer. Food and family were inextricably linked. But her food was never comfort food, plentiful but monotonous, steak and potatoes. She had too much style for that. Her Swiss fondue had to be liberally spiked with fine schnapps and a strong dose of garlic powder. The sourdough bread would be fresh and chewy. A good meal began with an appetizer, sliced baguette spread with chèvre and cloudberry marmalade, baked in the oven; or, another time, vegetarian paté garnished with peeled shrimp and caviar. There should be garlic and soy butter to go with the roast lamb. Not just dinner but breakfast was a family meal, the table set with three shades of dark bread, tubes of liver and cod-roe paste, cheeses, a tub of butter with a little wooden paddle to skim it out, soft boiled eggs nestled in egg-cups, herb salt, tomatoes, cucumbers, juice, and strong coffee as brown as mud. Now that the girls were grown, Bodi and Martin often drifted out of their cottage to join Lillemor and

Uffe for morning coffee. Lillemor's food was more than sustenance. It was a mysterious delight. You had the feeling that in every meal she prepared, there was an echo of the road not taken—the adventure in foreign lands, nude romps on the beach, intellectual disquisitions on art and literature animated by passion and cheap wine. By nature, she was restless and dissatisfied, a perfectionist, one of those women who at least once a year was overcome by a compulsion to rearrange the furniture. That was her destiny, to nurture others, sealed from the moment her mother named her. Lillemor, she liked to say, wistfully, meant "Little Mother." She had no choice but to become a maternal being, although her own version of maternity resembled not so much the virtuous, diminutive qualities conveyed by her Swedish name as the fiery Minoan serpent goddess of ancient Crete. On one of her many trips to Crete she had brought back a small, painted pottery reproduction of this goddess—bare-breasted, provocative, wearing the prototype of the Mona Lisa smile, clutching a writhing snake in either hand. This earthy image of femininity was the one to which she subscribed.

Lillemor Mattsson had grown up as the daughter of a warrant officer in the Swedish cavalry, turned private security consultant, and had internalized, as the wives and children of officers everywhere traditionally have, a subtle sense of aloofness, grace, decorum, mixed, perhaps, with a touch of entitlement. Her family might not have been rich, but her father was an officer and a gentleman, part of the warrior aristocracy, valued and respected by society. Hers was not the housewifely temperament, but the artistic one, with all the mercurial highs and lows that that entailed. Now 56, she had come of age in the '60s, and the restlessness of that generation suited her. In the guestroom, old necklaces made of seashells, amber, glass, turquoise, and silver hung on pegs like ornaments, mementos of her youth and travels. She had coveted that water bed, and still liked to lie in its heated expanse in winter with the window cracked open to let in the frosty night air. Her treasures were her books, high and low literature from John Grisham to Karen

Blixen and Bo Carpelan; the smooth gray pebbles, each a perfect oval, collected from a beach in Crete; the abstract paintings done by friends. Pick a book—*Smilla's Sense of Snow,* maybe—she had read it and would like nothing better than to talk about ice, murder, Greenlanders, depression. Maybe she identified with Smilla, the smart, discontented, eccentric Scandinavian. She liked to say that she subscribed to Cicero's maxim: He who has books and a garden is content. But with Lillemor, being content was relative.

Her children were accustomed to her days of manic activity, when she was shot through with inspiration and anything seemed possible. At the Lyceum, the exam-based high school for Aland's brightest students, she was a passionate teacher of English and Swedish literature, a demanding taskmaster who pushed her students to the limit, whose message, when students thought they had done as much as they could humanly do, was—do more. For those students who burned the midnight oil, rose to her standards, and discovered that they were smarter and more capable than they had imagined, she was one of a kind, a teacher to be remembered and cherished for the rest of their lives.

But her family had also learned to brace for the crash that sometimes followed the intensity of her commitment, when she collapsed in bed of exhaustion and could not get up. Once, recovering from illness and sunken in a black funk, she stayed in bed for days, not speaking. Helena Lundberg—her friend Nena—came and sat by her bedside, sharing her silence, not needing to know why or attempting to shake her out of her despair. "She was willing to wait," Lillemor said. She had never forgotten that. Nena liked to drop in unannounced, walking to the red farmhouse from her home a kilometer away along the winding country road. For the return, when it would be dark, she wore a reflective belt around her waist, fastened just under the tips of her long mane of wavy hair, and carried a flashlight.

On springtime visits, Nena observed a well-honed routine. First she did the circuit of Uffe's garden, checking for any new buds and leaves.

Should the browned and wilted leaves on last year's lavender be sheared? "It is better to wait first and see what happens," Nena said. (Her grandfather had been a gardener; old women used to come to him in spring to buy flowers to plant on graves.) She was always patient.

She and Lillemor sat at the kitchen table and talked until late at night, sharing a bottle of red wine. From time to time, one of them would get up and walk over to the stove, light a cigarette on the lighter Lillemor kept on the stove, and stand there smoking it, guiltily, cigarette hand cocked under the exhaust hood.

The Grussner household was a society of women—Lillemor, her three daughters, sharing intimacies, the father an interloper to be affectionately teased, though in the last years, Uffe had found allies in his two sons-in-law. The circle opened easily to encompass Nena. When the Bronx kids visited, she was 45 and unmarried. But like so many Scandinavian women of her generation and younger, she had maintained a marriage-like relationship with the same man, a guitarist, for twenty years. They had two daughters, Nelly, 6, and Karin. Like Lillemor, Nena appreciated cultivation, but was bored by convention. She had the independent thinker's knack for finding meaning in the most banal circumstances. She advised that it was not so bad to leave the wine glasses standing on the kitchen counter unwashed until morning, their residue of Beaujolais coagulating like blood. "They will remind you of what a good time you had with friends the night before." But she was not sloppy. Before she left, Nena, the daughter-in-law of a dairy farmer, made sure to put the milk in the refrigerator, where it would not spoil.

Nena's serenity was a good foil for Lillemor and her daughters, especially the flirtatious Bodi, who most resembled her mother, in appearance as well as personality. They suffered moods as far beyond their control as the shifting tides. When the moon was full, they assembled for breakfast with swollen eyes, and revealed that they had been up all night, weeping. They had vivid, prophetic dreams. One morning, Lillemor came down to the breakfast table looking particularly haggard, her mouth slack, her eyes puffy. "I had a nightmare last night," she reported, bracing one arm against the butcher-block counter. "I was on a trip. I lost my purse. I couldn't find my keys, wallet, money—nothing." This was the morning when she had planned to talk about her past, but now it would be much harder than she had anticipated, for her identity had been stolen by the thief of her dreams.

Uffe came down to breakfast in his country gentleman's uniform, green twill slacks, plaid flannel shirt, to take his place at the head of the table, already set with a white cloth and burgundy placemats to match the heavy curtains at the kitchen windows. He listened without comment, his reserve enhancing his air of sagacity. Within the family, Uffe was the steady one, with his dry sense of humor and businessman's bonhomie. He and Lillemor balanced. When the women cried over the full moon, he made them laugh by jauntily reciting doggerel he learned in high school English classes: "Cook took a look at her cookery book," he began, in a starched British accent. "Mr. Knox keeps his socks in a pale-pink chocolate box. Bennie lay in bed and covered up his head. His mother said: Pet, out of bed you must get!" While Lillemor spoke English fluently, Uffe mangled nearly every sentence, but gamely plowed ahead.

He was a self-made man, who started two enterprises from scratch— a tourist café in 1965, when he was 25, followed by a bus company fourteen years later—and had been shrewd enough to make his fortune at them. He was reputed to have inherited his mother's drive, single-mindedness, and spirit—she raised her children alone, taking in laundry, running a bakery, overcoming the hardship of having her house confiscated by the Russians after World War II, in retaliation for her husband being a German national.

A generation later, Uffe's jaunty red buses had become a fixture of the Aland landscape. He began with tourist buses, and expanded to the municipal bus franchise in Mariehamn and surrounding communities.

But beyond the buses, Uffe himself was a local figure of almost folkloric renown, who, despite his admittedly suspect foreign paternity, had managed to construct an image as winning, distinctive, and pseudo-historic as a character in the Asterix and Obelix comic-book series. When he drove by in his Toyota jeep—red, naturally—children laughed and waved; he tooted the horn back. The jeep was decorated in red and white block letters with the legend "Röde Orm," the name of his bus company, and an homage to a historical novel of the same name, written across the front. The names of Kings and Vikings from the novel—Harald, Odd, Svarthofde, Loke, Toke—wrapped around the sides of the jeep.

Rode Orm, literally "Red Snake," and the name of the protagonist, was written by the Swedish writer and historian Frans G. Bengtsson. The book came out in the 1940s and was translated into English as *The Long Ships*. It is a heroic saga of tenth-century Viking conquests of land and women, set against the backdrop of spreading, missionary Christianity, told in the dense encyclopedic manner of a James Michener tale. It has become a modern Scandinavian classic. The paperback version is sold in every airport bookstore, the literary counterpart to the little china Viking figurines sold in tourist shops. It was easy to understand why Uffe Grussner, who fell in love—like Rode Orm—with a strong-willed Swedish woman, and set up house with a sweeping view of a twelfth-century church, would think of the book as a kind of bible. There is even a passing tribute to the seafaring skills of the Alanders, and a character called Glad Ulf, for his merry temper. It is, above all, a boy's book, in which one scene of battle, looting, and conquest follows another in an endless adrenaline rush, and the women—though independent, beautiful, and wily—are secondary characters, domesticated and left behind while their men strike out yet again for adventure.

Like that of his mythological hero, Uffe's life had not been short of adventure, beginning with the checkered history of his father, Albrecht. Given Albrecht's past, it was, perhaps, no accident that his son had steeped himself in the legend of the Red Snake and, consciously or not, cultivated his own image as a loyal Norse Viking, dedicated to preserving local tradition. For even within the Grussner family, there were suspicions that Albrecht had been a German spy.

Uffe had grown up thinking that his German father was a geologist, mapping expert, and diplomat. In the late 1930s, while working on his doctoral degree, Albrecht had spent time at the German embassy in Helsinki and then in Aland, working on a thesis about the geopolitical importance of the archipelago. In the event that Russia sought to invade Finland, Aland would be a crucial staging ground. In Kvarnbo, Albrecht met Anna-Greta Hagmark, the proprietor, with her mother, of a local boarding house. The couple married in 1938, and moved to Berlin when Albrecht was recalled because of the war. Uffe was the third of their four children, all born in Germany. In 1944, Albrecht marched to Stalingrad with the German army. As the allies bombed Berlin, Anna-Greta sold her silver spoons and managed to spirit her family out of Germany on the last train to Finland. Albrecht spent five years in a Siberian prison camp, and when the war ended, his family didn't know whether he was dead or alive.

By the end of the war, as the Russians began rounding up German nationals in Finland, Anna-Greta chartered a boat to take her family to Sweden under cover of darkness. During the crossing, they met refugees from Estonia who had run out of gas, and stopped to help. The Coast Guard intercepted them. They spent eighteen months in an internment camp on the mainland, along with other civilians from axis countries, before returning to their home in Aland, but not for long.

Uffe remembered the tension in the air as three black automobiles drove up to Solkulla, his mother's boarding house, a grand Victorian mansion with three chimneys, the wooden siding painted aristocratic yellow. The cars contained officials from the Russian embassy who gave Anna-Greta and her children seventy-two hours to leave home. The property was in her name, and she was a native Alander, but she had both German and Finnish citizenship, and this, apparently, was used against her. They were not permitted to take any of their possessions with them. Anna-Greta tried to salvage a piano, although she did not play it very well. But someone in the village reported her, and she was forced to leave it behind.

Rebuilding her life, Anna-Greta opened a bakery and then a laundry business and secretly divorced Albrecht. It turned out that Albrecht had, indeed, survived Siberia, and he returned to a government job in Bonn and remarried. Uffe and his siblings still thought of him as their father, and he sent them Christmas presents for many years. Uffe was 16 before he saw his father again.

The Russians denounced Albrecht as a spy, and Uffe himself had never been sure what to think.

"It was even in the papers," Lillemor said.

"And I think perhaps he was a little bit of a spy," Uffe added thoughtfully. "He thought himself to be an ordinary geologist, but I think he was used—of course he was used—to tell about things. I asked him, 'Were you a spy?' He said, 'No. If I had been a spy, do you think I should have written about it in the papers?' He had published an article for a German newspaper called 'The Question of Aland.'"

"Was he naïve?" Lillemor suggested.

"I think all governments wanted information from all lands at that time," Uffe replied.

"He wrote those articles because he needed money," Lillemor concluded. She would rather not think too ill of him.

Despite past hardships, Anna-Greta flourished. By 1955, she employed five or six people in the bakery and the laundry. "She ran her companies with a hard hand and a warm heart, that's what I remember," Lillemor said. "She really started with two empty hands. She was a proud woman who wouldn't take help from anyone. She's the one who always helped others."

As her business prospered, she became known for handing out baked goods at Christmas to alcoholics and street people. In the late 1980s, when unemployment was high in Helsinki, she organized a campaign to persuade companies in Aland to donate food for needy people in the capital. By then she was in her late 70s, and the efforts of this elderly businesswoman attracted the attention of the newspapers. "It was very humiliating, this little island sending food to Helsinki," Lillemor said smugly.

"She got a letter from the president of Finland," Uffe added.

"This is Johanna in many many ways—and her father too, of course—full of ideas," Lillemor said.

"We never felt our childhood was terrible," Uffe said.

"It was happy," agreed Lillemor.

"Happy," Uffe echoed, "because we were four and felt very close."

"Anna-Greta always said that with those three boys she had everything she needed," Lillemor recalled. "When I first met them I was fascinated. It was such an open house, all these friends working at the bakery in the summer. One of them is a doctor now, another a journalist. They had big parties."

"We had fun," Uffe allowed.

"There was always room for everybody all the time, day and night," Lillemor continued. "I think Anna-Greta slept about three or four hours a night, maybe a little nap before the fire."

Uffe snored, imitating his mother, then added: "Johanna is about the same."

Uffe's older brother, Knut, inherited the bakery, although he turned out to be allergic to flour and eventually gave it up, becoming a music teacher instead. But Uffe had his own ideas. In the early 1960s, given Aland's growing reputation as a tourist destination, Uffe, then working in a bank, and a friend, who was a doctor, started thinking about investing in a tourist café. The friend's father, Valdemar Nyman, a prominent local minister and writer, steered them to the perfect location, a forested mountaintop with a dramatic view of a sound connecting to the Baltic Sea, where the sailboats below looked like toothpicks. "From there," Uffe said, "you can go to America if you want." He was also drawn to the location by a sense of history, for this was the spot, legend had it, where a local man sounded the alarm as Russian troops invaded during the war of 1808 to 1809. An architect friend designed the café, tracing the first sketches in the snow on the mountain: an octagonal wooden structure, surrounding a central sunken fireplace. They named it Uffe pa Berget, Uffe on the Mountain, a reference to a popular eighteenth-century Danish comedy.

Everyone thought Johanna had inherited the entrepreneurial gene through her father. Johanna had considered taking over the café, but that would mean abandoning her music.

Uffe and Lillemor met as he was planning the café, when he was 24 and she was 20, staying at her parents' summer house in Aland. As practical as Uffe might be in business, he had a romantic side. Tucked among the cookbooks in the kitchen was a fake–leather bound Swedish encyclopedia called *1966, Biggest Events of the Year*, its glossy pages gray from being fawned over so many times by family members and guests. Flipping through photographs of prominent newsmakers of the year—Indira Gandhi, Ho Chi Minh, U Thant—you came to a black-and-white photograph of Lillemor and Uffe, bundled up like arctic explorers in furs, scarves, and goggles, stiff with cold, riding a snowmobile across a frozen stretch of the Baltic between Sweden and Aland. That winter, Lillemor had been studying in Stockholm, Uffe was working in Aland. Ice had prevented the ferryboats from sailing and there was an airport strike. Uffe, determined to see Lillemor, asked a friend who owned a snowmobile company to help him pick her up in Sweden and bring her back to Aland. The friend agreed, on the condition that Uffe notify the newspapers. The trip across the ice took three and a half hours (only an hour longer than the ferryboat), and the return took four, because the reporters, having been duly notified, insisted on stopping to draw hearts in the snow as the backdrop for a photograph. As romantic as the stunt may have seemed to the newspapers, it was not without discomfort for the participants. Uffe made the mistake of lifting his goggles to clean them, and found his eyes instantly frozen shut by his own tears. Lillemor spent the whole trip wishing she could stop to pee, and fuming at the reporters who surrounded them. Had she known the press would be there, she insisted, she would not have consented to playing the damsel in distress. Uffe, on the other hand, didn't mind the attention one bit. "I think he liked the notoriety," Lillemor said.

They married in 1967, and moved next door to Uffe's mother in Godby, but talked constantly about finding a house in the country. Like a guardian angel, the same minister who had suggested the location for the café steered them to an old house in rural Palsbole, which had been empty for years. They tracked down the owner, the custodian of the nearby church, and offered to buy the house. The old man looked at them for a long time, apparently thinking this over, then said gruffly: "Well, it's not for sale—but why not?" He seemed to have made up his mind on the spur of the moment. "He fetched the key and we went there and we just thought, 'Oh, this is the place,'" Lillemor said.

They bought the house, which came with the carriage house and an underground root cellar, in 1970, two years before Johanna was born, and spent a year restoring it. Originally, it had been painted yellow. But they repainted it red, in part to match the outbuildings and in part because they liked red better. They furnished the house with a bed, a table, two chairs, and a Christmas tree and moved in, with 3-year-old Cocki, on Christmas eve, 1971. As they settled in, Uffe chose the room on the ground floor, overlooking the old stone church, to be his study. The view had survived untouched by development for nine centuries, and was still intact when the Bronx kids came to visit. By that time, though, development threatened, and Uffe was fighting to prevent the open land around the church from being sold to build a golf course.

As Mr. Benardo shrewdly deduced, family tradition—the house, music, charity, and, yes, Mr. Benardo's own highest value, loyalty— mattered deeply in the Grussner family.

The sisters paid homage to their father in the name of the singing group they established, as a common calling, for love and money. They called it Ulvens Dottrar, "Daughters of the Wolf," a winking allusion to Uffe's name, Ulf, literally "Wolf." They sang medieval and ethnic music, their voices rising into animal keening, trilling, and jazzy bird cries, sometimes a cappella, other times accompanied by flutes, fiddles, a Jew's harp, cymbals, tambourine, and digeridoo. Their sisters' voices harmonized easily, because they sounded so much alike, and the group was well known at county fairs. Cocki asserted her seniority by carrying the melody. Bodi was the most versatile musician, composing and playing her exotic instruments one-woman-band style, like Bob Dylan. Johanna had the deepest voice and the widest range.

While the Bronx kids were visiting, someone asked Uffe what he hoped Johanna, his enterprising middle daughter, would achieve. "I wish for her to get married and have children," he said. Lillemor, who knew how hard her daughter had worked, was livid.

CHAPTER EIGHTEEN

ℭℕ

Bronx Bombers

Their first morning in Aland was Mother's Day. Johanna couldn't sleep and rose at 6 A.M. to find that her father was already awake as well. They went out to the grassy front yard, gray and dewy in the first morning light. Sitting at two wooden chairs next to the table fashioned from an ancient stone mill-wheel propped on an obelisk of a stone base, looking down the gentle slope to the stone church below, they talked about the day ahead. Just being able to talk about routine, innocuous matters, like the logistics of transportation, with her organized, methodical father was comforting.

It had been nine years since Johanna left Aland for Boston, and every one of those years she had gone through the same wrenching ritual. By June, the end of the school year, her heart was breaking with the ache of missing her home and family. She couldn't wait to return. She had idealized everything that she had left behind. She wanted to be able to pick up the telephone and call her mother without worrying about how much it would cost. She wanted to be able to drop in for dinner unannounced. She wanted to sit on the couch at night watching the local news with her father. She wanted to play the djembes while Bodi played the didgeridoo and Cocki sang the melody to a song that only Bodi could compose. All the ordinary things that families did when they lived nearby, when they had not been cruelly separated by time and distance, by their own selfish choices. She didn't even mind the thought of taking orders and washing dishes at the café, the long drudgery of a restaurant night. But then she got there and poof! The opposite happened. Over the course of the summer, she found herself missing her new life in Boston, or New York, even the Bronx, longing to go back. How could she have ever craved domesticity? Wasn't the life of the working girl so much more fulfilling? What about her responsibility to the children? Vincent's pre-adolescent crush. The feelings he didn't understand yet. How could she let him down? And her band—she missed Gary backing her up on trombone, Mika's fingers tripping over the piano, Andreas on bass. Crooning "Angel Eyes" for the summer crowd at Saratoga Springs. Reaching for the brass ring, too young to doubt that she would ever grab it. The tension was neverending, irresolvable. Johanna had a need to break with her past, with her upbringing, over and over again. And she had a love–hate relationship with the freedom and promise of her life in America. Her way of grappling with this conflict was to try to have it both ways, to bring the Americans she loved home to Aland. First Gary, her boyfriend at Berklee, who went home with her every summer during the three years they were together, then James, whose trip had turned out to be such a disaster.

She had brought musicians, too. One summer, she arranged for one of her roommates, Miles Okazaki, to spend a month on the road with her in Aland. He was a guitarist, and she conceived a gig where they would give concerts one summer in every medieval stone church in the archipelago. They called it the "Stone Church Tour." They traveled by boat and by car to six different islands, staying overnight in little cottages along the way. Mostly she sang Swedish folk music, accompanied by Miles. In their first concert, she innocently sang a popular song about an Alander who lived off the land, building his own house, growing his own food, taking a local wife, and distilling his own liquor. The reviewer for a local newspaper took her to task for promoting alcohol under a church roof. At first, Johanna was crushed by the negative publicity. But the song was well known, and readers began to write letters to the editor defending it—and her. After that, every concert was packed with people curious to hear this sacrilegious singer, and Johanna learned that controversy was an asset to marketing. Having Miles along attracted audiences as well, for they were intrigued by this local girl who had brought back a Japanese-American to perform in their midst. She was familiar; he was not—an enticing mix.

But her most ambitious attempt at cross-fertilization coalesced around her master's thesis. A condition of graduation was to present a two-hour concert in front of a jury. The typical arrangement for a singer like Johanna involved putting together a trio—maybe piano, bass, and drums—as backup. That was not how Johanna saw herself. This was her chance to realize her ambition of being a big-band singer, the Scandinavian Ella Fitzgerald or Peggy Lee or Sarah Vaughn. But to do that she needed at least fourteen guys who were of semi-professional quality, who would agree to rehearse week after week and then play for free at her graduation. What was in it for them? As luck would have it, the Aland jazz festival that year, in the summer of 1998, was going to have a big-band theme. She called the organizer, whom she knew well, and asked if he had booked an American big band yet. No. "I have a big band in New York," Johanna told him, bluffing. "They're really good. Basically professional. But because they're still finishing school you wouldn't have to pay them that much, which is the best part."

"Wow, that's great," he said. "What's the name of the band?"

"It's called the Johanna Grussner Manhattan Jazz Orchestra," she replied, the name, which she had rehearsed so often in her daydreams, tripping instantly off her tongue, though she had never spoken it out loud before. "We have our own arrangements."

She negotiated a deal in which the band would get airfare, lodging, food, and some pin money. The main condition was that they wouldn't lose money. Now she started calling friends to offer them the job. She hadn't told anybody in advance, so as not to disappoint them. Everyone she called wanted to do it. She lined up eighteen musicians, including her new boyfriend, Nick (a big band doesn't usually need a vibraphone, but she couldn't very well leave him out.) They performed at her graduation, then every night for two weeks at the festival in Aland.

The boys were great musicians, touchingly handsome in their mismatched black shirts—a T-shirt here, a buttondown there, a turtleneck and blazer on someone else—cradling their golden horns as debonairly, as deftly, as girlfriends they had touched so often they knew their every hollow. But they were still kids, and they acted like kids, totally dependent on her, and she almost blew it, big-time. On the Fourth of July, she bought hot dogs, Coke, and beer, and enlisted her father, her uncle, and Cocki's husband, who all had boats, to take the band to an uninhabited island. They went skinny-dipping, ate every last crumb, and returned to the mainland, where Johanna discovered that she was missing an envelope stuffed with $2,000, their pin money. Her father found her sobbing in her attic room. "Where did you use it last?" he asked. "To buy food." Taking Bodi with him, Uffe set off for the island. Several hours later, they came back, their hands filthy, having retrieved the ketchup-stained envelope, cash intact. Johanna had thrown it in the garbage with the hot dog wrappers.

On their last night, everyone went barhopping in Stockholm before the SAS flight to New York. At 7 A.M. the next morning, Johanna looked around the hotel lobby at the boys in their rumpled clothes, groaning from hangovers and three hours sleep, and realized that Brett, the trombone player, was missing. She panicked. They had to be at the airport in an hour. "Where's Brett?" she demanded. Several of the guys had seen him with a Swedish girl, a gorgeous black woman, exotic in a roomful of blondes. A couple of boys dug into their pockets and found the girl's phone number. "I'm going to stay here a few days," Brett said drowsily, when Johanna tracked him down at the girl's apartment. "Great. You can take care of your own ticket. We're leaving," she snapped back.

Before disbanding, the group played for several Scandinavian organizations in New York, at some restaurants, and one night at Birdland. In the end, Johanna discovered that running a big band was not as easy in reality as in her fantasies. Singing over eighteen musicians was hard on her voice; but coordinating eighteen people was the real killer. She was happy to have had the experience, and to have taken them home with her. But she never wanted to go through that kind of stress again. It was the best and worst thing she had ever done.

Now here she was, breaking her promise to herself. She was doing it again, this time with real children, not semi-professionals who acted like children. She and Uffe looked at each other and laughed, then Johanna got up to take Mother's Day breakfast to Lillemor, and to sing her a song. But as she climbed the creaking wooden stairs with a tray, she found Lillemor already on the way down.

At least this time, Johanna was not the only one responsible for the kids. She had arranged to meet the others at the harbor in Mariehamn, where they would inaugurate their first full day in Aland with a cruise on a two-masted wooden sailing ship, the *Albanus*. This was, after all, billed as an educational trip, with every hour of time accounted for to the Board of Education.

The children arrived at the harbor with their host families, and Jeremy immediately breathed in a tangy smell of sardines, or maybe herring. "Is this salt water?" he asked. "It's not strong salt water," Margaret replied. "It's fed by rivers. It's soft salt water." Dorothy Pack, a cashmere sweater thrown across her shoulders, interjected, refusing to patronize the kids: "Brackish. It's brackish water. They might as well learn the vocabulary."

The original *Albanus* had been built in 1904, and carried firewood between Aland and the Swedish and Finnish mainlands until the 1940s. This one was a replica, built in the 1980s, but otherwise unchanged from the original. The husky, bearded skipper, Allan Palmer, told them that the ship could hit speeds of 8 or 9 knots in open sea, and would take twelve hours to reach Stockholm, about six times as long as the ferry. Palmer came from a sailing family. His father was a mate on cargo ships sailing from Aland to Australia, and his confidence showed as he turned the tiller over to the children. Vincent steered the longest of all, feeling the suck of the waves under the hull, thrilled to be in control of such a powerful vessel. Priscilla, pale, seasick and homesick, was the first casualty of the trip. Going below, she flopped down on a bunk and refused to eat, despite the entreaties of Emily Coca. Mr. Benardo and Johanna's father sat side by side on a bench along the perimeter of the boat, deep in conversation, as if they were old friends, although they had hardly met. As the boat turned back to the harbor, Vincent reluctantly gave up the tiller. All of a sudden, the wind caught his sports cap and whisked it away before he could react. He yelped and watched it drift away and then sink in the choppy green waters of the Baltic Sea, his face clouding. For Vincent, whose moods were as fickle as the wind, the exhilaration he had felt while steering the boat vanished with his hat.

A local newspaper photographer waited on shore as the boat returned. Johanna tried to oblige her hometown paper by organizing the children to sing "Vem Kan Segla," while standing picturesquely in the anchored craft. But Vincent was sulking over the loss of his cap, and stomped to the other end of the boat, refusing to sing. Erica Davies, slender but with a will of steel, closed her eyes and delivered the female solo that began the song. Then it was Jamie's turn to chime in, but Vincent's truculence had infected him. He couldn't allow himself to be upstaged by Vincent. Jamie opened his mouth but nothing came out. He started again, only to clutch his throat after a few bars, as if he couldn't go on. Johanna cut him short and, with the other hand, signaled impatiently to the bigger group to fill in. Their voices swelled obediently, picking up the words where Jamie had left off with the perfect Swedish accents that only children, maybe only children with musical ears, could muster. To the crew, the spat passed practically unnoticed.

But Johanna was beside herself. This had been the first test of their discipline as a chorus since they had arrived, and Vincent and Jamie had botched it. As they left, Vincent, still uncooperative, refused to sign the guestbook, posterity being a concept with which he was unfamiliar. "I ain't signing anything," he snarled, his street smarts telling him that any document requiring a signature was likely to have dire consequences. When you lived on welfare in the Bronx, it was prudent to slip through life under the radar. Ashley, on the other hand, had seen a guestbook before, and knew that signing it would not be the same as creating a paper trail for the benefit of the Bureau of Child Welfare, especially not when they were thousands of miles away in Finland. "I'll do it for you," she said, taking pity on Vincent, and wrote his name in the book, under her own.

Everyone crammed into the bus for the second stage of the voyage, their five-day stay at Lembote, the Lutheran-run camp of Johanna's childhood. They wouldn't be seeing their host families again until the final concert in Mariehamn, on the eve of their return home, when the families would once again become the bookends of the trip. Lulled by the movement of the bus, and still jet-lagged, the children began looking drowsy. But Johanna, undeterred, launched into a scathing lecture on proper behavior. The kids listened grimly while the teachers grinned broadly. In their view, Johanna had never understood the value of discipline, always leaving the classroom teachers to impose order and good behavior. No wonder the kids adored her, in the way a pet favors the one who feeds it. The teachers were happy to see her play the heavy for a change.

"I understand that you lost your Yankees cap," Johanna said, addressing Vincent. "Is it worth destroying the whole trip for that? Maybe we'll put you on the plane back tomorrow. By being mad right now you're making me mad. You're making me in a bad mood. You are spreading a bad vibe among the chorus. The chorus sounded terrible on the ship."

Mr. Benardo was the only one who appeared distressed by Johanna's loss of composure. Just as she feared that Vincent's breakdown would ruin the trip, the principal seemed worried that Johanna was going to crack. Trying to restore equilibrium, he took off his own baseball cap and extended it to Vincent. Vincent stonily refused.

Emily Coca warned the principal not to get involved. "Take it back," she muttered, as Benardo proffered his cap. Her guidance counselor instinct told her there was more to Vincent's temper tantrum than met the eye, and the principal was only inflaming it. Even Vincent, who had the hair-trigger temper of the bad guy in a spaghetti western, would not get so upset over losing a Bronx Bombers cap.

"Leave him alone. Don't give him a window."

"He got the window already," Mr. Benardo said.

"But he got it on his own."

Miss Coca was right. That cap was more important to Vincent than they could know. What he stubbornly refused to confide in them, as he sat there scowling, was that it had not been the Yankees cap that everybody was accustomed to seeing him wear. Just before the trip, his mother had given him $25 to buy a 76ers cap, an authorized team cap, a street-culture status symbol, which he had coveted for weeks. His heart sank as he saw the princely sum of $25 lost in the waves. But it wasn't just the money. His new cap, like his old one, had become his lucky charm, his version of a rabbit's foot or religious medallion. He put it on in the morning and took it off only to go to sleep. It made him feel powerful, good-looking. He didn't feel complete without it. Perhaps unconsciously, it was a link to his father's alternate world in Allentown, a promise that he would move there some day. The 76ers were a Philadelphia team, and Allentown was a satellite of Philly. His father's aura, his father's shamanic protection, had drowned with that cap in the brackish waters of the Baltic Sea.

And Mr. Benardo was the last person Vincent would allow to fill his father's shoes.

Johanna, holding the microphone, hardly noticed Mr. Benardo's intercession, her anxiety expanding as rapidly as one of those tiny paper pills that unfurls into a lurid, luxuriant flower when dropped in a glass of water.

"If you don't appreciate the things that we do, then we won't give you any more liberties. If you don't work with us, we won't work with you. You don't understand this sailing ship we traveled on is very very expensive. We got it for free. They are a very experienced crew, working for free. Our host families made us lunches and we were very lucky with the weather. The only thing I wished for was for you guys to show smiley faces and sing out strong for one photograph at the end."

The children looked relieved when their arrival at the camp forced Johanna to end her sermon. Lembote was as austere as a monastery, clean and restful, a spa for the soul: pine floors, white walls, slatted furniture. There was a stainless-steel kitchen and a large refectory, where the children would be served meals—whole-grain bread, lots of butter, yogurt, cold cuts—three times a day. Rooms were assigned, boys in one dormitory, girls in the other, with the nametags of the children in each bedroom affixed to the doors. Each room was equipped with two to four cots or bunkbeds, a few shelves, and a desk. The campground was set in a clearing amid the shelter of towering pine trees, and a lake stretched out behind it. A wooden boardwalk connected two sauna houses, one for men and the other for women, to the lake. Beyond the enclosing wall of forest, the farmlands began.

"Nobody under any circumstances goes near the water," Mr. Benardo warned. "Stay away from the water." He meant the children, not the adults.

After the others had gone to bed, Shelly Benardo heard music coming from the grand piano in the main lodge, and wandered in to find Johanna. She was playing fiercely, obsessively, blowing off steam. He sat down on one of the white couches, and waited for her to stop playing and join him. "What's wrong?"

Johanna was still angry with Vincent and Jamie for not singing. What if they choked up on their last night, when they would be giving a concert before the whole town? They were her main soloists, and for them to fail would be the ultimate humiliation, for her and for them. Maybe her confidence in Vincent had been misplaced, she told the principal. Out of his element, Vincent seemed small and scared. Jamie was a different case. He should know better, should understand perfectly well what was at stake for her. She feared he was manipulating her, that the attention had turned him into a prima donna. "I'm going to tell Jamie that I have a backup," Johanna said. "If he does that on Friday, he can't sing. It's like anorexia, you have to shake them out of it." There it was. She had unwittingly blurted out a shameful fragment of her own past. She had been anorexic in high school, driven to succeed, afraid that she wasn't good enough.

Mr. Benardo listened quietly, alertly, absorbing the veiled cue about Johanna's past. He was surprised at the depth of her rage until he realized that she was fighting her own inner demons, her own struggle with the impossibility of perfection. He recognized that this was about Johanna, not only the children. She was the one who felt tested and judged. She had dreamed of a triumphant homecoming, and now she saw her dream slipping away. She was the one who needed to put things in perspective. "These people have known you since you were 2 years old," he told her, gently. "Anything you do will look good to them. It doesn't matter whether Vincent moves his legs. Jamie is meek. He won't cause any problems."

∾

While Mr. Benardo comforted Johanna, her father sat in the kitchen of the red house. Lillemor wanted to know everything. What did Uffe think of Mr. Benardo? She already felt defensive toward him, because she knew he had criticized her daughter, and she was bracing for the moment when she would finally meet him.

"I liked him," Uffe said. Shelly Benardo had told him a story about a fire drill, praising Johanna's conduct. Hundreds of children had to descend the staircases and gather in the yard. Johanna had brought her guitar. While the children waited for the all-clear signal, she distracted them by playing her guitar and coaxing them to sing along with her. Mr. Benardo told Uffe how impressed he had been by her poise. Uffe recognized a type, the manager who has learned, through painful experience, to keep his counsel. Like Uffe, Mr. Benardo was parsimonious in self-revelation, waiting to test the waters of his listener's psyche before risking any confidences, and then saying only what seemed safe to say. But he did not hesitate to talk about Johanna, and what he said was kind. He seemed to care about her, and to want her family to be proud of her. It seemed that Mr. Benardo had been something of a father-figure to Johanna. Maybe he had been hard on her sometimes. But that was to be expected. Unlike a father's, a boss's love is never unconditional.

CHAPTER NINETEEN

ᘓ

Johanna's Secret

Johanna called a taxi to take her home. Letting herself into the red house, she climbed the stairs as quietly as she could. It was nearly midnight, and she didn't want to disturb her parents, but her halting step was hard to miss, especially for Lillemor, whose nocturnal hearing was still attuned to the weight and rhythm of each child's foot on the creaking wooden staircase, even now that they were all grown. Rising into half-consciousness, she registered that this was not the effervescent step of Bodi, but Johanna, her middle child, whose footfall echoed a fraction longer tonight than last night.

Gripping the wooden banister, Johanna pulled herself up one stiff leg at a time, pausing on each step to catch her balance. It had been a long day; the trouble with Vincent had slowed her down.

"What is her secret?" someone asked during the trip, marveling at Johanna's drive and ambition. People often asked that question, in the same rhetorical spirit as "I don't know how she does it."

But Johanna did have a secret that she tried to keep from all but a few close friends. She had been in her early 20s when she first learned that she and her two sisters had muscular dystrophy, the degenerative muscle disease that would shadow them for the rest of their lives. Against the odds, they had lost a statistical lottery. The disease afflicted all three sisters through a recessive gene transmitted by both of their parents, who had been unaware that they were carriers.

At times Johanna struggled to keep her secret even from herself, to ignore it, forget it, pretend it didn't exist. All that activity, that relentless pursuit of her goals, helped her to forget. Her weakness drove her.

But at home in Aland, Johanna found her illness easier to confront in the company of her two sisters. In fact, it was hard not to think about it, when every time she came back, Cocki, as the oldest, seemed to have deteriorated a little more. By now, Cocki had made a habit of hiding her atrophied legs under long flower-child skirts, and had a handicapped parking permit, though people often glared at her when she used it, not understanding how a woman so youthful and healthy looking could be disabled.

The conversation turned to their illness the next morning at breakfast, as the sisters had their first chance to be together since Johanna's arrival. Bodi and Martin staggered out of the carriage house where they lived for a cup of coffee in Lillemor's kitchen. They were still groggy from a late night tending Uffe's café. Cocki drove in from her home twenty minutes away. Nena also came by for the reunion.

As far back as Johanna could remember she and her sisters had had leg pains, which they had learned to dismiss as growing pains. Johanna remembered Bodi waking up in the middle of the night, crying, and being given hot baths to soothe her cramps. But these pains had never seriously hindered their activities. If anything, the sisters overcompensated. They skated and skied.

"We could run fast," Bodi recalled, as the three of them reminisced around the kitchen table.

"Not that fast," Cocki demurred.

"I was strong," Bodi insisted. "I could hit a baseball, and in arm wrestling, I beat all the boys in my class."

But they tired quickly.

"I was always the last one picked for games at school," Johanna recalled.

When she couldn't keep up with the other children, her coaches accused her of being lazy.

"They never thought there might be more to it," she said.

In high school, she pushed herself to keep up. She began swimming three times a week to strengthen her muscles. Then she would be in agony all weekend.

"The thing is, we all thought it was normal," Bodi said.

"I remember every year, from first through sixth grade, we had to go for a community walk—five kilometers. The night before that day I was so nervous because I knew my legs weren't going to manage."

"I felt it in discos," Cocki added.

If anything, their growing pains were dwarfed by Bodi's childhood blindness, a much more dramatic discovery, and by a normal amount of sibling rivalry.

Bodi was a clumsy, backward baby. She learned to walk and talk late. She tripped on stairs and showed no interest in books or television. She spent a lot of time sitting at the piano in the parlor, picking out tunes. Lillemor became protective, carrying her everywhere to keep her from falling. But in most ways Bodi was a lively, curious child. So with the laissez-faire attitude of an experienced mother, Lillemor never suspected that anything was wrong.

Then when Bodi was about 4, she accompanied a cousin on a visit to the eye doctor. While there, she took the eye test herself, just for fun. The nurses were flabbergasted to discover that little Bodi was nearly blind in one eye, and had very poor vision in the other. The doctor first prescribed a patch for the blind eye and, later, glasses with mismatched lenses, one thick, the other thin. The glasses made her appear to be a homely child. But her vision steadily improved. Finally, in high school, she went for a checkup and discovered that her sight was 20–20. For the first time she could remember, she was able to take off her glasses, and at that moment, she turned from an ugly duckling into a swan.

Telling the story, she went to a kitchen drawer and, laughing, pulled out a souvenir of her childhood, a child-sized pair of silver-rimmed spectacles, the left lens so thick it looked telescopic, the right one thinner.

Bodi's blindness drove something of a wedge between her and her older sisters. Lillemor showered her with maternal attention, and the other girls noticed.

"We were jealous, Mamma," Cocki scolded, looking back on their childhood.

"You gave all your attention to Bodi," Johanna seconded.

"You were never angry at Bodi," Cocki said.

"You were always angry at me," Johanna added, petulantly, only half in jest.

"She never said a word until she was 8," Lillemor put in.

"You can see why, because everybody else talked," Bodi retorted.

Johanna tried to compete with Bodi by demanding medical treatment of her own. Once, her mother persuaded her to go to a regular doctor's visit by promising that she would receive a polio vaccination. But when they got there, the nurse looked at her chart and announced that she had already been vaccinated; there had been some misunderstanding. Johanna threw a fit and would not stop bawling until the nurse agreed to give her another shot, a measles vaccination, instead.

"I have no memory of my childhood at all," Johanna said, perturbed, as her mother told the story.

Cocki was the opposite, always well behaved, the perfect older sister. It wasn't so much that she wanted to be Miss Goody Two-Shoes, but everyone seemed to expect and demand it of her. "I pierced my nose when I was 14," Cocki recalled. "No one I knew had a piercing in the nose. Everyone was so shocked, especially daddy. But I didn't want to be the princess anymore."

By the time Bodi was old enough to rebel, her parents hardly noticed, just as they had, for a while, been sanguine about her blindness.

"Now she's got piercings and tattoos and nobody says anything," Cocki said.

"You have changed the most of all of us," Cocki said, addressing Bodi. "You were so wimpy. Now you're this tough girl."

"It's hard to be the younger one," Bodi objected, bridling at the attack.

At this, Nena, who had been listening quietly, weighed in on Cocki's side.

"It's harder to be the older one," she declared.

"I had to fight with both of you," Johanna pointed out.

"Mmmm. The double fighter. Up and down," Nena mused.

☙

In spite of their competitiveness, the sisters were close, and they grew closer when Cocki discovered the truth about their childhood growing pains. It was 1993, just before Johanna left for Boston. Cocki was 25. Her first child, Olivia, was a year old. As the pregnancy had progressed, Cocki had found it increasingly difficult to climb stairs. She asked friends whether they had experienced similar symptoms during pregnancy, but they had not. She did not become very alarmed until she found that she could no longer carry Olivia and walk upstairs at the same time. Her doctor ordered tests, and her muscular dystrophy was diagnosed.

Neither Johanna nor Bodi bothered to go to the doctor for confirmation that they were affected. They knew immediately, without being tested, that they had it too.

"Bodi and I kept on going with our lives," Johanna said later. "I never thought about getting myself checked, since I already knew.

I moved to Boston, and I never took it very seriously until years later, when I saw what was happening to Cocki. It's not something you can imagine until it happens."

Uffe handled the news stoically and, in his rational way, focused on treatment and solutions, like designing a handrail on the front steps for Cocki. Lillemor was devastated. Her hair, which had always been a pretty light auburn, turned gray—overnight, it seemed to her.

CHAPTER TWENTY

∞

Paradise

The chorus woke up to find that they were front-page news. *Aland-stidningen* chronicled the arrival of the kids under the headline, "Close to Nature with Aland," and played the story above the fold, more prominently than an article entitled "From Pig to Sausage in the Same House" or the latest news about a virus that was killing farmed fish. Johanna was pleased. She was counting on the publicity to drum up interest in their concert.

The kids might as well have been visitors from outer space, alien, dark, fascinating to the locals in their mix of childish innocence and untold danger. Even to the most sophisticated Scandinavians, who consciously knew better, the Bronx was the iconic New York, a code-word for abandonment, crime, devastation, otherness. North Bronx, South Bronx, those were incomprehensible distinctions, academic nuances. By comparison, the rest of the day's news was tediously parochial, the daily gruel of country life.

Over the next few days, the kids didn't take their growing celebrity to heart. Reading about their adventure in the newspaper paled compared to the experience itself. They were exhausted, happy, relaxed. Mr. Benardo was proud of his energetic young teachers. One afternoon, he threw his arm around Emily Coca's shoulders like a shawl, as they walked to the main camp cabin side by side. Heads together, they seemed comfortably lost in some confidence, secure in the knowledge that all was in order.

Each day, they would follow the tourist routine that Johanna had promised to the Board of Education, and then retreat to the camp as if it were their home. The Spartan cabins and grassy fields became their private space, walled off from the tensions of a strange land. But after dinner, the kids missed their real home, and found the quiet—no traffic noise, no sirens or flashing lights—unsettling. They congregated by the single telephone in each cabin, waiting for their parents to call. The boys heard tapping on their windows, and a rumor spread that there was a bear or a burglar on the prowl.

In the eerily prolonged daylight, Ashley Alvarez and Jheanamer Hernandez asked Johanna to explain the difference between wildflowers and cultivated ones, so they would know which ones they could pick. Johanna laughed as they filled the empty Pringles potato chip cans they had brought with them with flowers. Ashley had saved three Pepsi bottles, the glass a novelty, as souvenirs. Eralis collected live snails. She stepped on one and was panicked that she had killed it until she saw two antennae peek out. Then she carried it around in the palm of her hand like a pet.

"I've seen the child side of them," Johanna told her mother. "In New York they have to be so grown up, keeping a set of keys, finding a way home. What time to do this, what time to do that."

The adults, tired of spending hours a day in the company of children, found more adult ways to amuse themselves. Someone showed them how to fire up the sauna, which was nothing like the electric saunas in American locker rooms. Each wooden cabin was equipped with a pot-bellied stove, stoked with firewood and newspaper. The stove heated a pot of hot water, which was ladled onto a pile of smooth black pebbles to create steam. In Scandinavia, the Finns told the Americans, taking a sauna was a macho spectator sport, like cockfighting or a Golden Gloves boxing match. Finns competed against Swedes to see who could withstand the greatest extremes of temperature—heating up in the sauna, then jumping into icy water—while consuming large quantities of fried Baltic herring and cold Schnapps. Shelly Benardo and company didn't achieve quite that degree of authenticity, but they were tickled to be able to do something truly Finnish, not to mention having a chance to relax. In a steam-room version of the faculty lounge, they sat on the frigid dock wrapped in towels, gossiping about the kids, the school, one another. Their sauna became a nightly ritual. Only Margaret and Dorothy stayed away, not quite part of the club, though Margaret, amused, took pictures.

On the third night, as the children were being put to bed at camp, Nena dropped by the Grussner's house. It was the night before the long-awaited dinner with the chorus, and she found Lillemor in the kitchen marinating pork loin and snipping parsley for the potatoes. (After seesawing between rice and potatoes, she had decided on potatoes.) "So you're the one who made the big meat order," Nena observed. "The butcher had nothing left to sell."

"Stay for dinner," Lillemor said.

"No thanks," Nena replied. "I'm making myself a nice lamb with potatoes, mushrooms, and cream sauce."

"Will you be back tomorrow then?" Lillemor coaxed. She might need the moral support.

"I'll see."

Uffe meandered in next, part of the constant parade, pacing the room like a lion in a cage. "I'm hungry, wife," he barked, hoping a little comedy would soften her up.

"Have a banana," Lillemor said coolly, picking up a banana from the counter and handing it over.

CHAPTER TWENTY-ONE

❦

Edible Flowers

With Johanna's father at the wheel, the red bus cruised through an idyllic rural scene, past antique red windmills with missing sails, cows lazing in a pasture. Johanna pointed out the pond where she had skated as a child. "I love ice skating. I can't really do it anymore," she said wistfully.

The bus pulled to a stop along a grassy field studded with yellow dandelions, where a double-file of children—students at Palsbole Skola, the village school—waited excitedly behind Ester Miiros, their principal. With unconscious drama, Miiros had led her flock out into the fresh air and across the sweeping hillside for their first meeting with Johanna, who might have been a pretty young governess, and her troupe. The children were introduced to their penpals, and everyone tromped together across the field to the school.

Chatting with Mr. Benardo as they walked, Miiros, a pretty, ivory-complexioned woman in her late 30s, with a soft cloud of brown hair, told him that she had just been appointed principal of this and two neighboring schools. But even as she had been adjusting to her new job, she confided, she was juggling a new baby, her third child. She had returned from maternity leave only yesterday, but she didn't feel too bad because her 9-month-old son was home with his father, rather than a babysitter. Being childless, and male, Mr. Benardo didn't pick up on her frank maternal anxiety. But he did absorb that she was a novice administrator, not up to his level. "I've been in the job ten years," he said, a bit smugly. "That's why I have gray hair."

Mr. Benardo had pegged Miiros as a small-town school mistress, holding down a job much less cutthroat than his own. Her genteel style and conservative clothes only added to the impression: loose flowered skirt to her ankles, black pumps, white lacy blouse, green jacket, and, of course, glasses. Next to her, the teachers from the Bronx, Fiona, Michelle, and Emily, looked tough as nails. In their formfitting jeans and tight knitted shirts they might as well have been dressed for a visit to a bar or a disco.

All the adults assembled in this grassy field seemed to be actors in different plays, as if Miiros had come prepared to co-star in a gauzy production of *Brigadoon*, all romance and idealism, while the Bronx teachers had stepped out of the wardrobe section for *Saturday Night Fever*. The contrasts gave the encounter a bizarre air of dissonance. The Finns were on their home turf, so they seemed comfortable in spite of these early warning signs. But on the American side, everyone, both teachers and students, looked a bit shell-shocked. This was the first time since their arrival on Finnish soil that they had been called upon to be not just passive tourists but active participants, forced to interact with their hosts. They hadn't bothered to study the rules of the game in advance.

◌♉◌

The outside world was intruding on Aland in ways that many of its inhabitants didn't like. When Shelly Benardo met Ester Miiros, misjudging her as a mommy-track principal, she had just been assigned to a challenging job as troubleshooter and peacemaker, dividing her time between three regional schools. The small, idyllic Palsbole Skola was undergoing profound upheaval. The days Johanna remembered, of an independent country school, hardly bigger than the proverbial one-room schoolhouse, where teachers nurtured children as if they were their own, had begun to fall prey to many of the same pressures that Mr. Benardo faced in the Bronx: centralization and loss of local autonomy and standardization and testing.

As part of the increased central supervision, the province of Finstrom had proposed to consolidate three small country schools of fifty to sixty students each into two larger ones, one in Palsbole and one in Godby. Administratively and financially, consolidation made sense. The existing schools were so small that it was hard to equalize class sizes. Depending on the birth and mobility rates, a class one year might be much smaller than a class the next, sometimes forcing teachers to change grades or classes to include more than one grade.

Teachers feared that the consolidation would disrupt the separate culture that had grown up around each school, and that they had had a hand in creating. Anne-Charlotte Haggblom, the longtime English and Swedish teacher, was one of the most skeptical. The essence of the education that Johanna remembered so fondly—the individual attention, the devotion to play as well as to lessons—was on the way out, Haggblom warned her younger colleagues. Bur Miiros argued that in struggling to remain independent, the smaller schools had starved themselves of money and resources that would be available to a larger school through economies of scale.

If anyone could steer the schools through these debates, it would seem to be Miiros. She took an appealingly modest view of her abilities, saying that she had gone into teaching because she was not brilliant but could do many things competently. She soon discovered that although she was on her own behind the closed door of her classroom, she was not totally in control of her destiny. She was part of a bigger organization, in which decisions were made for her by her superiors within the school system and by politicians outside of it. To be effective, she felt that she had to become one of those people. Some of the older staff resented Miiros, the hard-charging working mother (she kept a yellow cellphone for family calls, a gray one for work calls). They saw her as the hired hatchet, too acquiescent in the drive to shake up the established way of doing things.

But she still believed in the intimate, informal kind of educational philosophy that Mr. Benardo had thought would be so difficult to sustain at his big institution in the Bronx. Like progressive educators in the United States, she lamented that the central government was trying to wrest control of the schools away from local administrators like herself. Aland's schools had been unfairly maligned, she thought, for having lower test scores in Swedish and mathematics, on average, than schools in Sweden, where the curriculum was similar. But what the government had not sufficiently taken into account, Miiros believed, was that students in Aland had better attitudes toward education than those in mainland schools.

For the time being, the government was focusing its attention on testing students more—and evaluating teachers by test results—in the older grades. Miiros feared, however, that this method of judging schools would inevitably drift downward to the earlier grades. She predicted that too much emphasis on testing would undermine the confidence of teachers, would dampen their willingness to take chances, to have fun, to leave the classroom and romp around in the forest. Had he known Miiros's point of view, Shelly Benardo probably would have approved.

Palsbole Skola, built in 1966, was only one story high, a modest yellow-brick rectangular building with floor-to-ceiling windows all around it. The schoolyard was spacious and inviting, equipped with tire swings, wooden climbing bars, soccer fields, and a grassy lawn. It would have looked at home in one of New York City's smaller, more exclusive suburbs, Briarcliff Manor, perhaps, or in the hills of Vermont. The effect was charming, rural, intimate, an architectural homage to progressive education and implicit repudiation of the factory model the P.S. 86 children knew so well. For Vincent, brought up in the arid brick canyons of the Bronx, this verdant hamlet and quaint little school were bizarrely intimidating. He walked cautiously through the school door. Sneakers and sandals littered the foyer, where the students and teachers had shed their shoes before going to class. Even though Vincent had had to take his shoes off at Tomas's house on that first night, he had not realized then that this was a universal custom, which would be enforced in public and private settings alike. "That's ghetto," he said, grimacing, as he reluctantly added his sneakers to the pile.

He felt exposed, a dangerous feeling for a tough kid. Walking around in athletic socks took a little bit of the edge off his strut, as if he had been handed a pair of bunny slippers and told to put them on. American sneakers were a status symbol, but what good was a weapon if you had been disarmed?

In the hallway, sunlight streamed through windows filled with spider and snake plants. The linoleum floors and '60s modern furniture were in perfect shape, and stylish enough to look at home in a Third Avenue doctor's office, or maybe a retro furniture showroom in trendy Soho or Tribeca. Looking down the corridor, the children could see a succession of comfortable places to sit: a green vinyl bench, a brown leather bench, and a blue cloth bench. The very idea of upholstered furniture would be anathema in a New York City public school, where indestructibility was the goal. The esthetics of the Board of Education had more in common with the esthetics of a county jail than of a family dwelling, and students, like inmates, were viewed as wards who must be tamed rather than civilized.

It was true, as Johanna had told them, that her old school had just fifty-six students and six teachers in first through sixth grade. As in an old-fashioned country schoolhouse, some teachers taught two grades in the same room. The Bronx children sat on the bright-orange linoleum floor in the doll-sized gymnasium and studied their Finnish counterparts sitting opposite them, like two sports teams divided by hair-color, one uniformly dark, the other uniformly light.

Anne-Charlotte Haggblom, the English, French, and religion teacher, dressed in a sunny yellow suit, asked each class of Finnish children to stand and recite their names, one by one, so the American children could hear what Finnish names sounded like. The children were less impressed by the names than by the large size of the Finnish students. Jamie, who was on the short side, pointed to a first-grader and marveled: "Look at her. She's about my size. I'm a midget. My God, Eralis is shorter than the first-graders." Eralis, a basketball player, was considered fairly tall by P.S. 86 standards.

Describing their schoolday, Haggblom mentioned that the children went out to play twice a day, in the morning and in the afternoon, on top of the short breaks between each lesson. To the Bronx children, for whom going outside even once a day was a luxury, and who were sometimes punished by having recess withheld, so much playtime was nirvana. "I hope I get lost so I can stay here," Jamie whispered to Krysten.

Mr. Benardo put on his diplomatic hat and rose to the occasion with a long, gracious speech of his own, a virtual tour of P.S. 86, which he described as a much more daunting environment than Palsbole Skola. Mr. Benardo's amateur-psychologist persona kicked in, as it had so often on this trip. He had a knack for echoing back what others told him, making them feel appreciated and understood, and it was a skill he put to good use while visiting Johanna's old school.

"First, I apologize for not being able to speak Swedish," he began. "Everybody here speaks our language. That's something perhaps that we have to do a little bit better." The children on both sides of the

Atlantic had a lot in common, he noted: They listened to the same music; they worried about boyfriends and girlfriends; they surfed the net. But their schools were very different.

"Let me tell you about our school and our day. First, we have 2,000 kids in the school. Our main school building is five stories tall. We had to build two other buildings, one that took up our schoolyard and one many blocks away. Most of our kids walk to school, some take the subway. We start at 8 in the morning. We have breakfast for half an hour. Our subjects go 'til 12:30, then we have lunch 'til 1:30. We return to our subjects until 3 o'clock. Most of the students at 3 o'clock begin another part of the schoolday that goes until 5 o'clock.

"In our school we have 200 teachers. You're really fortunate that you get personal, caring attention that enables you to learn so much. I see you call your teachers by their first names. In New York, everyone is called 'Miss,' whether they are a grandmother or married. Maybe I can learn something by being here. Maybe a school works better when a teacher is called by her first name."

It was a good speech, humble and deferential, and the Finnish teachers were visibly moved. He had left them feeling slightly superior, and he seemed genuinely interested in their way of doing things. They were convinced that he would try out some of their methods in New York—the first names, perhaps.

The big culture shock came when the children sat down to lunch in what passed for the cafeteria, an airy space off the gymnasium, flooded with light by a full wall of windows, in contrast to New York school cafeterias, which were typically buried in the gloomy basement level. The lunch tables were small and round, a communal shape, not the long rectangular kind in the Bronx, the kind that forced kids to lean over their neighbors to talk. Each table seated just six or seven people. The tables were set with white china plates, silverware, and bunches of freshly picked yellow wildflowers in glass vases. Each table had been equipped with a bowl of butter, another bowl of beets, a carton of milk, a metal pitcher of cold water, and a roll of paper towels. There was a certain delicacy about the whole arrangement. None of the teachers assumed, it seemed, that anything breakable would inevitably be broken, would cut someone accidentally or, worse, on purpose—or if they did think of such things, they seemed prepared to cope. There were no disposable cardboard trays. There were no plastic sporks, a spoon with a jagged tip like a dull fork, the hybrid parody of an eating utensil that has been inflicted on American schools and prisons, eliminating the need for separate spoons and forks, and, presumably, reducing the risk of someone using the fork as a weapon. The napkins were not wrapped in sanitary plastic and carefully rationed. And there were no lines for food so long and slow that some children ended up with only five minutes to wolf down their lunch— a problem that was once cited as the cause of a choking death in a Manhattan public school.

Adults and children ate together, family style. Even the kitchen staff and the cleaning woman, Britt-Viola Johns, who had picked the flowers and had sewed the printed fabric curtains for the classrooms, joined the students for lunch, fanning out among the tables. When a teacher was absent, the cleaning woman, who knew the children as well as anyone, often doubled as a substitute teacher.

Despite the hospitality, the American students felt disoriented. They stood uncertainly as the Palsbole students said a short prayer—translated into English for the benefit of their guests—over their meal of boiled potatoes and fried whitefish. "In the name of Jesus we sit down at the table. God bless the food we receive. Amen." But the moment passed quickly.

Over lunch, the children got to know their penfriends, as the Finns called them. Two crew-cut, giggling boys, Rasmus and Emil, "full of sausage," one of the adults joked affectionately, had been paired with Priscilla and Jamie. Priscilla had recovered from her homesickness on the boat, but was not impressed by her penfriend, the well-fed, moon-faced Rasmus. Rasmus had said something insulting to her that she would not repeat. But she did not hesitate to tell her classmates what she thought of him. "He's rude and big," she said. "I expected to get somebody cute and nice, not large. He's overweight, he's larger than I expected. My sister's not even that large." So much for cross-cultural friendship.

☙

Priscilla had no way of knowing that the impudent Rasmus Kytomaki was the grandson of one of Aland's biggest industrialists, Trygve Eriksson, the chief executive of Eriksson Capital. To his classmates, he was a smart student with a sly sense of humor. Asked what he wanted to be when he grew up, he quickly replied, "Bigger!"

Even at the age of 11, Rasmus had seen more of New York City than the average student at P.S. 86. He had been to New York the year before with his grandmother, taking in a Rangers game at Madison Square Garden, but never venturing as far north as the Bronx.

His favorite writer was P. G. Wodehouse, because he was funny and because he wrote about golf, a sport that Rasmus played with his older brother.

They lived in a newly constructed pale-blue house with an Italianate tile roof, a greenhouse, a skylit garret, a two-car garage, and a foyer strewn with children's toys. Every night, Rasmus climbed, like Heidi, up a blue ladder to a sleeping loft. Lying in the loft, he gazed up at a ceiling decorated with phosphorescent constellations.

Rasmus's best friend (besides the eerily twin-like Emil) was Christoffer Blomqvist, who had been placed at a different table with Rickey Colbourne. Although Rickey had corresponded with Christoffer, he felt scared the first time he saw him. Christoffer had classic country-bumpkin looks: beanpole tall and lean, with a bowl-trimmed head of carrot-red hair and a field of freckles across his rosy cheeks. Maybe people looked like this in Idaho, but not in the Bronx. Christoffer's size and foreignness were intimidating, and hard to interpret. Rickey could read the subtlest cues about disposition on the streets of the Bronx, judging in a split-second—by the rhythm of a step, a fleeting moment of eye contact—who was a threat and who was harmless. But here in Aland, he had been disarmed, his usual survival tactics almost irrelevant.

But Rickey's fears were misplaced. Christoffer was a sweet, precocious kid who had taught himself English before he was old enough to go to school, by watching cartoons with Swedish subtitles on Nickelodeon. He had read all the Harry Potter books—in English. Collections of vintage Donald Duck comic books and empty Coke bottles lined the shelves of his room at home. He was fairly thrumming with anticipation, and couldn't wait to try out his English on a real live person.

There weren't many opportunities to meet Americans in Bartsgarda, the tiny village that encompassed the Blomqvist family farm. The road to Christoffer's house meandered through acre after acre of neatly mapped out apple orchards, then across a bridge over a rushing creek to a lush stretch of rolling hills. Going from Mariehamn to Bartsgarda was like crossing a space-warp and leaping from New York to Kansas— the traveler experienced the compression of distance and rapid shift of terrain that often characterize small places. The houses were spread far apart; the nearest grocery store was Sarling's, owned by Cocki's in-laws, across the street from the Grussner house, 8 kilometers away. The isolated setting seemed to portend a simpler life and gentler manners.

And Christoffer did, indeed, have an unpretentious decency, perhaps born of husbanding farm animals. He had grown up in a modern white-stucco trailer-sized house on a hill. To the left of it stood the original red farmhouse, with a corrugated metal roof, built by his grandfather. His mother had grown up in the old house, but now it was sagging and had been relegated mainly to storage.

Like Rickey's father, who worked in construction for the money and designed leisure clothes as a passion, Christoffer's parents led dual working lives, one motivated by economics and the other, at least in part, by sentimental attachment. His father, Kurt, managed tax-free shopping on the Viking Line ferry. But Kurt and his wife, Marina, were also vegetable farmers—growing onions, cucumbers, melons, peas, cabbages—on the land she had inherited.

Christoffer had gone moose and bear hunting with his father, but never killed an animal. He preferred target practice with his bow and arrow. He knew the foibles of every farm animal: Olga, the little white chicken with the golden breast, who considered herself the queen of the roost; the bunny, Elvis, who had a habit of tunneling into the ground; the Shetland pony who constantly escaped his stall.

To Christoffer, Rickey represented an exciting world outside Aland, a world he planned to explore someday as a pyrotechnics expert. So far, he had been to Morocco, Egypt, and the Canary Islands. Comparing notes with Rickey, he learned that they both liked Gameboy and Pokeman, and that they shared a favorite television show, *The Simpsons*.

At lunch that day, Christoffer told his American tablemates that the wildflowers, gullviva, were edible, and daring to munch on the yellow blossoms became their lunchtime entertainment.

Vincent's attitude improved after lunch, when the children went out for some playtime. He grabbed a basketball and initiated a pickup game, as if he were back with his buddies on the sidewalk in front of his building in the Bronx. Malin Jansson, Vincent's penfriend, who had asked whether he had a girlfriend in her letter to him before the trip, immediately joined in. Malin, a 12-year-old Pippi Longstocking looka-like with flaming red hair, had had her eye on Vincent since lunch. Rickey and Christoffer followed, along with Bisola Bruno, Eralis, and their Finnish counterparts. The game reflected their off-court personalities. Vincent focused on showmanship, dribbling the ball between his legs, while Rickey concentrated on winning, tearing toward the net. The Bronx kids used their superior technique to make up for the Finns' taller stature. While the Finns played silently, the Americans talked trash. "A girl is beating you and you moving nowhere, Vincent," Bisola taunted, until Vincent, stung, dunked the ball.

Malin was smitten. "He's cute," she said, admiring his big dark eyes and baggy hip-hop pants.

As the Bronx kids gathered to leave, Mr. Benardo and Miiros talked about the possibility of the Finnish children making an exchange trip to New York. Unexpectedly, Mr. Benardo dropped a hint, loud enough for everyone to hear, that he was not sure Johanna would be returning in the fall. "One thing you have to do for me," he said to Miiros. "You have to convince Johanna to come back to our school in September. If you do that, I'll make sure you're invited."

Listening, Johanna felt a pang of anxiety. He knew. Those seven suitcases had been an omen, an unspoken clue that she might not be returning. He had not said a word to her directly, but he wouldn't. This was all the acknowledgment she would get. She realized, to her surprise, that in spite of everything, Mr. Benardo valued what she had done.

CHAPTER TWENTY-TWO

∾

A Scarlet Letter

As the chorus left Palsbole Skola, Benardo was in an irascible mood. Despite his self-effacing speech, he hadn't liked the implicit comparison between the Finnish school and his school. He hadn't liked being patronized by the Finnish teachers, and he worried that his students felt inferior. P.S. 86 was a well-managed school, and he resented any implication—even unintended—that it was not. But hadn't he himself stressed the contrasts? What about the admiration he had professed for the Finnish way of doing things? He had sounded so sincere. What about calling teachers by their first names? Hadn't he said he might try that at home? The fact was, that would never really work. He was only being a good guest. His speech had been a kind of Kabuki theater, a stylized dance of politeness, not to be taken at face value.

No one was more loyal to P.S. 86 than Benardo. Soon after taking over the school, he had been through more than most principals go through in a lifetime: a corruption probe that could have ruined his reputation and ended his career. After that experience, some colleagues thought he had become hypersensitive to criticism. But in a way, they understood his position. Anything that reflected badly on him or his school might raise the specter of that investigation, which, though closed under the law, was as fresh to him as if it had happened yesterday.

In December 1993, Edward F. Stancik, the city's special investigator for schools, announced the results of a ten-month investigation accusing New York City's Board of Elections of "gross mismanagement" of the city's community school board elections the previous May.

The report, called "From Chaos to Corruption: An Investigation into the 1993 Community School Board Election," described petition fraud, political coercion by school officials, and, in one part of the northwest Bronx, a scheme to deliver phony absentee ballots on behalf of certain candidates. Despite the allegations, it was unclear, Stancik conceded, that fraud or corruption had changed the outcome of any of the elections.

In District 10, which encompassed P.S. 86, Stancik accused James P. Sullivan, director of pupil personnel for the district, of orchestrating a ballot-stuffing scheme. Stancik said the motivation for that and alleged corruption in other parts of the city was to protect the jobs of political allies and to maintain control over school budgets in the $100 million range. The attempt to influence the elections, the investigator said, had everything to do with politics, and nothing to do with the education of children.

Sullivan, the report said, had engineered the "most egregious fraud" of that year's election: Under Sullivan's direction, two Fordham University students, working as temporary district employees, had filled out 117 absentee-ballot applications using the names of unsuspecting fellow university students and cast them on behalf of Edward McCarthy, a school-board candidate. McCarthy won the election.

∽

In the wake of that report, Stancik and the U.S. attorney for the southern district conducted a joint investigation that lasted more than two years and involved hundreds of interviews and the review of thousands of documents. During federal grand jury proceedings, hundreds of witnesses gave hundreds of hours of testimony and thousands of documents were introduced into evidence. At that point, the federal authorities decided that they lacked jurisdiction to prosecute and turned the case over to the Bronx district attorney.

The investigation ensnared one of Shelly Benardo's assistant principals, Lorraine Pacheco, and turned P.S. 86 upside down. Pacheco had been a popular assistant principal at P.S. 86 until 1993, when she was promoted to interim principal of a school in Manhattan. She was accused of helping to carry out the ballot-rigging scheme.

Although Benardo had not been mentioned in the Stancik report, he was among those called to testify before the grand jury. He admitted that he had been given absentee ballots to fill out, but denied that he had done anything illegal. When the investigation was over, he believed that he had only narrowly escaped being indicted himself.

On April 24, 1996, five high-ranking officials of District 10 were charged with participating in a scheme to rig the 1993 school-board election.

Prosecutors portrayed a school district riddled with political rivalries and connections to city and state legislators, in which the school system functioned essentially as a big patronage hiring hall. The goal was for the defendants to preserve their own jobs, which depended on which of two factions controlled the school board, and for their political allies to maintain control over patronage in the schools.

The indictment charged that Sullivan and the other four defendants duped college students, homeless mothers, elderly residents of nursing homes, colleagues, and relatives into casting more than 250 fraudulent absentee ballots. Their goal was to control the majority on the board, so that John Reehill, the district superintendent, would keep his job and they, presumably, would keep theirs.

Two juniors at Fordham University, who were working as secretarial assistants in the district office, testified that they had coaxed fellow students into signing ballots.

Investigators said nursing home residents signed the absentee-ballot applications even though the nursing home was a polling place, and residents could simply have gone downstairs to vote.

At P.S. 86, the only school named in the scheme, Pacheco was accused of filling out absentee ballots for school aides and parents. An investigator told the *New York Times* that the pressure to deliver ballots was so intense that once, when a mother came to Pacheco's office to discuss her son's progress in school, Pacheco asked her to fill out an absentee-ballot application.

In a motion to dismiss the charges, Pacheco's lawyer denied that Pacheco had tricked or coerced anyone into filling out ballots, saying that they had done so willingly. Pacheco was exercising her right to participate in the democratic process and, to that end, had a right to rally voters in support of candidates she believed in, her lawyer said.

In the end the voter registration effort was a failure. Only four of the candidates on the Sullivan-Reehill slate were elected, one short of the majority needed to control the nine-member school board. The new board ousted Reehill, and Sullivan lost his position as director of pupil personnel.

One of Sullivan's alleged partners in the scheme was Joseph McCarthy, the district's director of special education, whose brother, Edward McCarthy, a lawyer, was running for re-election to the school board at the time of the alleged election fraud. (Edward McCarthy was never implicated, and said he knew nothing of the ballot fraud.) McCarthy was another Bronx political operative; he had been the north Bronx coordinator for Rudy Giuliani's campaign in the 1993 mayoral race. The others were Edward McFadden, the district director of substance abuse programs, and Inez Adan, who was in charge of making sure that children in homeless shelters attended school.

In lengthy indictments, all five defendants were charged with forgery, conspiracy, and election-law violations. If convicted, they faced a maximum of seven years in prison on the most serious charge of forgery.

Although these were white-collar crimes, when Pacheco turned herself in she was paraded in handcuffs in front of the TV cameras.

Two days after the indictments were handed down, the *New York Daily News*, in an editorial headlined "A is for Apathy, B is for Bums," demanded: "Need more proof that the upcoming community school board elections are a farce? The number of names on the ballots is the lowest in 25 years. In at least two districts, there are more open seats than there are candidates. Voters have always been apathetic. Now, even candidates are. Still need more reasons why the whole system must be overhauled? Here are five: James Sullivan, Lorraine Pacheco, Edward McFadden, Inez Adan, and Joseph McCarthy. These current and former employees of Bronx District 10, the city's largest, have been indicted in a voting fraud scam that allegedly helped McCarthy's brother, Edward, win a seat in '93."

⌀

The city's thirty-two community school boards had been created in 1969 and were born out of the explosive mix of idealism and racial politics of the 1960s. The idea was that if community leaders were given the chance to shape educational policy in their own neighborhoods, the schools would improve.

In some communities, the boards were more or less true to that idealistic mission. At their best, the school boards functioned as the voice of the community that elected them. In middle-class communities, like the Upper West Side, the Park Slope section of Brooklyn, or Bayside, Queens, the boards helped shape schools in the image of the people who lived there. They became a potent line of appeal for parents who wanted programs that met the needs of their children: programs for gifted students, or progressive teaching or instruction that alternated between English and Spanish.

Activist parents often ran for the school boards and won. Some of those parents used the boards as launching pads to higher office, like state Senator Guy J. Velella, a Bronx Republican, or Ruth W. Messinger, a Manhattan Democrat, who went on to become a member of the City Council, the Manhattan borough president, and a candidate for mayor.

In poorer school districts, however, the boards sometimes were perverted into more virulent forms. Unscrupulous politicians managed to stack the boards with their own loyalists. Political clubs were more interested in using the school boards to hire friends and relatives than in helping children to learn. For those who wanted to exploit them, the boards offered a lucrative patronage mill, through their ability to hire and fire district superintendents and, through them, the principals and assistant principals of elementary and junior high schools. Ultimately, the boards held sway over hundreds of positions, from administrators to the paraprofessionals who helped teachers wipe children's noses and take them to the bathroom.

Winning a seat on a school board was hardly a paying proposition in and of itself. School-board members were reimbursed for expenses but did not receive salaries. They were elected for three-year terms on a nonpartisan basis. To run for school board, one had to be altruistic and committed to education, or to have ulterior motives, or sometimes a little of both.

The politicization of the boards was exacerbated by the well-intentioned but ill-conceived system used to elect them. The system was so convoluted that it was hard for any layman to understand. Political organizations were able to manipulate it not only because they understood it but because it was designed to favor slates of candidates over individuals.

The nine-member boards were elected through proportional voting, rather than through a simple system of majority rules. The system was intended to enhance the chances that minority candidates—blacks, Hispanics, and Asians—would win seats. But under proportional voting, a candidate could win a seat on the school board with as little as 10 percent of the vote, as long as he or she was allied with a winning slate. The election process was so Byzantine that it took six weeks to find out who had won. While every other New York City election used voting machines, school-board elections still relied on paper ballots.

By the early 1990s, when Ed Stancik began investigating corruption in the school boards, good-government groups and editorial pages were already calling for change.

After being appointed in 1990, while Shelly Benardo was still an assistant principal, Stancik used his office to investigate political patronage, theft, gang warfare, and school security, often winning praise from parents and public officials. At the same time, he was widely feared and loathed within the school system for his Javert-like pursuit of more sensational crimes like corruption and sex abuse. The impact of his reports tended to be magnified by his knack for packaging investigations so that they had maximum impact, and for releasing them on slow news days when they would be most likely to make headlines. Stancik, who died in 2002, was sometimes criticized for bundling up many small incidents of wrongdoing to make them look more systemic than they really were.

In an unusual arrangement, the special schools investigator had the power to subpoena, investigate, and hold cases up to public scrutiny, but not to prosecute. The ultimate burden of proof was left to others. This meant that his office sometimes seemed more intent on winning its cases in the court of public opinion than in a court of law.

At the time of the ballot-fraud report, much of the city's political and educational establishment had joined forces to make the case that the thirty-two neighborhood school boards were too powerful. Business and good-government groups argued that only mayoral control of the city's schools would provide the accountability needed to reform the unwieldy school system. While the city teachers' union fell short of advocating mayoral control, it had always favored more centralized power, because central authority was easier to influence than thirty-two unruly local school boards.

In December 1996, the state legislature voted to shift control of the schools back to the central administration, through the chancellor and the central Board of Education. The lawmakers stripped the local boards of most of their power, including the power to hire and fire superintendents and, through them, principals, giving it to the chancellor instead. Stancik's investigations played a major role in achieving that legislation.

⁄∂

In the meantime, several factors made District 10 ripe for political intrigue. It was a vast district, the size of the Buffalo school system, with more than 30,000 students, stretching from the leafy upper-middle-class precincts of Riverdale, where people lived in single-family Tudor mansions, to the housing projects of Marble Hill and the working-class blocks of Kingsbridge Heights, near P.S. 86. In New York City, schools dominated by poor children and those dominated by affluent ones often had very different needs and priorities. Although the northwest Bronx was, like New York City generally, traditionally Democratic, it had been split between rival Democratic clubs. Political alliances were often based on tribal loyalties—whether one was Catholic or Jewish—though there were exceptions.

During the mid-1980s, the District 10 board was split between Democratic factions connected to Stanley Simon, the borough president, and G. Oliver Koppell, a state assemblyman. The *Riverdale Press*, an enterprising community newspaper, found that twenty-five of the forty-eight assistant principals and principals appointed between 1982 and 1986 were relatives of politicians or affiliated with political clubs. There was no evidence that these administrators were unqualified, but it was said that they needed to "buy insurance" for their promotions by supporting one political club or the other.

In a December 1989 interview with the *New York Times*, Koppell said he felt compelled to support some candidates for principal and assistant principal as a matter of political survival. "The whole school establishment was being used to try and defeat me," Koppell said. "They were standing on street corners handing out flyers at polls urging people to vote on primary days. Many of these were teachers and assistant principals."

These were the years when Benardo's administrative career was on the rise. He was the assistant principal at P.S. 7, under Milton Fein, the powerful chapter leader of the Council of Supervisors and Administrators, the citywide principals' union. Fein was an ally of the then-superintendent, Fred Goldberg, who had a reputation as a professional who tried to navigate the political shoals in a way that put the needs of children first.

Jim Sullivan, a school-board member in the 1980s, also served as the $93,000-a-year director of pupil personnel for District 10, a job that put him in charge of all school employees except teachers. "Jim used his board position to get the district job," one former school official said. "It's clear he tried to influence people in the system to be his political adherents. People who weren't campaigning for his board nominees were in trouble because of that. Alliances shifted. Once Jim got into a position of power, people who were against him gravitated over to him."

Sullivan worked hard to depose Goldberg as superintendent, orchestrating a campaign charging that the district under Goldberg's leadership discriminated against Irish-American applicants for supervisory positions.

When a state law was passed making it a conflict of interest to serve on a school board while working in the school system, Sullivan stepped down from the board but maintained his pupil personnel job and remained politically active. In 1991, he helped engineer the appointment of John Reehill, an activist for Irish causes, as district superintendent, succeeding Goldberg. Reehill had worked as a supervisor of teachers assigned to tutor disabled students at home and in hospitals.

When Rehill took over, six principals, including Ray Osinoff, the principal of P.S. 86 at the time, had announced their retirements, as had at least twelve assistant principals. More principal positions were expected to become vacant in the near future.

Although Benardo was never officially named in the ballot-fraud investigation, investigators dropped his name behind the scenes. On May 13, 1996, the *New York Times* quoted unnamed investigators insinuating that Benardo had benefited from his connections to the local political machine, and had been privy to the alleged ballot fraud. The article, headlined "Students Lag in Districts Where Patronage Thrives," quoted investigators saying that Sullivan was a friend of Benardo's brother, Steven, and that the two of them had worked together in politics. Sullivan "and other district officials then hired political allies," the story went on to say. "For example, at P.S. 86, Sheldon Benardo became the principal."

The *Times* account did not explore the connection between Steven Benardo and Jim Sullivan any further, but people who knew the two men assumed that it had a personal component. Steven Benardo and

Jim Sullivan were neighbors in Riverdale. Like Sullivan, Steven Benardo had been a District 10 official, a superintendent of special education who went on to run a special public school district for handicapped children at Kiryas Joel, a Hasidic enclave in Orange County.

In closed testimony to the Bronx district attorney's office on March 14, 1996, during the ballot-fraud investigation, Shelly Benardo acknowledged that he owed his job to the Sullivan machine, but said he had not been asked to repay the debt in any way. He described how he began his career in 1972, teaching mentally retarded children at Junior High School 80 in the Bronx, then emotionally disturbed students at another school in Manhattan, before rising to assistant principal of P.S. 7 in the Bronx in 1985.

A prosecutor took it from there, according to the transcript of the interview.

Q. How did you obtain your assistant principalship at P.S. 7?

A. I went through an interview process.

Q. Could you explain that for the record, please?

A. I was told prior to the interview process that I would be the recipient of the assistant principal job, and I applied for the position. I came for the interview.

And the superintendent recommended me to the school board. And the school board voted publicly in March of 1985, and I was appointed.

Q. Who told you that you would be the recipient of the assistant principalship?

A. Sullivan.

Q. Who do you mean when you say Sullivan?

A. Jim Sullivan.

Q. What is Jim Sullivan's position, if any, with the Board of Education?

A. He was removed from his position I knew that he had. I don't know what his position is today.

Q. What prior position did he hold in the Board of Education?

A. In District 10 he was the Director of Pupil Personnel Services.

After a short digression, the interrogation returns to the subject of Sullivan.

Q. What was your conversation with Jim Sullivan that you would be the recipient of the assistant principalship in P.S. 7?

A. He told me to apply for the job and that I would down the road become the assistant principal there, and it happened.

Q. When you say down the road, do you mean in the immediate future from the time that you applied?

A. He told me prior to there being an advertisement for the job when the job is advertised I should apply for that job and that I would become the assistant principal.

I didn't ask him the mechanism by which it would happen. He just told me it would happen.

Q. Did your brother have anything to do with your getting the assistant principalship?

A. I would say to the extent that he had a personal relationship with Sullivan, was a booster of mine, and would always speak highly of me, in that way.

But to my knowledge, there was nothing offered or given or sold or promised to Sullivan for that end.

If there would have been, I wouldn't have gone along with it because I wouldn't allow him to have sold a piece of himself.

Q. Meaning your brother?

A. Yeah.

Q. What is your brother's name?

A. Steven Benardo.

A similar exchange ensued on the subject of how Shelly Benardo advanced to become principal of P.S. 86.

Q. How did you obtain the principalship at P.S. 86?

A. I was put in as interim acting by John Reehill, the superintendent, in August of 1991. There was an advertisement some months later. I applied for that advertisement.

I was interviewed by a committee made up of about eight parents, an administrator in the school, and an administrator selected by the superintendent who worked in the district, and those people determined who would be interviewed and who the top five candidates would be.

In the end, Benardo said, his name was the only one recommended by the superintendent to the elected school board, which unanimously approved his appointment in a public meeting in March 1992.

Q. How did you obtain the position as interim acting principal at P.S. 86?

A. I was placed there by Reehill after a very brief not substantive interview.

Q. Did your brother Steven have anything to do with your getting the principalship at P.S. 86?

A. I would have to say that his personal relationship with Sullivan was the reason because I did not have a positive personal relationship with anyone who was in the decision-making category that could have seen to it.

But he told me, as in the assistant principal job, that nothing was offered. There was no quid pro quo between Sullivan and him.

Q. And again, him would be your brother?

A. My brother.

Q. At the time you were applying to be principal, did you have a conversation with Sullivan?

A. Sure, I had several. And he kept on telling me that he was willing to accept the fact that I had not been loyal to him in the past, that I better remember to be loyal to him in the future.

Q. Did he indicate to you at all that you would be the recipient of the principalship at 86?

A. He couldn't control the level of the parents. The parents were an independent group who made their decision based on I hope what they saw me doing as the interim acting, that they liked the job I was doing.

Beyond that, he had to my knowledge the control of the school board. Not that he was on it, but that he could get them to vote for people who he wanted them to vote for. I don't know why, but that's what he represented himself as.

In his testimony, Benardo seemed to accept the inevitability of the political process, while not defending it. Reehill, he noted, promoted him after a perfunctory interview, and showed little "substantive" interest in his ability to do the job or in his level of commitment to children.

To some degree, politics played a role in selecting principals in the northwest Bronx; but this is not to say that educators caught up in politics, even dirty politics, didn't have the best interests of children at heart. That may have been true of Lorraine Pacheco and Shelly Benardo.

Were they captives of a system in which the fate of children was indirectly determined by patronage and factionalism? Did they have no choice but to deal with political hacks at high levels of the bureaucracy? By all the evidence, Benardo ran a clean, orderly school, hired skilled teachers, and cared about the children in his charge. But in the end, the job security of a typical principal in the Bronx may have been determined not by his dedication and competence as a manager but by his willingness to play the political game.

About a year after the indictments were handed down, Thomas A. Tormey Jr., Pacheco's lawyer, wrote a letter to Justice Richard Lee Price of Bronx County Supreme Court. "It has come to my attention," Tormey told the judge, that a handwriting expert hired by the Bronx district attorney determined that Shelly Benardo had forged Lorraine Pacheco's name on numerous absentee-ballot applications.

Mr. Tormey suggested that Benardo had coerced Pacheco to participate in the ballot-stuffing scheme.

If his client had known about the handwriting analysis, Mr. Tormey said, she might have testified before the grand jury. Pacheco had not testified, the lawyer said, because she thought that any allegations she made against Benardo would not be corroborated.

The allegation of forgery and coercion went nowhere. In November 1999, Pacheco pleaded guilty to falsifying ballots, under an agreement to sentence her to a $2,500 fine and 200 hours of community service. A year earlier, McFadden and Adan, two of the other defendants, had settled their cases by pleading guilty to forgery. They were each fined $2,500 and ordered to perform 100 hours of community service.

The alleged ringleaders held out for trials and fared better. On June 23, 1999, Sullivan was acquitted of 57 of the original 104 counts, including forgery, conspiracy, and filing false election papers. The other counts had already been dismissed. Justice Lawrence J. Tonetti said there was no proof he had forged ballots, presented false documents to the Board of Elections, or conspired with anyone else to do so.

Sullivan's actions, the judge said, amounted to run-of-the-mill political dirty tricks, not violations of the law. Prosecutors, he said, had "proven beyond a reasonable doubt that the defendant manipulated the political process and schemed and connived to get votes from people who . . . had no idea who the candidates were and couldn't have cared less."

But Justice Tonetti said that there was "not a scintilla of evidence" that Sullivan had acted illegally. The people who signed absentee ballots did so willingly, he said, and those who forged them committed forgery on their own, not under orders from Sullivan.

"Like too many of our politicians today, Mr. Sullivan lives on the edge, very frankly," Justice Tonetti said. "But being the shrewd political figure he is, he seems to know when to draw the line."

Seven months later, Joseph McCarthy was acquitted in a bench trial. McCarthy, choking back tears, said he felt "affirmed, validated." He said he had a 15-year-old child with Down syndrome, and would return to working in special education.

Though Benardo escaped prosecution in the voting scandal, it was as if he wore an invisible, self-imposed scarlet letter on his breast for years afterward. Like Hester Prynne, he seemed to wear the badge of sin with a kind of defiance, with the conviction that what had really transpired had been grossly misunderstood by people who were too self-righteous, indecent in their eagerness to pass judgment.

In more than one conversation around the time of the trip to Finland, Benardo volunteered his version of what had happened.

He had been given absentee-ballot applications to hand out to his friends, family, and colleagues during the 1993 school-board election. He didn't want to fill them out, but he felt under enormous pressure to do so. If he did not comply, he feared retribution against his wife, more than against himself. She was a special-education teacher, working in a so-called resource room for children in regular classes who need extra help to keep up with their peers. Special education was under the jurisdiction of Joseph McCarthy, who was working with Sullivan to promote the Reehill slate on the board. "They could take my wife's job away," Benardo said.

Anguished over what to do, he took the ballot applications down to Chinatown and threw most of them in the trash. He gave the handful that remained to friends and relatives—his mother-in-law, brother, sister, uncle.

"I was in considerable danger," he recalled. "People pressured me to do things. If I only did a little, they would leave me alone."

He testified before the grand jury for five hours, he said. He found himself worrying about who was minding the school during his testimony, because eight of his staff were on holiday. He was, he recalled, the only target of the investigation who was not indicted. He seemed to think the outcome might just as easily have gone the other way. "I had a good lawyer," he said. "A very good lawyer."

His sense of relief was still palpable five years later.

A decade after the Stancik investigation the jury is out on whether the school system is better now than it was before. Bowing to years of pressure, the legislature completed the recentralization of the New York City school system in 2001, putting it under direct mayoral control. Though the avenues of patronage have been blocked off at the community level, it would be naïve to think that higher levels of patronage—in the City Council, the state legislature, and the mayor's office—might not move in to fill the vacuum. In July 2002, Mayor Michael R. Bloomberg chose Joel I. Klein—the chairman and chief executive of Bertelsmann Inc., the financial and legal arm of the German media giant, and a former assistant attorney general in the Clinton administration—as the first chancellor under the new system of mayoral control. Klein embarked on an immediate, corporate-style shakeup of school administration. But two years into the new experiment in mayoral control, the impact of those changes on children in the classroom remained uncertain.

One thing is sure. At the school level, Shelly Benardo remained the ultimate authority, a complex figure who had done good and bad things, hurtful and helpful things.

It would be hard to overestimate the power of the principal in any school. Benardo was no exception. He was like the CEO of a company town, a place in thrall to the bigger corporation, yet with a unique character defined by the idiosyncrasies of the children and adults who studied and worked there. No school-board member, no chancellor, could know the people in that school as intimately as he. He knew secret details of the private lives of many of his teachers: which ones had been treated for terminal illness, which ones had money problems, who had affairs, who had nervous breakdowns.

Chronically underdressed, sometimes ill-shaven, with a runner's gait, he prowled the school every day, popping his head briefly into every classroom, if only to say "How's it going? How are you?" He was likely to spend a few seconds more in the classroom of an inexperienced teacher than with the veterans. A savvy principal like Benardo could take the pulse of a school almost by osmosis, the way an experienced mother won't bother with a thermometer but will tell a fever by kissing a child's forehead. And there were some things—like a teacher yelling at the kids—that were more likely to be detected by an impromptu walk down the hallway than by a scheduled visit to a class.

Benardo was judicious in his flattery, as if his own cynicism made him wary of arousing any suspicion of insincerity in others. He was more likely to convey a compliment from someone else to one of the teachers than a compliment of his own directly. He was less sparing, however, in his criticism, and some teachers quaked when he passed.

Not so the children. Although the school was big he seemed to know almost every child by name, and they knew him and felt comfortable in his presence. He made a habit of standing on the sidewalk in the morning as children streamed into the central entrance of the double-winged building. He did not feel compelled to interact; he got more out of observation. Here, too, he had become an astute observer of subtle signs. He made a mental note of which children looked happy, which ones sad; which parents dropped off their children, which children came alone, perhaps clinging to the hand of an older sibling; whether children looked attentively dressed or as if they had dressed without any adult supervision; whether they looked hungry or well fed.

He spoke fluent Spanish, which he attributed to his Sephardic Jewish heritage and his exposure to Ladino, the language of the Spanish Jewish diaspora. On a more practical level, speaking Spanish allowed him to communicate with the many immigrant parents in the school. During open-school nights, Mr. Benardo made announcements in both English and Spanish.

He consulted with teachers on the lives of troubled children, who were truant from school or embroiled in violent families. He picked up the phone and made clincher calls when promising students needed help being admitted to a good middle school, rather than the ghetto school down the street.

Benardo was proud of the dogged fight he had waged, shortly after becoming principal, to remove a teacher who, he said, invited little boys to sit in her lap and wore a wedding dress to class. New York City teachers are tenured after five years, and the process for removing an incompetent teacher is so cumbersome that principals rarely muster the stamina to invoke it. Benardo spent days testifying against the teacher, who was allowed to collect her salary for three and a half years without setting foot in the classroom before she negotiated a settlement and resigned.

Some teachers found him intimidating, autocratic, and vengeful. But others acknowledged that he had a tender side. Benardo once confided that he saw his role as protecting and comforting the afflicted, not affirming the strong.

"I go to forty funerals a year," he said. "A parent dies, a child, a mother-in-law. I don't go to weddings, bar mitzvahs, confirmations. People need support in pressure situations."

He played a regular game of cards with a group of friends, and was reputed to be a master of the high-stakes bluff. He traveled frequently and his dressed-down style belied a taste for expensive food. Friends joked that he could recommend a first-class restaurant anywhere in the world, from the Champs Elysees to Lake Geneva to Helsinki.

He contributed occasional crossword puzzles to the *New York Times,* more for the mental exercise than the $75 fee. (He kept his first puzzle framed in his office.) So far, his puzzles had been printed only on Mondays, the easiest day of the week, but he aspired to advance through the week, composing ever more difficult puzzles. (Much later, to the consternation of the puzzle editor, he submitted essentially the same puzzle twice, with minor variations. Both versions made it into the paper, seven months apart, and the duplication was noticed by diligent crossword-solvers. Benardo said the repetition had been an oversight.)

He was a creature of a certain era in the history of New York City schools. He had come up through the ranks of an intensely feudal system, where you advanced through either connections or political deals, or, if you weren't lucky enough to have connections, through a civil service system that cared little for merit and treated you like a name, rank, and serial number. In such a system, even very intelligent people were caught up in forces they couldn't control.

Benardo was smart enough to negotiate his way through that medieval system. But understanding the role of personal fealty in the school system—and having nearly become a victim of it—had also imbued him with a strong belief in the value of loyalty.

He took pleasure in seeing his protégés flourish, but could be paranoid and vindictive toward people he thought had betrayed him. He hired many young teachers, nurturing them and building up their self-esteem. But in return he demanded that they give him absolute allegiance. "Loyalty" was a word he used often.

Incidents that might have passed unnoticed, or merited a gentle reprimand in another school—like Johanna's giving private lessons to the daughter of a teacher—were magnified at P.S. 86. Veteran teachers suspected that Benardo did not want to be twice burned, and was trying to avoid putting the school at risk of another painful scandal.

It was hard for an outsider, Benardo once said, to understand what it meant to be responsible for 2,000 children and a staff of 250. He had to maintain an equilibrium between the needs of all those people, allowing them to feel creative while still maintaining his authority. If he was strict with them, it was because they all had to play by the same rules; he could not run a school effectively while playing favorites.

Perhaps because of his run-in with a grand jury, Benardo sometimes seemed harder on Johanna than he was on himself, at least his younger self.

As a young teacher, Benardo had hardly been above reproach, recalled one of his former colleagues, Irving Newman, who had been a floor supervisor at Junior High School 80 in the Bronx when Benardo was just beginning his teaching career. Newman often had to drag Benardo out of an ongoing card game in the teachers' lounge in which the players became so immersed that they lost track of time.

It was a pinochle game, Benardo confirmed, adding dismissively: "I was 22."

CHAPTER TWENTY-THREE

❧

"All the Small Things"

At the house, Lillemor's nerves were frayed. Until now, she had been a second-hand participant in the trip, listening to her daughter's accounts of events, but staying at a remove from the action. Now her turn on stage had come.

She had been looking forward to meeting Mr. Benardo and the children in the chorus with almost as much anxiety as she had felt over Cocki's wedding. Now twenty-four kids, the principal, and four teachers she had never met before were coming for dinner.

It was as if Johanna had eloped and Lillemor were finally meeting the in-laws. Would she like them? Would they like her? This would be a day of judgment. She had invested much of her last-minute insecurity in how to wear her hair. In the morning, she had gone to Sickan to have her shoulder-length tousled gray hair bobbed to chin-length, a more coifed and matronly look. Now she was having second thoughts, lamenting that she had gone too far in the direction of stodgy.

As the bus approached, Lillemor was taking several rolls of meat out of the oven. "Mamma, Mamma," Johanna called from the front yard, arriving like the pied piper with the chorus straggling behind her.

At the sound of her daughter's voice, Lillemor wiped her hands and dropped the towel on the counter. Not bothering to put on her shoes, casual but chic in a purple and blue striped Marimekko tunic over blue jeans, she dashed outside barefoot to greet them.

Intercepting Johanna just outside the front door, she wrapped her in a motherly bear hug, then looked up to see Shelly Benardo right behind.

"Oh. You are the principal," Lillemor said, peering quizzically at Mr. Benardo.

"And you're the mom."

Flustered, Lillemor abruptly ended the exchange and turned to the others. "I hope you are hungry, all of you."

Mr. Benardo was hardly more composed, for this was the first time he had truly seen where Johanna came from, had seen her in a context outside the leveling influence of the school, had looked at her as someone other than just another teacher. He wasn't sure what he had expected the music teacher's house to look like, an ordinary suburban tract house, maybe. Whatever he had imagined, he wasn't quite prepared for this, the sprawling red frame farmhouse on a hill, the expansive views, nearly unchanged for hundreds of years, the wildflowers in bloom—a breathtakingly beautiful setting. He walked up the three steps into the mud-room, stepped onto the woven rag rugs, and removed his shoes. Ignoring the crowded kitchen to his right, he advanced straight ahead to the parlor and stood surveying the room, as if he were admiring a lushly painted canvas at the Met, a scene as carefully composed and as crammed with eye-catching detail as a nineteenth-century still-life by Severin Roesen.

He took in the elaborate lute casually propped in its open case. The black piano carved with cherubs. The antique wooden table and buffet carved with birds and fruits. The lace curtains fluttering in the breeze. The china tea service, decorated with pale-blue flowers, each saucer crossed by a silver spoon. On close inspection, the doorframes had been hand-painted in trompe l'oeil wood grain, by a violinist friend of the family. Around the corner, in Lillemor's study, stood an old pot-bellied wood-burning stove. The room was warm and homey. Yet no casual accumulation of objects could be so artful. Every object must have been carefully considered, placed just so.

"Some house, huh?" Mr. Benardo muttered under his breath.

He was stunned by Johanna's privileged upbringing. How could she handle moving from a place like this? Why would she ever consider it? He squinched up his eyes, stuffed his hands in his pockets, and withdrew into his inscrutable Yoda mode, pondering the meaning of what he had just learned. Johanna had been rootless, contextless, in the Bronx, one of Mr. Benardo's large stable of pretty young teachers. Now he knew that she was upper middle class, that she had grown up surrounded by art and culture, that her parents were members of the local elite. This house sent a message that she was not cut out to be a schoolteacher in the northwest Bronx. No wonder she had demanded so much, conveyed such a sense of entitlement.

Back in the kitchen, Cocki, the Madonna, washed salad leaves while a blond toddler clutched her long skirts. Bodi, her flaming hair streaming down her back, dressed in black leather pants, her midriff winking through a black mesh T-shirt, bounced in followed by Martin. They had just returned, astride Martin's Indian motorcycle, a bright-orange antique, from a day's work at the café.

On any other day, Johanna would have registered Cocki's toddler and Bodi's fiancé as silent reproaches, reminders of her sisters' superior domestic achievement. This time she was too busy to notice.

Bisola, drawn by the perfumes emanating from the kitchen, craned his neck over Uffe's arm carving the pork loin. "What kind of meat is it?" Bisola asked. Hmmm. Uffe knew a leading question when he heard one. "What kind of meat is it—wife?" he punted to Lillemor, who was busy arranging the cucumber slices. When Lillemor ignored him, Uffe considered the options. No one had told him what kind of meat it was, so he could honestly answer almost anything. Bisola was obviously hungry, and this was the last good meal these children would have before bedtime. He opted for compassion. "I think it's cow," Uffe pronounced with a flourish of conviction. What if Bisola were a Muslim? Uffe would hate for the boy to leave with an empty stomach. Actually, the meat was pork, and Bisola was Catholic, the son of a homemaker and a businessman from Nigeria.

Uffe's brother, Knut, giving a tour of the musical instruments in the parlor, turned his story into a parable that illuminated Johanna's character as well. For some people, the paramount goal was to make money, he said. "But not our family. We want to save the culture." It was an attitude he and his siblings had learned from their mother, Anna-Greta, who always gave some of the bread from her bakery to charity. "She used to say it was more important that the people have the bread than that we have the money from the bread," he recalled. "I think a little of that is in her children, and also her grandchildren."

The guests served themselves buffet style from the parlor table, then took their food outside to eat on picnic tables set up in the yard. Mr. Benardo cornered Bodi and Martin and quizzed them on their perceptions of New York for what seemed like an hour, trapping them on a bench. "What do you think of New York?" he asked. "Do you think of it as all streets and sidewalks?" Bodi felt that she was being pressed to express a view of New York she knew was a caricature. She tried to tell him that both she and Martin had been there—twice actually—and knew what the city was like. They were not strangers to large cities, and knew London and Stockholm as well.

The encounter with Mr. Benardo was not a conversation, it was an interview, Bodi fumed. They felt patronized, defensive. As they chatted, one of the girls spilled her plate of food on the front steps. The girl froze, horrified by the mess at her feet. Martin jumped up to help, as Mr. Benardo scolded: "You had better behave yourself!" To Martin, he added: "Don't pick it up for her. She has to do it for herself." Feeling sorry for the girl, who was clearly mortified, Martin gave Mr. Benardo a dirty look and kept on plucking the meat and potatoes out of the grass.

"It's time for you to come back," Bodi muttered to Johanna as they bumped into each other moments later at the kitchen sink.

After the food, Mr. Benardo called for silence and gathered everyone around.

Calling Uffe over, he presented him with a red toy Corgi bus, a replica of the one Uffe had been driving. Uffe, rising to the occasion despite his limited English, pretended to drive the bus through the air, making sputtering engine noises as he did. The children laughed.

Mr. Benardo gave a potted white orchid to Lillemor. "This trip and everything we get out of it is because of your commitment to your daughter," he told Johanna's parents, standing in front of the house, framed by the leaded-glass windows as if they were posing for "American Gothic." "It's about family."

Cocki watched, fascinated. She liked the gifts, which were playful and personal but not extravagant. Mr. Benardo had adroitly built on what little he knew about Johanna's parents to make the selections. And that line, "It's about family," reverberated in her mind. He was right, of course. There was nothing the Grussners wouldn't do for Johanna, and for one another. They had gone out of their way to help her bring the chorus to Aland. Cocki knew that Johanna had mixed feelings about Mr. Benardo, but knowing her sister, she discounted some of that negativity. Johanna was a performer; she had always had a histrionic side.

Bodi and Martin disagreed. They had been appalled by Mr.

Benardo's outburst at the girl who dropped her plate. Johanna had told them how he had upbraided her in the privacy of his office, while preening over her accomplishments in public. To them, his praise of the Grussners rang hollow.

There was truth on both sides, Johanna thought. Sometimes, Mr. Benardo was perceptive and caring; other times, he had little faith in anyone. He seemed to go through life as if it were his regular game of pinochle with the boys. The stakes were high—career, reputation—and he kept coming out a winner. The point was to keep bluffing, or risk falling for someone else's bluff and looking like a fool. The last thing Mr. Benardo wanted, Johanna thought, was to be played for a fool.

"Put your hands in the air, wave 'em like you just don't care." The house mix of familiar rap music filled the air, and lithe, prickly Ashley Alvarez jumped onstage in the dollhouse-size gymnasium at Palsbole Skola, knees and elbows pumping, hair flying, as if she had been waiting for just this chance to unwind. Mr. Benardo had been watching her—and all the kids, for that matter—like a hawk. Still, she had been well behaved so far, and it hadn't been easy, staying calm so far from home, separated from her mother, unable to watch TV, unable to fight with her little brother or bake bread with her mother's boyfriend. They had been on foreign territory for four days, coping with an unfamiliar language, strange food, the sterility of the Lembote campground, compared to the pulsating grunginess of the Bronx. Ashley, always the clever one, had been forced to tiptoe around, one part of her wary of inciting Mr. Benardo's wrath, the other part busily trying to decipher the customs of the Finnish people around her. Should she help Johanna's mother wash the dishes? "No, no!" one of Johanna's sisters had said. "Go back outside."

With her stomach pleasantly full from dinner at the Grussners, she had half-dreaded returning to the Palsbole school, where all the children had seemed so exemplary—scrubbed, fair-haired, snub-nosed, tall, their faces blandly smiling or blankly neutral. The Finns were born to be popular, successful, presumably lucky enough to grow up in the kind of carefree families you saw on TV sitcoms, where life's traumas were reduced to glitches that could be resolved in less than half an hour. Probably none of them ever got into trouble.

At first, it seemed that she was right, the Bronx kids were doomed to play the role of underprivileged urchins being tamed by proper society. When they returned to Palsbole Skola that evening, after dinner with Johanna's parents, Ester Miiros, the principal, had a surprise for them. She invited them to dance a polka with their Aland counterparts.

Shelly Benardo shook his head in disbelief as Miiros lined up all the children and demonstrated the moves—do si do, swing your partner round and round, hand over hand around the circle—to the tune of old-fashioned accordion music. Vincent lowered his head in concentration as he skipped, grinning sheepishly, around the gym. He would never do anything like this at home. It was amazing what you could get kids to do when they were off their home turf.

The polka turned out to be just an appetizer. After a couple of dances, someone dimmed the lights. Someone else aimed a strobe light at the silver disco ball, and one of the girls dropped her house music CD into the boombox.

"Put your hands in the air, wave 'em like you just don't care," a rapper shouted over a heavy bass beat.

The students, Finnish and American, came alive. Ashley took the lead, spinning like a whirling dervish, intoxicated by the music, and the other girls—Erica, Priscilla, Keshauna, Samani—formed an impromptu backup group around her, chanting the refrain "Must be the money, Must be the money." Finally, they had a license to be themselves, and for once, the Americans—not the Finns—turned out to be in command.

Johanna watched enthralled, then stepped onto the dance floor herself, snapping her fingers, her stiff-legged gait keeping time to the beat. This was not the cultural détente she or Mr. Benardo had envisioned—their conception had been much more formal, scripted, down to the event, the day and the hour. But this was better than anything she could have engineered, because under the spell of the music, the children from the Bronx had discovered that they had something to share with the kids from Aland. They had become the embodiment of American youth culture, the epitome of hip.

Vincent, too gawky and self-conscious to dance, found himself stranded in the center of the room. Suddenly, four Finnish girls, all at least a half-foot taller than he, gyrated around him in a tight circle. These were the acolytes of his rival on the basketball court, the red-headed Malin, who had dispatched them like sirens to break down his resistance.

Eminem and Sisqo blared over the boombox, and the Finnish and American children gleefully shouted out slangy, sex-filled English lyrics. Vincent stood rooted to the spot as the girls plucked at his shirt. "I don't dance to hip-hop," he mumbled. "I only dance to Spanish music." Yet the dislocation of the last few days melted away: his first trip in an airplane, his first night away from home, his first glimpse of a land without tall buildings, his first taste of the black bread and pickled herring so different from the red beans with yellow rice and roast chicken with lime he was accustomed to at home.

His pants bagged around his hips and ankles, but Vincent was no longer the gap-toothed, sinister street kid who made elderly women flinch when they passed him. In this room, he had been transformed from principal's headache to international heartthrob. A shy grin crossed his face, and he worked up the courage to dance. Malin, wearing a red and blue Supergirl T-shirt for the occasion, elbowed her acolytes out of the way and moved in for the kill. As the other girls receded, still shaking their shoulders, Vincent found himself facing Malin, his feet moving clumsily to the beat.

In the background, Blink-182 sang "All the Small Things":

Late night, come home.
Work sucks, I know.
She left me roses by the stairs,
Surprises let me know she cares.
Say it ain't so, I will not go.
Turn the lights off, carry me home.
Keep your head still, I'll be your thrill. . . .

Where would they be in ten years, these innocent, opaque, hungry children? What kind of work would they do? Who would they leave roses for? "He's going to be a lady-killer when he grows up," Johanna said, watching.

ℛ

Some kind of second sense had told Malin that she and Vincent came from roughly the same social class, and that it was safe for her to approach him. This was not true of all the children. Unlike P.S. 86, where the students came from similar backgrounds, Palsbole Skola had all the hallmarks of a small country school, where the children and grandchildren of the very rich, like Rasmus, mingled with the children of the working class, like Malin.

New York City's politicians liked to brag that the city was a melting pot, but its schools could hardly have been more segregated. P.S. 86 was typical, a sea of black and Hispanic faces, punctuated by a sprinkling —less than 3 percent—of white ones. Those few white students were recent immigrants, Albanians and other refugees from former communist-bloc countries who had discovered the solid yet relatively affordable housing stock of Kingsbridge Heights. In the New York system as a whole, the biggest system in the world, only 15 percent of the

1.1 million students were white, and they typically attended solidly middle-class schools in solidly middle-class neighborhoods.

Counterintuitively, perhaps, it was Palsbole Skola that was the melting pot, at least economically. Still, even in tiny Palsbole, the educational system did not typically help students rise above their origins. Social class in Aland, no less than in New York, was a fairly rigid predictor of educational success. Only here it was the high school entrance exam, not neighborhood segregation, that served as the gatekeeper, typically steering more affluent children to the academic Lyceum and less affluent ones to vocational school.

What Malin had no way of knowing, never having experienced abject poverty, was how much more privileged her life was than Vincent's. She had two married, working parents to support her and her brothers, Markus, 14, and Mats, 7. Her mother, Chris, worked as a housekeeper in a nursing home; her father, Ingmar, designed and ordered prefabricated kitchens at Bygg VaruHuset, the Finnish version of Home Depot. He had designed the family kitchen, outfitted with sparkling white laminated cabinets and butcher-block counters. No roaches crawled across the kitchen floor; no trash blew across the yard, as it swirled through the courtyard of Vincent's apartment building.

By suburban American standards, Malin lived modestly, in a house about the size of a double-wide trailer, but it exuded a degree of warmth, permanence, and pride of ownership that Vincent's mother Ruth had not been able to muster. A still-life consisting of a birdhouse, red-glass lanterns, and a little windmill decorated the front yard. Inside, the house was spotlessly clean and crammed with family photographs, her father's deer-hunting trophies, her soccer certificates. Pots of orchids, African violets, and cactuses filled the windows. In the sauna, a basket of smooth gray stones waited to be doused with water from a copper ladle, and five bathrobes in different colors hung neatly on pegs. A huge, green-slate fireplace, obviously a point of pride, dominated the living room, where two pristinely white bearskin rugs covered the floor.

A home computer along one wall of the living room allowed Malin to send email without having to go to a neighbor's house, as Vincent did. Everything looked new and modern, except for a pretty carved wooden bench in the kitchen, an antique much like the one the Grussners had in their own kitchen, which had somehow stayed in the family.

Malin had no books of her own. But unlike Vincent, she did not have to share her room with anyone, and she had decorated it with a sense of permanence, not as if she had just checked in and would be moving on soon. She had a television set and a CD player. She had arranged cylinders of lipstick and glass bottles of nail polish and perfume on her lavender dressing table. On the wall, she had taped magazine cutouts of her teen idols: Tom Cruise, Will Smith, Dave Beckham, Enrique Iglesias, Nick Carter of the Backstreet Boys, and Fredrik Ljungberg, a Swedish soccer player.

On the surface, the lives of these small-town Finnish kids seemed quaint, parochial, vestigial. The Bronx kids, surrounded by everything New York had to offer, should have been so much more sophisticated. Yet the opposite was true. They were the sheltered ones, and the kids from Aland had the world at their fingertips.

For all the apparent raunchiness, the dance retained its essential innocence. Very young children mingled with older ones, skinny second-grade girls held hands and giggled as they watched the sixth-graders shimmy and shake. They drank Coke and munched potato chips and cheese puffs. The few adults behaved as nonchalantly as if they were at a church social. Dances weren't quite this free and unfettered in the Bronx, Shelly Benardo told Ester Miiros. He wished it could be different. But one mistake—a stranger entering the building, or a child hurt—could be catastrophic.

The children left the little school feeling as if they had changed.

Rickey was sure he would remember that day forever. Jamie felt more confident than before. "I'm not going to be shy like I used to," he said. "I used to be mad-shy. A new person would come in and I wouldn't say 'Hi' for like a week or two."

Before boarding the bus, Vincent pulled a postage stamp–sized school photograph of himself out of his wallet and gave it to Malin. Then Malin handed Vincent a scrap of paper and a pen and asked for his address. As the boy from the Bronx looked for a surface to write on, the girl from Aland turned her back and gestured for him to use that. He pressed the paper against her shoulder. "Grand Concourse," Vincent printed, in careful block letters, and in the glow of their teenaged romance, it didn't sound so far from the one-road town of Palsbole.

CHAPTER TWENTY-FOUR

❦

"The Trip of a Lifetime"

Wednesday afternoon, the chorus held its only full-court rehearsal with both the American kids and the Finnish adults in the pine-raftered living room of the main cabin. The children saw their host families arriving and registered with a slight shock that these people were their alter egos, Johanna's Finnish chorus, the friends she had grown up with in music camp every summer. Pierre and Jeremy smiled shyly at square-jawed Tracy Nyholm, the former Australian au pair, as she shrugged off her boots at the door. Erica and Priscilla got a reserved nod from the pointy-bearded Anders Hallback, his legs like two sticks in his stovepipe black jeans, the one who had let them fish in his backyard creek that first exhilarating night. Anders, a radio reporter, had already dropped by a few times, usually with his wife and cherubic toddlers, to interview the Bronx kids for his radio station. This time, he came alone, as if singing were a more single-minded pursuit than journalism.

So this was Intermezzo.

Sitting at the grand piano, Johanna drove the children hard, making them repeat notes, showing them where to punch the lyrics. She introduced them to a new song, "Going Up Yonder," an R&B-flavored Scandinavian gospel tune, which was part of Intermezzo's repertoire, but which her chorus had never heard. It was good to shake them up. They shouldn't be too complacent, too well rehearsed, too programmed, going into their big night. Serendipity and spontaneity, a little of the tension that came from a high-wire act, would add to the energy of the show.

She demonstrated the song for them, accompanying herself on the piano.

If you want to kno-ow, where I'm going, where I'm going soo-oon.
If anybody asks you, where I'm going, where I'm going, soo-oon.
I'm going up yonder. . . .

Breaking off the refrain, she said: "'Yonder' means 'up.'"
"Away," Bob Robertiello corrected her.

I'm going up yon-der, to be with my Lo-ord.

The children and Intermezzo joined in.

"Raise your eyebrows, stand up straight. Think high," Johanna exhorted her chorus. "These are tricky shifts between the soloist and the choir, back and forth."

During a break, Johanna overheard Ashley, padding about the cabin in her sock feet, singing the refrain to herself. This was not unusual. The children often could be heard singing the songs she had taught them—in the hallway between classes, on the bus. Snippets of song fluttered around them like butterflies. (Once after a shopping trip Keshauna burst out singing on the subway platform near Macy's at

34th Street, only to have a woman hand her a business card, saying, "Call me. I'm a talent agent." Keshauna never did.)

But there was something about the unconscious abandon with which Ashley sang the words "Going up yon-der," stomping on the d's, that made Johanna ask her to sing a duet with Anders the next time around.

Anders had a robust, resonant baritone, a voice that conjured the early years of radio, when newsmen wore fedoras and brandished microphones the size of Cadillacs. It was a voice that emerged like a gift from this pointy scarecrow of a small-town radio announcer. Instinctively, tall, lanky Anders and spunky, diminutive Ashley began to play off each other. They took turns belting out "Going up yon-der" at the top of their lungs, alternating bass and violin. First Anders, his baritone rolling like thunder against the rafters, would sing it. Then Ashley, her hoarse voice nasal, sinuous, as if she had absorbed some Middle-Eastern inflection from her mother's Moroccan boyfriend, would repeat the same phrase. Then their voices would meet and dive together into the hushed final phrase, "To be with my Lo-ord." Their voices penetrated the walls and ceiling, reaching back to the gleaming stainless-steel kitchen. Soon the camp kitchen and cleaning staff stood at the door listening, in a reprise of the way the custodians and kitchen workers used to listen to chorus practice in the Bronx. Only now those rehearsals in the Bronx seemed to have taken place 100 years ago.

Emboldened, Johanna tried another new song, "Soon I Will Be Home," a hymn by a Norwegian composer, Elisabeth Odegard Widmer. It was a difficult, intricate melody, tripping up and down like a stony mountain path, culminating in the yearning refrain: "Soon I will be home. Soon, I'll reach the promised land. Soon, I'll meet him face to face, and he will say, No-ow, you can rest."

Listening to the words, Pierre felt his chest about to explode. He wished he were home with his mom and dad, with his eight annoying brothers and sisters, in their two-bedroom apartment that was bursting at the seams. When Johanna finished singing, Pierre piped up: "Miss

Johanna, I think I can learn that solo." Johanna looked at him. She had never thought of Pierre, so quiet and unassuming, as a soloist. But he was so earnest, how could she refuse? She hesitated for a moment, then invited him to step forward and try it. Pierre sang the solo twice. He fumbled over the unfamiliar words, squinting at the lyrics in the three heavily annotated pages of sheet music Johanna had handed him. But his delivery was flawless. His phrasing was clever and light. He filled up the pauses with little jazz licks. "He's a natural," Bob Robertiello commented. Johanna agreed, quizzically.

"The funny thing is, I didn't know that until now," she said. Had Pierre heard this song before? That seemed impossible. It was Norwegian. Nobody sang it in New York. She fished a pencil from her bag and copied out the lyrics on a plain white sheet, four stanzas and the refrain. "Study this whenever you have a free moment," she told Pierre.

The rehearsal was over, and the children and Intermezzo went outside to grill sausages over an open pit, a treat for that night. But Pierre wasn't hungry. He was too homesick. He went straight to the boys' cabin and climbed into bed, clutching the words to his new solo like a security blanket.

Thursday morning, the children woke up to gray skies, the first rainy day. But nature in Aland did not seem like an alien force the way it did in New York. The spring drizzle smelled warm and loamy, and the kids lay in bed a few minutes longer than usual to listen to the soothing drumming of the rain on the cabin roofs. The teachers had planned a shopping expedition, so the kids would have a few souvenirs to bring home with them. On the way to Mariehamn, their bus drove over red granite roads and passed stone outcroppings made slick and shiny by the drizzle. Long-legged seabirds spiked the wetlands on the outskirts of town.

At a small tourist shop, Pierre picked out what looked like a diamond ring for one of his sisters. But first he asked Mr. Robertiello for advice.

"Do you think it's a real diamond?" Pierre wondered.

"Oh, yes," Bob assured him.

"It's a lot cheaper than in New York," Pierre said with satisfaction, laying a few small bills on the counter.

By now, the children's every move had been chronicled in the hometown paper. Everywhere they went, people recognized them. Alanders rushing about their morning business stopped to gawk and wave as the kids frolicked on Torggatan, the market street, a cobbled pedestrian mall lined with boutiques and outdoor teahouses. At a one-hour photo developing store, Anna Purtsi, the sales clerk, resolved to go to the Bronx-Intermezzo concert the next night after waiting on Keshauna and her friends. The American kids seemed so friendly, warm and open, less suspicious than most Alanders. Of course, these kids had dark skin, the clerk noted, but that piqued her curiosity, too.

In the last five days, the travelers had all grown closer, a family moving to one rhythm. Not the big institutional foster-family of P.S. 86, but more like a clan of cousins who might, in another setting, play football in Hyannisport or dance to bachata in Santo Domingo. They had played catch on the lawn outside their cabins, told ghost stories in their bunks, and traded Eminem and Azul Azul CDs.

They had exchanged small kindnesses. Mr. Benardo had assigned Margaret to be the housemother in the boys' cabin, and she had contentedly reverted to being the smoothly competent mother of boys. She set up a system to make sure all of them had a chance to use the bathroom at night, to brush their teeth, to exercise the hygiene that boys seemed basically allergic to without a mother's intervention. When Rickey woke up at 2 A.M. one night, Margaret diagnosed a night chill. She got him a blanket and tucked him in, and he went right back to sleep, almost as if she had been his real mother, she thought, gratified. After quelling a pillow fight, she began calling herself the pillow police. "The pillow police is coming," she would say if the boys got out of hand or made too much noise, and they would stop whatever they were doing. When Bob noticed Krysten scowling at mealtimes, he encouraged her to help herself to more sandwiches. Bob knew that Krysten's mother had taught her to associate food with love, and he grinned triumphantly, his pop psychology vindicated, as the pleasantly plump girl returned from the buffet table with a full plate and a happy face.

Bob Robertiello and Dorothy Pack had gotten to know each other during this trip, and had become constant companions, sitting together at mealtimes. They both had a low-key, observant manner and good listening etiquette. With the others, Dorothy had tried to stay in the background. But however inconspicuous she tried to be, she sensed that Mr. Benardo still thought of her as an extra responsibility and had never adjusted to her presence. His "girls," as Margaret called them, seemed to register Dorothy as an unwelcome mother-figure, watching and judging them. One time, Dorothy had made the mistake of criticizing the young women teachers for not keeping the girls in line, allowing them to leave their beds unmade and their clothes on the floor. The teachers had complained to Mr. Benardo. From then on, Dorothy kept her mouth shut, except with Bob. He commiserated when Dorothy felt excluded; she, in turn, listened to his confidences about how painfully estranged he had been from his prominent and disapproving father.

That night, Mr. Benardo interrupted dinner to make a speech. Pushing back his chair, he stood portentously among the tables and benches, and the children and their teachers looked up from their pizza expectantly, a little apprehensively, as if they expected the principal's voice to begin crackling out of a box in the wall, even though he was standing right there in front of them.

"Usually when I speak to you it's about a schedule, about behavior, about something that concerned me, something that I didn't like," Mr. Benardo began, as if reading their minds. "That's not tonight. I want to use tonight to set the record straight.

"I'm not sure when Johanna came to me with this trip. I put a lot of obstacles in her way. I wanted approval from this person and that person, letters from this person and that person. You know what? They all got solved the next day.

"I was reluctant to go to Hoboken, let alone across the globe. But she has the way, she has the heart, she has the purpose.

"We all had the trip of a lifetime.

"This trip, although it's to her home, was never about Johanna. It was about her choir, it was about you.

"She told me in New York, 'I'm going to have to be on my cellphone all the time.' But seeing her in action, making sure this flows, that goes right, has been amazing. It's all about you.

"That's a person who has committed her total being to you. It did not happen any other way than Johanna's standing in this community and Johanna's love and commitment to every person in this room.

"This is a very very special individual, and we have been very lucky to know her."

There was a long silence. Johanna sat stiffly in her chair, looking stunned. Finally, Priscilla was the first to react. "We love you," she said, and ran over to give Johanna a hug. The others followed: Matthew, Rickey, Jeremy, Jamie, Kimberly, Vincent. . . . Vincent enveloped Johanna in a smothering embrace, not just a hug, lingering over his teacher as if delivering the climactic kiss in *Casablanca*.

Mr. Benardo had taken his seat again, and had thrown back his head and half-closed his eyes, like a choreographer appraising the execution of his dance. Johanna rose to parry his tribute.

"You're growing. You'll go to college, have a salary and income of your own and you can save it so you can come and visit me. See? This trip wasn't only about you; it was about me, too. And if you have a connection with Aland, you will come and visit me. I'm glad Mr. Benardo made me cry tonight, so I don't have to cry tomorrow."

Mr. Benardo stirred. "Don't bet on it," he interjected.

There would be no more rehearsals, Johanna told the kids. She wanted them to rest their voices. This was their last night at the camp, their last night before the concert. In the morning, they had to pack for their final night with their host families. "It's our last big night. I want it to be perfect. There are certain things you have to do for me. All go to bed early. I really want you to sleep. If you can't sleep, please don't get up. At 10 A.M. we're going horseback riding. Then we'll go to the potato chip factory."

"Do we get potato chips for free?" Ashley asked.

As they turned in for the night, Emily Coca improvised a beauty salon in the girls' quarters. She wanted to do something for Keshauna, who had been hiding her unkempt hair for days under a red bandana. The girl needed a mother to braid her hair for her, and as the guidance counselor and a former hairdresser, Miss Coca was the next best thing. After she had fixed Keshauna's hair, the two of them went to work on Ashley, Eralis, and several other girls. When they were through, the girls looked like straight-laced boarding school students in their tight, glossy plaits. All they needed were the plaid pinafores.

In the other cabin, the boys washed up and then trickled into the living room in their nightclothes.

Johanna sat at the upright Yamaha, working individually with the soloists despite her caution that they should rest their voices. "There's one thing I've been thinking about you, which is that you let all the air out," she told Jamie. "Try to work with the stomach and let the chest stay high."

Overhearing, Vincent chose that moment to make Jamie feel even worse. "Erica did it nice today," he said, subversively.

Johanna jumped in to silence both boys and neutralize their rivalry. "I'm going to tell you not to talk to anybody the whole night. You've both been so active. You both got hoarse. Take this night to write in your journals."

Now it was Pierre's turn to feel left out.

"How about me?"

"I'd like you to do it, too."

Vincent set up a chessboard and challenged Matthew to play. Soon Bisola joined them, settling in to study their moves, his striped cotton pajama shirt flapping open over his bony chest. Jeremy came out of the shower wearing boxer shorts, a white T-shirt that looked as if it had been ironed, and glossy black leather slippers. Vincent reeked of Old Spice. The boys munched lazily on yellow apples from a bowl on the table as they scrutinized the chessboard. Lounging in their masculine underwear and cologne, they projected the incongruous suaveness of 1950s matinee idols, Gregory Peck or Cary Grant.

Sitting alone on a couch, Pierre pored silently over the words to his solo. Over the last twenty-four hours, he had caressed that white sheet of paper so many times that it had become as creased and soft as chamois. Mr. Benardo took it all in with veiled eyes, keeping track of the comings and goings. Noticing a shadow at the door, he barked, "You're up next, Pierre," the cue for Pierre to go to the shower room.

The ring of Johanna's cellphone interrupted their reverie. Distracted by the noise, Vincent jumped up from his chess game to pace around, then drifted out of the room, leaving Bisola and Jeremy to take over the board.

A few minutes later, Vincent wandered back in wearing a shiny silver taffeta robe. His skinny neck jutted out of a collar that looked like a floppy white linen napkin. The hem reached just above his bare knees and white athletic socks. It was one of the gowns that the friend of Lissette's mother had whipped up, so the children would look like a real choir, not amateurs in T-shirts. The warrior moms had prevailed. Mr. Benardo had thrown a small fit when he saw the gowns, but then relented. Vincent preened for his gaping audience.

"You look like a girl without hair," Jeremy needled.

"You look like an angel," Johanna said adoringly.

Vincent smiled good-naturedly. For once, his classmate's teasing rolled right off his back.

⁄⁄⁄

The last few days had put all of them in a meditative mood. Johanna dreamed of falling in love, having children. That part hadn't worked out in America. Maybe she was more foreign than she thought.

New York was a punishing place for a musician. The competition was fierce. Stockholm might be less pressured.

New York was also a tough place for someone who was handicapped, as she expected to be.

What if she moved, not to Aland, but to Stockholm, to try to settle down, have a family, her own kids, growing up the way she did? She would refocus on her own singing, too. The last couple of years she'd been so intensely working with the kids that she had neglected her own singing. She needed to find some kind of a balance.

In Stockholm, it would be easier for her to live on singing and teach less, although all the great musicians were in New York. She'd have to sacrifice that. She just didn't know whether she was more of an American or a Scandinavian anymore. When she was in New York, she was constantly thinking about how it would be to make a living in Stockholm, and when she was here, she was constantly thinking about New York. If only there were some kind of sign telling her what to do. Then again, the whole project had made her more attached to the school, the children, the teachers, and even Mr. Benardo. She looked at them in a different way. It would be so hard to leave.

Shelly Benardo, sitting in the boys' cabin waiting for the children to go to sleep, thought about Johanna. She didn't need to tell him that she was homesick; he knew that. In any case, he was more concerned about the children's future than Johanna's. She could look out for herself. His students had risen to the occasion. He marveled over Ashley's ability to dominate the dance. What a smart kid. If she picked up on the fact that her actions would elevate her then she would play it, and play it very well. She had talked him into believing that she was innocent of stealing money from her teacher's purse. He had known better, but he had let her go. If she can manipulate me in my home base, then she's pretty good, he thought.

How would these kids turn out? Every year, 300 or so children left P.S. 86 for the rest of their lives, and he was in some sense responsible for what happened. You can't take that lightly. He knew how much of herself Johanna had invested in the trip—here she was, coming home and presenting herself and what she did for the approval of her parents, her sisters, the community. He was sure the trip would stay with the chorus as a pleasant memory, but nothing more.

Why did Johanna insist it was such a big deal, a change of life for the kids? That was too ambitious, something out of a TV show: Maury Povich or Sally Jessy Raphael, "Incorrigible Teens," a lot of garbage. To think that somehow a few days could actually change not the pathology but the difficulties and lives that had made these kids who they were—that was impossible. But what it *would* do was validate these kids as important human beings. How often does that happen to any of us? If through the generosity and outreach of a whole community the kids could become a little kinder, a little more generous of spirit, that would be great. You couldn't expect more than that. You couldn't expect to change their lives because of one week in Scandinavia. It was all going to fade into a dream.

By the next morning, the rain had stopped, but the sky was still softly melancholy and gray. The children left their suitcases outside the main cabin, ready to be picked up. After breakfast, they marched about half a mile along the country road out of the campground to a municipal bus stop. For once, Uffe was too busy to drive them.

In just one week, with a boost from the spring rain, tender green shoots had sprouted in the furrowed black earth. As they walked along the deserted road, Mr. Benardo kept up a bantering conversation with the children.

Ashley, walking next to him, reported that the Finnish kids were not the saints that people made them out to be. Priscilla's pen pal, the worldly Rasmus, grandson of Erikkson Capital, had called Priscilla a bad name.

"He called her a beep," Ashley said indignantly.

"A what?" a puzzled companion asked.

Benardo grinned and, playfully covering Ashley's ears with his hands so as not to offend her sense of delicacy, translated for her. "A bitch," he clarified. Then he matched his stride to Priscilla's and had a heart-to-heart talk with her about the incident.

At the bus stop, the children boarded a bus that was already half-full, mainly with elderly women and children. With Finnish reserve, the passengers averted their eyes and said nothing to the noisy children from the Bronx.

When the children returned to camp that afternoon, Johanna's father was waiting, ready to pack up their bags—and them—for their big night. He turned to the principal.

"I have ties for you," Uffe said brightly, in the tone of a sergeant proudly reporting his mission accomplished.

He held a fistful of stripes and colors toward Shelly Benardo. Uffe looked as if he were trying to keep a straight face, to hold back the urge to recite some fitting doggerel for the occasion. ("Mr. Knox keeps his socks in a pale-pink chocolate box. Mr. Sty tells no lies, but he always forgets his ties.")

"I only need one. The dark one," Shelly Benardo said. He knotted

Uffe's tie under his beige raw-silk blazer. This was one of the few times during the last seven days that he had changed out of his usual Saturday tinkering-in-the-garage clothes—the "Only Natural Highs" warmup jacket or the "Delray Beach Florida" sweatshirt. He had remembered to bring the blazer, but had forgotten to pack a tie.

"The girls"—Emily, Fiona, Michelle—had dressed up too, in their Sunday finery: dresses, stockings, and jewelry. No tight jeans tonight. If Margaret and Dorothy were wearing something special, the change was too subtle to spot; they looked like grownups, which was to say their normal selves.

They were literally going to church, and that was the immediate trigger for this sudden wave of propriety. But they were also holding themselves up for the examination of the whole town, as the foreigners Johanna had brought home with her, foreigners from the Bronx no less, alluring yet fearsome, symbolizing everything that was bad about big bad New York.

The children wore their silver choir robes over their party clothes, which were poignantly formal. Under her robe, Eralis wore a mint-green spaghetti-strapped gown with appliquéd flowers that she had bought for a Sweet Sixteen party. Vincent had traded in his hip-hop pants and sneakers for dove-gray dress slacks, the cuffs draping over his shiny black oxfords. A large gold cross hung around his neck, a cloud of cologne enveloped him. Pierre dressed more modestly in black wool slacks and a green polo shirt. Johanna wore a tailored black pantsuit, vaguely reminiscent of a conductor's formal tails.

The Finnish choir, Intermezzo, waited for them outside the hulking stone Mariehamn Church. Except for the Australian-born Tracy, garrulous as always, the Finns showed no interest in small talk. Tomas Lundberg dragged nervously on a cigarette. The others stood in twos and threes, smiling politely, saying nothing. By now, the Americans had grown accustomed to the Finnish reticence, so notorious there was a joke about it: Two men have been chopping wood in the forest all day long when they come to a log cabin. They stop for a drink of vodka. "Skal. Kippis," the younger one says, in a toast. "Hey," the older one grumbles. "Are we here to speak or to drink?"

Mr. Benardo paced the sidewalk. If the children were nervous, they didn't show it. Their months of training had taken over. Looking to Johanna for leadership, they followed her every instruction.

At 8 P.M. church bells rang to herald the concert. About 400 people filled the wooden pews; another 50 or so had been turned away at the door. The front three rows had been reserved for Johanna's extended family. Mr. Benardo and the teachers from P.S. 86 sat five rows back. The children waited for their cue in the balcony. This was the first time that the New Yorkers had glimpsed the power of Johanna's homegrown celebrity and the ties that bound her to her neighbors in this town where anonymity was not an option.

"Det har ar Uffes dotter, Johanna," Guy Karlsson, the Intermezzo director and Johanna's childhood gospel mentor, told the assembled townspeople, inviting "Uffe's daughter" to open with a solo. Johanna repressed a smile. In Aland, you were not somebody if you were not somebody's daughter, or mother-in-law, or son-in-law. People recognized you by your relations. If you didn't have relatives in Aland, you were nobody. But this time, most of the audience had come to hear not Johanna but the kids from the Bronx. When their turn to sing came, they descended from the balcony in single file, chanting the call and response of "Siyahamba" as they walked down the aisle and took their appointed places in the front of the room, with Ashley at dead center.

The passionate, energetic children lit up the room. Despite their technical proficiency, the adults of Intermezzo looked wan and prim by comparison. They kept their elbows tight at their sides, while the Bronx kids swung their arms in exuberant arcs and stepped from side to side as their teacher had taught them. The Intermezzo singers looked all the same, oddly homogenized, one pallid face nearly indistinguishable from the other. The children looked radiant, telltale details of their features reflecting their ancestry in Antigua, Barbados, the Dominican Republic, Puerto Rico, Vietnam, Ecuador, Nigeria, and the Philippines, as evocative as a painting by Gauguin. They had the advantage of being in a place where they were not the norm, no longer ordinary, each transformed by differentness into someone special.

They plowed through their well-honed repertoire without a hitch: "Amazing Grace," "Every Time I Feel the Spirit," "Woke Up This Morning," "Joshua Fought the Battle of Jericho," "Come and Go with Me to that Land," "Oh Freedom," "Hold On," and the rest.

Jamie and Erica sang "Vem Kan Segla" in high, clear voices that hushed the house, except for a few sniffles and muffled sobs. Many people in the audience silently mouthed the words along with them.

Vincent, the hat that had blown into the Baltic Sea long forgotten, improvised fearlessly on "Oh Happy Day," then basked in two long minutes of applause. "It was perfect," Johanna whispered to him.

But it was Pierre the wallflower who brought down the house when he stepped out of the chorus line to croon "Soon I Will Be Home." He not only sang but acted, hamming it up with showmanship worthy of Al Green, arms outstretched, palms raised, face tilted ecstatically to the heavens. "I'm walking a path, following some steps. The road that I am traveling on, is rough but I am safe. . . ."

It dawned on Ashley, standing immediately behind Pierre, that he was stealing the show. Not to be outdone, she willed the tears to begin rolling down her cheeks one by one, as Pierre continued: "But there will be days my eyes become blinded. And I will stumble and fall. But then you'll fill my heart with peace. You'll touch my eyes so that I can see. The place made for mee—ee." By now, Ashley was sobbing, and Paloma wept along with her. "Soon I will be home. Soon I reach the promised land. Soon I meet him face to face. And he will say, No-ow you can rest." The spreading hysteria gripped Jeremy and Eralis, skinny as a coathanger in her Sweet Sixteen gown. A woman in the front row began to whimper, then another behind her. Soon the whole town seemed to be crying along with the kids, and Ashley doubled over with sobs.

The Finns rewarded Pierre with a standing ovation. Mr. Benardo, maintaining his professional distance, was the last to rise out of his seat.

Ashley recovered enough to belt out a spectacular rendition of "Going Up Yonder," wrenching the words from deep in her gut, harmonizing, as on Wednesday night, with Anders Hallback.

The vicar wrapped up the show by holding a traveling mike and interviewing the kids, Donohue style, beginning with the indomitable Ashley.

"Do you want to go home?" Rev. Karlstrom inquired.

"Of course," Ashley replied.

He turned toward Pierre. "After singing that song, of course I do," Pierre agreed.

"We have not prayed," the vicar said. "Let's pray."

The children obediently bowed their heads as the minister intoned: "Walk with these children in joy, love, and life. Lead them your way. Amen."

In the audience, Mr. Benardo rubbed his temples.

Nena walked out with Johanna's family. "This Pierre, he was so touching," she said. "I told my sister, remember that this is where we first saw him. I saw him in the choir earlier and thought to myself, that is the look of a real gospel singer."

Erica couldn't believe that all these people had come to hear them voluntarily. Not a single person had come to the concert out of a sense of obligation, because their children were performing and they had to show support. None of these people had to be there. They came because they wanted to be there.

Jamie Flores felt torn. "I'm feeling sad and happy," he said. "It's hard to explain. I have to leave this beautiful place and New York is missing something. I don't know what it is. But when I came here, it had something that New York was missing."

"Did you ever think it would turn out like this?" Mr. Benardo said, standing on the sidewalk outside the church, his eyes full of wonder.

In two weeks, the Aland choir would reciprocate, singing at P.S. 86 as part of an American tour. "The show will go on," Mr. Benardo said, already thinking ahead. He had invited the chancellor, and the whole prospect made him a little nervous. There would be plenty of opportunities for things to go wrong. He was temperamentally wary of too much attention, still stung by the memory of that phony corruption probe. Then there was the religious content of the songs, which might offend someone. It was almost graduation time, the season of tragedy and promise, the time of atonement in public schools when it is written who will succeed and who will fail. Oh, well, Shelly Benardo thought, philosophically. What is life if you don't take a few chances. Let the chips fall where they may.

CHAPTER TWENTY-FIVE

A Transient Person

This was not the way Johanna had pictured her last day of school. It had started out so well. Now Johanna was standing on the sidewalk in front of her beloved P.S. 86, tears flowing, in the ample arms of Rob Pape, the fifth-grade teacher, having just been fired from her job.

"There, there, Johanna," Rob clucked, in his funny working-class accent. She would miss his thirst for gossip and his hair moussed into little spikes, more becoming to one of his fifth-graders than to a middle-aged man with an incipient paunch. But that was part of his charm. He took so much pride in organizing graduation. Now she wouldn't be there. She buried her head deeper into Rob's shoulder.

How had everything unraveled so quickly? When the chorus returned from Finland, the bloom was still on the rose.

The kids developed the pictures they had taken on the trip (all but Vincent, whose mother put two disposable cameras in a drawer and forgot about them for the next two years). They described every moment, no matter how trivial, to their attentive parents. Erica's mother helped her put together a scrapbook. Among other souvenirs she had collected the many official letters about the trip that Mr. Benardo had sent home, preserving each precious page in a plastic sleeve and clipping the pages into a three-ringed binder. There was that first letter, on March 19, 2001, that began: "Your child has been selected to participate in a trip to Finland. . . . " Erica remembered how skeptical she had felt the first time she read it. Even now, she could hardly believe that things like this really did happen to the kids at P.S. 86.

A little further along in the album she had pasted a picture of the fish that she and Priscilla had caught, and named as if it were a pet. "This is Slippery," the caption said. She remembered the first question Anders had asked when they met.

"Did you picture us this way?"

Yes, she told him.

And she really had. "I wanted them to be nice, and I wanted them to be young. I sort of pictured them like my family."

She was relieved that her image of them had come true, because "Most of the time when you wish for something it's wishful thinking and you don't really get it." Erica, the A-student who felt herself to be such a misfit at P.S. 86, was a bottomless well of melancholy and promise.

Ashley stored all her souvenirs in a large lidded box under her bed. She had kept everything, no matter how trivial: postcards of the sailing ship *Albanus* and of yellow wildflowers like the ones they had nibbled in the Palsbole Skola dining room; colored pencils from the Finnair flight; the Viking line T-shirt; some gravel and dried flowers picked up on their walk to the bus stop on the last full day in Aland; Finnish coins; some beads that she and Keshauna had found in the camp closets and had strung into necklaces; two plastic tags labeled "Taffel," from the potato chip factory; a pack of Viking playing cards; and a wildflower, shriveled beyond recognition, that Johanna had picked and presented to her.

In a final rhetorical flourish, Mr. Benardo sent a thank-you note to Aland, which was printed in the newspaper: "In New York sometimes success is measured by the height of a skyscraper," he wrote. "We learned from interacting and living with your community that true success is goodness of heart and spirit."

As the concert in the Bronx approached, Mr. Benardo asked the parents to cook for the guests. He asked them to cook for four people each, knowing they would cook for eight. He knew from experience that whatever he asked, they would cook twice as much.

Ordinary life in the school went on as well. On Wednesday, May 30, Johanna directed the annual Spring Concert, her twenty-fifth concert of one kind or another since arriving at P.S. 86. As always, the children sang a medley of different songs and musical styles. The fifth grade sang "Erie Canal"; the fourth grade, the Simon and Garfunkel classic that had gotten her into so much trouble when Carlina sang it, "Fifth-Ninth Street Bridge Song"; the third grade sang "Rockin' Robin"; and not least, the Select Chorus sang a cappella, "Oh, Freedom."

In a one-page letter on the reverse side of the program, addressed to "Dear Family," Johanna plugged her program, sounding, at long last, like the teacher she had never intended to become.

"By supporting music and arts in the school, we encourage the children to be creative, positive, and productive," she wrote. "Music helps the children in other subjects like mathematics (learning rhythm), reading, language, speech, and many more. Music is the universal language that connects us with people all over the world."

The trip, she said, had taught them that: "Traveling to other countries makes us wiser. It opens our mind and helps us understand the world a little better. Home is always home, but by seeing other parts of the world we can appreciate what we have, and therefore show more respect and gratitude for our home community."

In closing, she tried to tell the families that it was their children, not she, who had made the experience special: "I wish you all a wonderful summer, and I thank you for letting me enjoy every day in music with your beautiful, beautiful children. They have given me more joy and happiness in life than I will ever be able to express."

Margaret asked Mr. Benardo whether he would like to compose a new motto for her Project Arts spring memo. For more than three years, she had been using one that she had written herself: "Thanks to ProjectARTS we are exploring exciting realms in music, visual arts, theater arts and dance." But now, she thought, Mr. Benardo might want to take more credit for the program. He agreed, surprising Margaret with his erudite result.

"Education can only be considered comprehensive if it includes a significant arts component. Remember. Ars longa, vita brevis. S. Benardo. Principal P.S. 86."

Like life, though, this honeymoon was shorter than anyone expected.

Sunday night, two weeks after the return from Aland, Johanna's friends from Intermezzo touched down at John F. Kennedy Airport. There were many more of them than the number of Bronx kids who had gone to Aland—forty five of them including Anders' and Siv's 16-year-old daughter, who had come to see America. They would repeat their performance with the P.S. 86 Select Chorus, then swing through the South, hitting Atlanta and Charleston, on their own gospel tour. That was a sight to imagine, the wide-eyed Alanders visiting Baptist churches to sing Norwegian gospel.

Tomas, the footloose bachelor, was planning to return to New York after they played the gospel circuit. He had asked Johanna to recommend a cheap hotel, and she had booked him a room at Jazz on the Park, a hostel on West 106th Street a block from Central Park. It was dear to her, since she had often performed there. Tomas was delighted to hear that in a former incarnation, it had been a brothel and crackhouse, a real slice of New York. Tomas had a taste for the noir.

But for now, the group was staying at the Vanderbilt YMCA in midtown Manhattan, which was more fleabag than noir. When Johanna met up with them at the Y, they were exhausted by the flight and a series of misadventures. A woman in the chorus had suffered a diabetic attack on the plane and was taken from the airport by ambulance. Their rented bus broke down on the way into the city and they had to wait for jumper cables to arrive. When they finally made it to the hotel, they found that they were being charged $85 a night for a 5-by-7-foot room that smelled recently fumigated—for what? roaches? mice?—with bunkbeds climbing the wall and a shared bathroom in the hallway. Tomas took one look at his room and announced that he was going out in search of a beer. He sallied forth into the neon-colored night, apparently undaunted by anything he might have heard about crime in New York.

Returning the Finnish hospitality, Mr. Benardo, ever the operator, pulled what strings he could. He invited Schuyler Chapin, the arts commissioner, to the concert, and dropped a hint about how the Aland chorus could hardly afford subway fare. Chapin rode to the rescue once again, obtaining free subway passes from Cristyne Lategano-Nicholas, president of NYC & Company, the city's conventions and visitors bureau. Margaret spent the weekend making Aland flags for the audience to wave. "I feel like Betsy Ross," she said dryly.

As Mr. Benardo had predicted, the mothers cooked enough food for an army: heaps of carne molido, pork rinds, rice and beans, Mexican tortillas, spring rolls, lasagna, steak and onions, corn bread. . . . One mother couldn't sleep and was up at 3 A.M. cooking shrimp, fried rice, and yellow noodles. They arranged the food in foil dishes on the long tables in the cafeteria of the mini-school, propping Margaret's flags around the room for decoration, the way you would put a little paper parasol in a cocktail glass.

On Monday, the chancellor was a no-show at the long-awaited New York City engagement of the Intermezzo–P.S. 86 Select Chorus. Meeting the chorus had been good enough for the governor of Aland, but back in New York, the normal hierarchy reasserted itself. Mr. Benardo had been crazy to think 110 Livingston Street would care about a school in the northwest Bronx. He was, after all, a speck of dust. Hell would freeze over before the chancellor, or even a deputy chancellor, walked the halls of P.S. 86. How had Mr. Benardo forgotten that? But if he felt snubbed, Mr. Benardo kept his disappointment to himself, and nobody else really noticed or cared. There was no dearth of dignitaries. More important people filled the auditorium than P.S. 86 had seen in a long time. Maybe since Howard Pack's time. There were dignitaries from the Finnish consulate, City Council aides, Bronx school officials, and the ever-loyal, ever-gallant Schuyler Chapin.

The Select Chorus looked heavenly in their gowns, although Lissette's mother clucked over the wrinkles in the tafetta, which nobody had thought of ironing after the trip. The members of Intermezzo, on the other hand, did not wear gowns. They gamely took the stage draped in the turquoise P.S. 86 T-shirts that Mr. Benardo had given them as a welcoming gift. Pierre reprised his star turn on "Soon I Will Be Home." As he sang his paean to Webb Avenue, his eyes flickered between Johanna, conducting, and his mother, Candi, sitting in the second row surrounded by her ducklings. "Did you see me?" Candi said afterward to another mother. "I was going bananas." Actually, all eyes had been on Pierre, who got his second-ever standing ovation, studded with whoops and whistles.

After Pierre finished, Anders, in his radio voice, and Ashley, belting her heart out, wrapped up with "Going Up Yonder" twice, once as an encore. As good as the kids were, everyone knew that they could not have done it without their teacher, and chants went up of "Jo-han-na! Jo-han-na! Jo-han-na!" as if she had just coached the winning game of the World Series.

But their performance this time lacked the fairytale perfection of the one in Aland. Here on Reservoir Avenue, reality had a way of intruding. The standardized test results had been waiting for them when they returned, and in the end-of-the-year ledger Ashley's name had been written on the negative side. The sparkling Ashley had flunked the fifth-grade test and would have to go to summer school. Mr. Benardo was crestfallen; he had such high hopes for Ashley, in spite of everything.

While Benardo cared about his students, he sometimes seemed to have the jaded attitude of many New York City educators toward academic failures. He sincerely mourned when students he knew were bright did not live up to their potential. Yet he did not blame his teachers. He seemed to take the conventional view that schools could change performance only at the margins.

During the year the chorus went to Finland, one out of three fourth-graders at P.S. 86 passed the state's English test, up from one out of five the year before. How did they do it?

"You want to know the truth?" Benardo shot back.

"We took the children who were borderline and worked with them to move them up a level."

In other words, he seemed to be saying, the improvement was due to something of a parlor trick. The teachers had worked hardest with the children who were just a hair below passing, to nudge them over the threshold. But for children who were far below, nothing changed. There were no overarching changes in teaching methods, curriculums or understanding of how best to help children learn. It was, he implied, a Pyrrhic victory.

Things weren't going any better for Ashley at home. Her mother, Ileana, was bankrupt. The pet shop had failed. Ileana had racked up $4,000 in credit card debt and $65,000 in rent arrears on the pet store. At night, they heard gunfire outside their building, as gang warfare infiltrated the block. Ashley's psychiatric counselor, with whom they had forged a relationship over nine months, had been promoted and replaced by a total stranger who had to learn Ashley's story from scratch. The system had backfired once again. It was time to leave New York, Ileana said. She had made up her mind. She was getting out. She planned to buy a house in the Poconos, hoping that small-town life might offer more security and support for her four children.

Vincent was acting up again. He was graduating only on the condition that he pass summer school. Jamie, his histrionic streak in full flower, had been telling people that he was planning to move to Aland permanently some day. "I want to go back too," Ashley said, and the two of them broke into a verse from "Vem Kan Segla," standing right there amid the long formica tables in the lunchroom.

Worst of all, the children and their parents had learned for the first time that their seemingly indomitable teacher had muscular dystrophy and expected to be crippled by it some day. Now Vincent understood why Johanna had been so grateful to have him carry her guitar upstairs for her, why she had leaned so heavily on the banister. Yet, when he heard that she was thinking of leaving New York, he couldn't help feeling a pang of abandonment, not the first in his life, or the life of many others in the choir.

"It's sad, so, so sad," Rickey said, standing in line after the concert to give his teacher a hug.

"She's the one who has helped them grow," Ileana said. "You could see them looking at her for direction. They were disciplined. She made them a team."

Was the rumor true? Was Johanna planning to move back to Aland? Johanna said she wasn't sure yet. Jennifer Padilla's mom, Wilma, still holding an Aland flag, buttonholed Johanna: "I'll speak to the mayor about you, so you can return to us," she promised, evidently assuming that only a force much more powerful than any in the Bronx could wrest their music teacher away.

Johanna smiled. "It's more my decision than Giuliani's," she assured her.

Her passion for her students had turned them from rough, street-smart city kids into a disciplined, technically proficient, soaringly beautiful gospel chorus.

But the visit from Intermezzo only stiffened Johanna's resolve that, like Mary Poppins, her work here was done, and it was time to go back where she had come from. To sail away on the north wind.

Singing a solo with her Finnish choirmates, she felt the tug of home. It hurt to leave the kids, but when she sang with Intermezzo, she felt that these were her people. She was one of them. They were home for her.

She had already rented an apartment in Stockholm for $300 a month. She had bought two cheap but roomy vinyl suitcases on 125th Street and booked a flight to Stockholm for Tuesday night. Although there were still three weeks left in the school year, she had always left P.S. 86 in the first week of June, because the flurry of end-of-school obligations—tests, graduation, cleaning out the desks—tended to eclipse everything else. She had never stayed for commencement. This year, though, she planned to return at the end of June to say her final good-byes to the sixth-graders in the chorus. They'd been through so much together. It didn't seem right to let them graduate without being there to cheer them on.

Would she come back in the fall? She was already plotting ways to maintain the connection. Maybe Margaret would let her be an artist-in-residence, returning for a month or so. They could put on a spectacular show, a musical, say, like the one she had directed at Aland's Lyceum. She had so many ideas to discuss with Margaret and Mr. Benardo. The six-hour flight between New York and Stockholm was nothing, really. She could make up for lost time in her singing career without sacrificing teaching, without giving up the students who made her feel so much alive, or the school she had come to feel so much a part of.

If Shelly Benardo was surprised by her plans to leave, he didn't show it. "I read the tea leaves," he said, slouching against the auditorium wall, shoving his hands deeper into his pockets. He did not foresee hiring anyone to replace her. "This is not an assembly-line talent."

∞

The next morning, Johanna returned to say good-bye to the kids and to make sure the music room was in order. She had an odd feeling as she walked around the school. There was something in the air, but she couldn't put her finger on it. Other teachers gave her curious, probing glances.

"Did you read the newspaper?" the secretaries asked, with studied casualness, when she stopped in the office to check her mail. She hadn't, actually. She knew there was a story in the paper about yesterday's concert. But she figured she would get to it at the airport. She had never been much of a reader. She read so slowly, line by line, and this was not a morning to waste time on the *New York Times*.

At chorus time, the kids came down loaded with teddy bears, flowers, and other going-away presents. Instead of holding class, Johanna sat with them in the hallway outside the auditorium, and they talked and laughed and cried. When the bell rang, Johanna carried the stuffed animals to the security desk, where Danny could look after them until she was ready to leave.

"Johanna!" Mr. Benardo loomed at the top of the stairs. He tipped his head toward the main office, beckoning her to come up. She walked behind him down the hall and through the gate that walled off the secretaries from importuning parents. Before Mr. Benardo closed the door to his inner office, she once again felt all eyes on her, that unsettling curiosity, that straining to read her face and body language. Realizing that she was still clutching a teddy bear to her chest, she set it down on the conference table. Mr. Benardo took his customary place behind his desk, and she sat in her usual chair opposite him.

"Have you read the paper?" he asked, his voice calm.

"No."

He ignored that.

"Have you ever heard the word 'loyal'?" he demanded, his voice tightening.

She hesitated, uncertain what he was driving at. (Where was she supposed to have heard this word? She searched her brain, as if he had just told her that he had mislaid his keys and she should try to remember where she had last seen them.)

"Do you know what the word 'loyal' means?" he persisted, his voice hardening. "Do you know how you behave when you are loyal?"

Johanna was starting to regret that she hadn't read the paper this morning. Had the subject of loyalty come up during the concert yesterday? This was worse than the time he had yelled at her over Carlina's solo, because at least then, she knew what he was talking about. "Mr. Benardo," she protested. "I don't understand."

He picked up the newspaper on his desk and read just one sentence out loud: "Almost from the beginning, Miss Grussner and Mr. Benardo clashed. She thought he was sadistic; he thought she was arrogant."

How could she call him "sadistic?" Mr. Benardo demanded. After all he had done for her? This was the height of disloyalty. He didn't deserve it. He had been unwaveringly loyal to her, and this was how she repaid him. His wife and mother were upset. He was upset. "You talked too much," he said.

She tried to tell him that "sadistic" wasn't a word she would use, that this was the journalist's word, the journalist's interpretation of what she had said.

"I never told bad stories about you," she said.

A familiar helpless feeling washed over her. Any time she experienced a moment of triumph, like the concert yesterday, Mr. Benardo ruined it by ripping her apart. What hurt her the most, she said that night, describing the conversation to a friend from a payphone at Kennedy Airport, was Mr. Benardo's accusation that she had engineered the trip only to make herself look good.

"He said I had abused the children as a ticket to my own success. He said I should never ever contact the school again. I should not email, phone, or fax."

When he was finished speaking, Mr. Benardo opened the door and ushered Johanna out. Clutching the teddy bear, tears running down her face, she left without saying good-bye.

Carol, her favorite secretary, stood up and gave her a hug. That took guts, Johanna thought. Wiping her tears, she walked slowly back down to the security desk. She saw Rob Pape, and told him she would not be there for graduation.

After dismissing Johanna, Benardo went looking for Margaret. He was removing Margaret from her position as arts coordinator, he told her, because she was responsible for hiring Johanna.

Johanna flew to Sweden that night. Benardo was still seething. "I felt incredible anger, disgust, disloyalty," he said, when friends tried to intercede on Johanna's behalf.

He had gone out of his way to help her succeed, building schedules around her, allowing her to have an accompanist, and then supporting her when she proposed the trip to Finland. He had defended her from the jealousy of the rest of the staff when she asked for special treatment. She had never appreciated his position, the pressure he encountered daily as an administrator trying to balance the needs of so many people.

"She did many positive things for the school," he said. "But when you make priorities for some people, other people feel slighted." Too much attention had been focused on the chorus, at the expense of the classroom teachers. It was a case of "the tail wagging the dog."

In fact, he argued, Johanna was not the most significant teacher in her students' lives. "To characterize her as the main professional in Vincent's life—she's not there six and a half hours a day, through breakfast, lunch, meetings with his mother," Benardo fumed. "Vincent comes in after beating up his sister. The classroom teacher is putting his heart and soul and free time into it. It's the classroom teacher whom the meetings are with."

A school was a fragile organism, more easily thrown off balance than outsiders could imagine. "You have no ability to recognize the dynamics of the school," he said. "Years ago, I had a lot of problems." The Stancik investigation had made him appreciate how vulnerable a school could be. He did not need this kind of negative attention.

"She's no longer a priority," Benardo said. "Did she do good things? Absolutely. Do I admire her talent? Absolutely. Did she have a good relationship with the kids? Absolutely." But she was dispensable. "She's a transient person. An important transient person."

At this point, Benardo muttered the line beloved by James Bond fans, spoken by Sean Connery as he is about to be sliced in half by a laser beam in the 1964 movie *Goldfinger*. "If you kill me," Benardo paraphrased, "M will send in 008." (In the movie, Bond says: "You're forgetting one thing. If I fail to report, 008 replaces me.')

Bond is trying to persuade the villainous Goldfinger to spare his life.

It's pointless to try to destroy me, Bond is saying; headquarters will always send another agent into the fray after me.

It was as if Benardo were composing one of his crossword puzzles, and challenging the listener to fill in the blanks. Did Shelly Benardo see himself as 007, virtually indestructible, a bit reckless, but on the side of good, one of an infinite army of secret agents, working to save the free world? He had, after all, emerged unscathed from the corruption scandal. Whatever this upstart music teacher, Johanna, tried to do to him, he would still be the principal.

After a pause, he added jauntily, as if trying to console himself: "No matter what, the sun is shining."

Why did he send Johanna away? Why was he crushed by one negative word in a long, glowing newspaper article that had described how he and Johanna had banded together for the sake of the kids and accomplished something extraordinary? Why, after being so elated by the trip and the concert, did Mr. Benardo suddenly want to cut down everyone in sight?

In a way, this was the story of every graduation, a textbook case for the education journals. Every year, in every school, the teachers and the principal put their blood, sweat, and tears into the kids. Then, at the end of the school year, they hold commencement. The kids graduate, and the faculty, no matter how smart, fabulous, and charismatic, are left behind.

Johanna, 28 and still young, was graduating. She was about to go on with the rest of her life. Mr. Benardo, 50 and middle-aged, was staying at P.S. 86 for the rest of his career, until he got his pension. Johanna had brought grace and purposefulness to everything she did. She had brought down the house. For a brief, shining moment, she had brought out the better side of Mr. Benardo. Now she was moving on to a second act, a whole new world of possibilities.

And the morning after, Shelly Benardo was still stuck at P.S. 86. Only now, he was stuck there without her.

∽

When Johanna walked out of P.S. 86 after Mr. Benardo told her never to come back, she found Vincent sitting on the front steps, waiting for her. "Do you need help?" he asked, jumping up.

"Yes," she said, forcing herself to smile at him. Dear, sweet Vincent with his puppy love. It was good to see him there. She didn't have her guitar for him to carry. But he helped her load the stuffed animals and cellophane-wrapped flowers into Margaret's car. Margaret had promised to drive her home that night. Going back and forth to the car, she started to calm down. "I'm going to miss you," Johanna told Vincent. She didn't say anything about what had happened between her and Mr. Benardo. Vincent was just a kid. There was no need to trouble him with that.

Margaret came out and offered to drive Vincent to the Grand Concourse before taking Johanna home. In the car, Vincent, sitting in the backseat behind Johanna, asked: "Would you like me to sing you a song?" Then he did, a rambling love song that she had never heard before.

Somehow, the kids always came through for her. She remembered those early days of teaching, when she would drag herself out of bed after a gig, dreading going to work. The kids had so much energy, and it was always infectious. The car pulled up to Vincent's apartment building. They both got out. Johanna gave Vincent a hug, right there on the Grand Concourse.

"Wait," she said. On impulse, she popped the trunk and pulled out her keyboard. "Could you keep this for me?" she asked. Vincent took the keyboard in his arms, and she watched him walk away with it.

Some day, she might come back for it.

◎◎

A Letter from Mr. Goodfellow

Johanna left telephone messages for Mr. Benardo, asking to be allowed to go to graduation. Finally, Emily Coca, not the principal, called back. Johanna could go to the ceremony, which was being held at a nearby middle school, but only as a guest, not as a teacher.

Johanna flew back from Stockholm and was so intimidated that she retreated to the last row of the balcony, where she was unlikely to draw attention. She saw Mr. Benardo circulating far below, but was not sure whether he spotted her. The boys wore blue gowns, the girls yellow, the school colors. For the first time, Johanna realized that there was a school song.

Hail to thee Oh halls of learning
That echo in our youthful years.
You have been an inspiration
You have sheltered all our tears.

Hail to thee Oh 86,
You have taught us many things

When the time comes to say farewell
Your praises we will sing.

Hail our blue and gold school colors
Our spirit of unity
Here we stand your loyal students
We give our hearts to thee.

Hail to thee Oh 86
You have taught us many things
When the time comes to say farewell
Your praises we will sing.

The kids sounded awful as they sang it, listless and fuzzy—their voices had been pitched too low. After a long time, Johanna recognized the melody; the words had been set to the tune of Bette Midler's torch song, "The Rose."

From her lonely perch in the back balcony, she hummed the original version under her breath. Without risking a broken heart, there can be no love, the song said. She knew that now.

She waited until the ceremony was over and the children streamed out to the sidewalk. Then she darted through the crowd searching for the faces she knew so well. She had printed certificates on heavy gray stock—"Music Awards" said the title across the top—listing the performances of the "P.S. 86 Bronx Select Chorus," and honors they had received. She had signed each certificate, "with love always, Johanna Grussner, Choral Director, New York, June 22, 2001." It might seem hokey to someone else. But she remembered how much that kind of recognition had meant to her as a child, how she had framed every one.

✍

In the few days that Johanna stayed in New York after graduation, she focused on Vincent, worried that he would be lost if forced to go to the neighborhood middle school. With Margaret's help she arranged auditions for him at three music schools, two private and one public.

Johanna had performing dates lined up in Aland, so Margaret agreed to stand in for her, escorting Vincent to his auditions. Vincent was summarily rejected by the first school, a private school in Manhattan, where he hoped to win a scholarship. At the Professional Performing Arts High School, a Manhattan public school for children who showed talent in music, acting, or dance (a former student was Britney Spears), he was taken more seriously and seemed to have a shot.

The principal, Mindy Chermak, a petite but vigorous and cheerful woman, met them at the door, shaking hands all around. "President Clinton addressed our graduation on Tuesday night, and everybody is still high," she said. ("I love it all," Mr. Clinton had said, after sitting through the ceremony. "I love the Shakespeare. I love the skits. I really love the gospel. I love the dance. I love—I love it all.")

As Vincent and Ruth waited in the cafeteria, Chermak spoke with Margaret in her office. "What he needs is some reason to exist," Margaret said apologetically. "His strongest teacher was in the first grade." Chermak knew enough to realize that that was because Vincent had been tracked into lower-achieving classes after that.

"We have a lot of force in the current sixth-grade class," Chermak said. But she added that Vincent's bad grades would not be held against him. "Academics don't affect admission. We take any kid no matter how much they struggle." On the other hand, she said, most of the children came in with strong family support. "I'll be really honest with you," she said. "Most of our kids are middle class, or upper middle class."

After the audition, though, she reconsidered. The feedback from the teachers who auditioned him, a voice teacher and a keyboardist, was negative. It wasn't just his lack of musical training, she said. He seemed to have severe emotional problems.

"If he came in here off the street he would never be taken here," she said bluntly. "He's completely disconnected. They tried to draw him out in different ways. It's not happening. He's going to be in with a group of kids who are extremely social and extremely charming. They have personalities that are huge. They are triple threats. They can sing, dance, and act. I'm afraid he'll feel completely inadequate. The worst thing we would want to do is to have him come in here and feel worse about himself."

She did admit him to the remedial summer program, which was mainly academic. But by the end of the summer, Vincent had only managed to confirm her worst fears about him. "Although he did not pass the audition, I thought I would try to see what you and others have seen in Vincent and try to find a place for him," Chermak wrote to Johanna. "Unfortunately, that did not happen. In fact, he presented behavior problems that were not acceptable. Vincent needs much more attention than we can offer."

The third school, the Harlem School of the Arts, was willing to take a chance on Vincent, but offered only after-school classes. For the regular academic year, he had no choice but to attend the school Johanna had feared most, the neighborhood middle school.

On Saturday, July 14, about three weeks after Johanna returned to Stockholm, she received a mysterious email from someone by the chipper name of Art Goodfellow, sent from a yahoo address. As she scrolled down the email, she discovered that the tone of Art Goodfellow's message did not match his name, unless the reader had a highly developed sense of irony. Art Goodfellow said he had read the newspaper articles about Johanna that appeared on the website where she promoted her musical career, and he was responding to her invitation to viewers to write in their comments.

"The feedback I would like to give you is this," Art Goodfellow began:

The picture of you that emerges is of a very selfish, ego-driven, immature, and highly manipulative person who, whatever the praiseworthiness of her motivations, is a person who has little or no respect for those in positions of authority, or those who host her residency in their land.

You came to a country very different than your own, Ms. Grussner, and to a city of 8 million people with some 157 cultures represented. This is quite a dramatically different reality than a very small, primarily Finnish village of just some thousands of small island inhabitants. So far, no problem.

However, you had the nerve to assume that somehow you, at a mere 28 years of age, are smarter and wiser about the education of children in this country, and the administration of public schools here, than are the native citizens of my country and the education professionals who have lived here all their lives and who have trained extensively for the complex, serious, and very challenging tasks of running a huge school with thousands of students, thousands of parents, and many dozens of teachers and other employees.

If I were to come to Finland and were to behave as you did here, namely arrogantly, highly manipulatively, sanctimoniously, and with unsupportable condescension toward the administrators in charge, I am sure I would be told, and would be CORRECTLY told, to please shut my mouth and go back to my country . . . that I have no business telling Finnish school administrators and educators how they should run their schools and teach their children.

Ms. Grussner, I am very glad that you are back in Finland and out of my city and my country. In fact, I hope you do not return here. Not because you are an evil person, which I do not think you are, but because I regard you as a person who has cleverly used a good and noble idea and deed (the field trip for some children at P.S. 86) as a prop in a larger egotistical and self-serving effort of yours, one that is quite apparent from a visit to your website.

Even more disturbing, you brazenly and manipulatively trampled

upon the well-intentioned efforts of the school principal and endeav-
ored to portray him as a real jerk who was barely tolerable.

Ms. Grussner, in my humble opinion as a longtime resident of New
York City and as a professional, I think you were INCREDIBLY
LUCKY that Mr. Benardo even hired you! I'm sure that now, after your
disgusting behavior and remarks, he wishes that he never heard the
name Johanna Grussner, and never took the huge risks inherent in hiring you. And I'm sure that any other principals you approached here
about a job, who DIDN'T offer you one, are congratulating themselves
that they avoided a real personal nightmare such as the one with which
you obnoxiously rewarded Mr. Benardo.

After your nasty and highly publicized characterization of Mr. Benardo
that appeared in the third *New York Times* article, no American school
principal (or other administrator) who read the article and who is in his
or her right mind would want to expose himself or herself to the serious
risks of such a needless and embarrassing character assassination.

Hopefully, your strident and thoroughly repulsive behavior toward
the principal who gave you the job will convince other principals to not
take such risks in the future.

Now you are back in Finland or Sweden . . . what good news for us
here in New York! I hope your body feels better there, and that you can
make a decent life for yourself as a self-supporting musician. Enjoy your
family and your friends, and be sure to take many opportunities to tell
them, in great detail, how strange, stupid, and backward are the people
of New York City—in particular, the school officials, the teachers, many
of the students, many of their parents, the school system, and American
society in general.

Be certain to let them know that you were terribly mistreated in
America, abused and psychologically tormented by a "sadistic" school
principal, and nearly tortured by the awful American society and most
of the people in our wicked country.

But do me and my countrymen and countrywomen, who are just as proud of our nation as is any Finn of Finland, one favor: Stay in Finland or Sweden, and don't come back here.

It's perfectly reasonable for you to adore your own country and your countrypeople. It might even be reasonable for you not to be comfortable in another country. So just stay there in Finland or Sweden and keep celebrating things Scandinavian, instead of coming to my country and endlessly polluting the air here with your ethnocentric and arrogant denunciations.

Good-bye, Ms. Grussner. Thanks for coming to America and giving us these valuable lessons . . . and thanks even more for leaving.

Art Goodfellow,
New York City

Johanna felt herself going rigid as she forced herself to keep reading. She was stunned, frightened really. Was this what people meant when they talked about celebrity stalkers? Worried, she showed the email to her mother. "It's him," Lillemor said grimly, the instant she finished reading. The principal. Neither one of them spoke his name. Could it be Mr. Benardo? The name was too good to be true. It sounded phony. Art Goodfellow—those words sounded like clues. The writer of the email obviously wanted to point up the contrast between his compassionate nature and Johanna's evil one. He was a good fellow; she was the "sadistic" one, whatever she might think of herself. Even the first name seemed freighted with layers of meaning. Was it Art, as in Arthur, or Art as in music and art? Or as in Project Arts? Whoever Art Goodfellow might be, he or she identified with the principal. Art Goodfellow wanted Johanna to feel Mr. Benardo's pain.

Was Mr. Benardo himself capable of writing such a venomous screed? She couldn't ask him because he wouldn't take her calls. But Johanna found that hard to believe, even after the way he had treated her. The letter was so personal, so insiderish, that it seemed to come from someone connected with the school. But it didn't have to be the principal, Margaret suggested, when Johanna consulted her. It could be his agent, someone familiar with his point of view. A relative. They had no way of knowing the true identity of Art Goodfellow. Johanna tried to banish the email from her mind.

෩

That summer, Johanna spent most of her time with her family, reacquainting herself after the years away. One rainy day, she and Lillemor cleaned out all the closets in the house, filling eight large trash bags, which Uffe drove to the Red Cross for delivery abroad. They laughed and cried as they sorted through Johanna's old books and toys. But when they were finished, her room no longer looked frozen in time. Now it looked neutral, almost impersonal. Johanna felt that she could breathe again, as if by cleaning her closets she had swept out her soul.

She went fishing for flounder with her dad. She felt liberated, unfettered, for the first time in many years. She enjoyed being single. She forgot about the pressure to have babies before it was too late, before she was a cripple. She felt whole, all by herself. "I just got back from a seasonal 'cousin party,'" she emailed a friend. "We all grew up together. We're basically the same age, and we're almost all girls. We have so much fun together. Two of them are pregnant now and in the midst of building their new houses. I used to feel stressed about building a family soon, like them, but not anymore. There has always been a boyfriend in my life, and now I feel like I really have time and energy to do my own thing and focus on just what I want to do. It's nice. Tomorrow I'm singing at my friend's wedding, and I'm going to the party alone. It'll be fun to see all my friends again. It's been so long."

෩

Not long after, Johanna fell in love. She and her sisters, the Daughters of the Wolf, did a concert tour of Aland that summer in one of her father's old buses, converted into a trailer, with a kitchen, bathroom, and nine sleeping compartments. Uffe came along as their chauffeur. Cocki brought her husband and three children. Bodi brought Martin. At a concert in Kumlinge, a small island in the archipelago, Johanna looked into the audience and noticed a wiry young man with a shaved head looking back at her with particular intensity. After the performance, he came back stage and invited her for a walk. His name was Magnus Danielsson. He was Swedish, an investment consultant, and he summered in the Aland Islands. Johanna and Magnus stayed up, talking, until dawn. She told him of her illness. "My legs are strong enough for both of us," he said.

૭૪૭

Johanna returned to New York at the end of the summer to record an original operetta based on the Moomins, the antic trolls created by Tove Jansson, the Finnish children's book writer and artist. The score had been written by Johanna's friend Mika Pohjola, and they recorded it in his bathroom in lower Manhattan. Johanna sang six different voices, laying down tracks to harmonize with herself. She spent the day recording, then spent the night at a friend's apartment on the Upper West Side.

On the morning of September 11, 2001, Johanna had just woken up when Mika called to tell her that terrorist hijackers had flown two jet planes into the World Trade Center. "Don't go outside," he told her.

Over the next few days, Johanna tried to do something useful. She signed up to give blood, but, since there were so few survivors, her blood was not needed. She called elementary schools, thinking that she might be able to comfort small children by playing guitar and singing with them. She could not get through.

Her family and Magnus, worried about her safety, begged her to leave New York. "I want you here," Magnus said, in a telephone call from Stockholm. "I want to be with you," Johanna replied. The next day, he called back. "I'm coming to get you," he said. Within twenty-four hours, he had flown into Newark. In his pocket, he had a ticket for her return. Lillemor cried when she heard that Magnus had gone to find her daughter, just as Uffe had ferried his true love across the frozen Baltic thirty-five years before.

◎◎

Magnus insisted that Johanna face up to her illness and consult a doctor in Stockholm. She went to University Hospital, Karolinska Sjukhuset, where a general practitioner examined her. He asked her to lie down on the floor and then watched her get up, to see how she did it. Then he asked her to climb a small steel staircase, noting that she favored her right leg, and it was stronger.

"What do you think?" she asked. "Should I get a formal diagnosis, or is it pretty obvious that I have this?"

"Are you kidding?" the doctor replied. "If you get a diagnosis, your case will be in the files. You can get continuous information as studies develop. You'll be entitled to physical therapy and all the benefits for handicapped people."

A muscle biopsy in her thigh and an electromyography test confirmed the diagnosis and found that she had limb girdle muscular dystrophy, the same kind as Cocki. Her shoulders and hips would be affected first. The neurologist sat and talked for as long as Johanna needed to, answering her questions.

"I can't promise anything," she remembered him saying. "But animal testing has been very successful. In ten or fifteen years we might be able to do gene manipulation. We could start rebuilding the sick muscle with healthy muscle genes."

The Swedish doctors gave her hope, and bolstered her resolve to stay strong in the meantime. Cocki's doctors had told her not to strain herself, and she had grown progressively weaker. Now the doctors in Stockholm told Johanna that she was probably lucky to have lived so long in New York. Without realizing it, she had been exercising more than her sisters. She didn't have a car. She took the subway. She was forced to walk up and down stairs.

The doctors encouraged her to continue walking and swimming at a pace that would raise her pulse. They also assigned her to a physical therapist who taught her isometric exercises with giant rubber bands.

Her co-payment for each visit was only about $12. "I'm so incredibly grateful," she said.

She couldn't believe how wonderful socialized medicine was. Taxes, taxes. Perhaps that accounted for the lovely dining room, with real china, at her childhood school. She had never thought of it before.

As she anticipated, Stockholm was paradise for a handicapped person. She was reminded of that every time she crossed the street and heard the streetlights beating out the time for the blind, sounding like grandfather clocks ticking or timpanis, depending on how urgent it was to cross the street before the light changed.

She still expected to be in a wheelchair some day. But if the doctor's prediction was right, she would be middle-aged by the time animal testing resulted in the real possibility of a cure for muscular dystrophy in people. Maybe 45 years old. Not so bad.

❦

Music brought the sisters back together again. Rehearsing for their performances as Ulvens Dottrar, they could fight over little things—matters of timing or harmony—without serious consequences. There would be tears, but then the moment passed. Sometimes, Lillemor listened to them rehearse and could not resist joining in, her own voice full, throaty, and sweet.

Johanna was finding her place at home, either defying or succumbing to the Law of Jante, she often wondered which.

The sisters bestowed one of their nonsense nicknames on Magnus.

"Magnus-Bagnus," they teased.

It was about time, they told Johanna when she visited Aland on weekends, for her to settle down with someone who appreciated her.

"I was 18 when I met Martin," Bodi said, tauntingly.

"At least you found one right away," Lillemor agreed, soothingly. "You must have been kissed by a prince."

"And Johanna brought home a whole frog farm," Bodi said.

"I was 20 when I met my husband," Cocki interjected.

"But Johanna never did things the easy way. Remember when you cut your hair? Did you regret it?"

"I don't know."

"Magnus likes you," Bodi told Johanna.

At that moment, Magnus and Uffe walked into the kitchen, returning from a day-long ice-fishing trip.

"Did you get any fish?" Lillemor asked.

"No," Magnus said, defiantly.

"The ice was knuckly," Uffe added in their defense.

"Good thing I cooked," Lillemor said, smiling.

Johanna jumped up and pulled on her coat. She and Magnus had to catch the ferry back to Stockholm. She was happy to be home, and just as happy to escape.

POSTSCRIPT

Vincent Maldonado

Vincent thrived at the Harlem School of the Arts, where his fellow students teased him for not knowing a word of French and admired his spunk. The music director, Bernard Phillips, asked after his homework and his family, and chose him to sing "The Star Spangled Banner" during a charity tennis event at Arthur Ashe Stadium. When he saw 14,000 people in the stands, Vincent had an attack of stage fright. He managed to squeak out only a few bars before stopping. "Open your mouth," he imagined Johanna telling him, and he started the song over, to cheers from the audience.

But after about a year, Vincent tired of the subway ride from the Bronx to Harlem and stopped going. His reputation as a troublemaker followed him to Middle School 399, where he earned poor grades. His mother found marijuana in his book-bag.

In eighth grade, he auditioned for a newly created small high school, the Bronx High School of Music. More than 370 children tried out for just 40 openings in the choral program. Vincent was asked to sing "Happy Birthday," but to give it a bluesy interpretation. Everything he had learned from Johanna came back to him, and he passed the audition. By the end of the year, however, it was clear that he was flunking eighth grade, and the school threatened to withdraw his admission.

Ruth feared she was losing Vincent to the streets, and called Ralph.

Vincent now lives with his father, his father's companion, Evelyn, and her six sons in a single-family house in Allentown, Pennsylvania. He has joined a naval junior ROTC program at his new high school. His first report card showed B's in English, History, and Algebra, and an A in Biology.

He misses his mother, and he keeps a snapshot of Johanna, beaming, tucked into the frame of his bedroom mirror.

Soon after moving to Allentown, he wrote Johanna an uncharacteristically ebullient email from his new home. It said:

> "I go to william allen high school and getting strait a's just for you and
> i joind a navy program called the NJROTC, I not sure what it meens
> yet but its fun. I love you and miss talking to you.
> LOVE ALWAYS,
> VINCENT MALDONADO."

Pierre Marquez

After Pierre's success at the final concert, Mr. Benardo helped secure a last-minute placement for him in a Bronx middle school with a performing arts component. There, Pierre discovered that his true calling was not singing but acting. He performed in school productions, and during a field trip met the actor Liev Schreiber, who was playing Henry V in Central Park. When Pierre graduated from middle school, his teacher gave him a volume of Shakespeare and told him that he was going places. He attends Legacy High School, a small school for academically motivated students on Manhattan's Upper East Side.

Jamie Flores

Jamie's mathematical ability took him, as his parents had hoped, to the competitive Salk School of Science in Manhattan. He rose at 6:00 every morning to ride the subway from the Bronx to East 19th Street. He stopped singing to concentrate on his studies. Surrounded by other bright, hard-working students, many of them the children of Manhattan professionals, he found some of their confidence rubbing off on him. In high school, he passed the audition for the Bronx High School of Music, and found his voice again. He taught himself to play piano. As his voice matured, he sang lead tenor in the high school choir, earned a 95-point grade average, and shot up from the shortest kid in the class to 5-feet-8-inches.

As for "Vem Kan Segla," it still holds a place in his heart. "I think I'll be 70 and still remember the words," he says.

Erica Davies

Erica no longer has to worry about being tormented for being the smartest girl in her class. After finishing Prep for Prep, she was accepted by Fieldston, a top private school in the Riverdale section of the Bronx. She can't wait to go to school every day, and pines for Fieldston during summer vacation.

Ashley Alvarez

Ileana Alvarez moved her family to a gated community in the Poconos, near the Delaware Water Gap. It is one of many former summer resorts now populated by commuters, many of them cops and transit workers, to New York City. Pocono housing developments have been in the news, because scores of working-class, black, and Hispanic Bronx homeowners have joined lawsuits claiming that they were lured there by unscrupulous real estate interests, promising bargain housing, then pushed into foreclosure.

Ileana was resourceful enough to avoid being victimized. With help from her mother, she paid $64,000 cash for her house, an alpine-style timber cottage with strings of decorative white lights framing the porch. She works at service jobs within the housing development, as a housekeeper or minding the recreation center. The wages are low compared to New York, but she has sworn off credit cards and is leading a quiet life for the sake of her children.

Ashley attends Lehman Intermediate School. She complains that the school has a conservative dress code—no tank tops—and that the principal is not nearly as understanding as Mr. Benardo. "He was the best principal I ever had," she says. She takes chorus, but it is not the same, and she is finding herself drawn to basketball instead.

She keeps her souvenirs of Finland in a box under her bed in the room she shares with her little brother. She dreams that some day her singing talent will win her a spot on the television show *American Idol*.

Malin Jansson

Malin keeps the picture that Vincent gave her of his 12-year-old self in her wallet, next to the photographs of her best girlfriends. She still doesn't have a boyfriend.

Her favorite television show is *Fame Factory*, a Swedish show that takes ordinary people and turns them into singers and dancers. It's the Scandinavian version of Ashley's favorite show, *American Idol*.

Malin has chopped off her red pigtails and let her hair, now short and spiky, revert to its natural brown. She wears two earrings in each earlobe, a black leather bracelet bristling with silver spikes on her wrist.

She plans to enter Aland's vocational school, Yrkesskolan, to study hair-dressing. Her ambition is to work in a unisex salon, but not in a small town. Only Stockholm will do.

She is saving up for the day when she can leave home. By the time she turns 18, she plans to have enough money to buy her own car.

Ester Miiros

Ester Miiros is no longer wearing her frumpy school-marm clothes—the elastic-waisted flowered skirt, the prim blouse. In hind-sight, the image she presented had more to do with her return from maternity leave than with being parochial. Now she's more likely to be found in a trim navy suit, an Armani knock-off, paired with a flowing light-blue shirt, untucked at the waist. She could stride into any office on Madison Avenue and look like she belonged. The burlap and felt patchwork quilt that the children had made in Margaret Bartelme's art classes, and which they presented to the Palsbole school, still hangs in the hallway near the dining room. The images on the quilt are like tourist snapshots, perfect in their corny evocation of New York City: a Yankees logo, the Kingsbridge Avenue el track, the Statue of Liberty, a silhouette of the lower Manhattan skyline, the twin towers rising up in the middle. A dusting of glitter covers some of the squares.

"This is typical America," Miiros said, admiringly, two years after the Bronx kids visited. "I have never been there. But this is my picture of America. Glittering."

Strolling out to the schoolyard, Miiros pauses to watch a new genera-tion of little girls playing jump rope during recess. Then she blurts out a question that has been vexing her for the last two years, ever since Ashley lit up the stage of Palsbole Skola.

"Did the journey make a difference? Did it give them some sort of hope? Hope for the world?"

Margaret Bartelme

Mr. Benardo apologized to Margaret and offered to restore her position as head of Project Arts if she wanted it. After giving the matter some thought, Margaret agreed. She has never found another Johanna. "I haven't even tried," she says. "Johanna was one of a kind." But art, dance, and music continue at P.S. 86 with the help of teachers and artists-in-residence, some quite prominent, brought in by Margaret. One of Johanna's old friends from the Manhattan School of Music has taken up her position as a singing teacher. The P.S. 86 gospel chorus has faded into school history.

Howard and Dorothy Pack

As long as Margaret remains at the school and his foundation money holds out, Howard Pack continues to support the arts at P.S. 86, his alma mater, and to enjoy being a big fish in a small pond. Dorothy sees Margaret often, but keeps in touch with the rest of her traveling companions from P.S. 86 only indirectly, by doing Mr. Benardo's latest crossword puzzles in the *Times*.

Sheldon Benardo

Mr. Benardo is still the principal, and by all accounts, he seems happy and mellow. On April 24, 2002, near the one-year anniversary of the trip to Finland, the *New York Times* published Mr. Benardo's third crossword puzzle. It marked his advancement from Monday, the easiest day of the week, to Wednesday, a more challenging slot. Dorothy Pack solved the puzzle and concurred that Benardo deserved the promotion, on the strength of No. 39 across, which seemed like a tacit memento of the chorus's Aland adventure. The clue was: "Helsinki mother's exhortation?" The answer was: "Finnish your meal."

Johanna Grussner

Johanna and Magnus were married on September 6, 2003, in the twelfth-century church below the house where she grew up. Sickan, the hairdresser who cut off all Johanna's hair when she was 9, highlighted and styled her now-long tresses for the wedding. Johanna wore her mother's wedding gown, indelibly marked with a red wine stain. Lillemor helped her disguise the stain with an appliqué of cloth flowers.

She keeps in touch with the kids who made up the Select Chorus of P.S. 86, and they often send her emails. Johanna's childhood chorus director grew tired of gospel, so Johanna and Anders Hallback, Ashley's singing partner, formed an offshoot of Intermezzo to continue the repertoire. They are now the co-directors of a new gospel choir in Aland, called "Good News."

She has never gone back to P.S. 86 or made up with Mr. Benardo.

ACKNOWLEDGMENTS

As I was writing the story of the chorus of P.S. 86 for the *New York Times*, songs echoed in my ears. I heard Vincent Maldonado pouring all the heartbreak of his 12-year-old life into "Oh Happy Day," and I knew that, in spite of the title, this was not a happy song. I heard Ashley Alvarez, a spunky but mysterious girl, belt out "Going Up Yonder."

I was working on a three-part series about Johanna Grussner and her chorus after years of covering education and before I went on to write a weekly column for the *Times*. But as I explored the lives of Johanna and the children, they opened up a world that moved well beyond the original series, into territory ranging from the state of public education, to how personal chemistry shapes the dynamic of a school, to family relations.

P.S. 86 is in some ways typical of public schools across the country, from the only school in the smallest Midwestern town to the neglected schools in the inner-cities of Los Angeles, Chicago, Boston, and of course New York. In that way, what happens at P.S. 86 is, I think, instructive for public education in general. At the same time, P.S. 86 is incontrovertibly unique, a precise constellation of personalities, events, history, and hope that can be found nowhere else in the world.

In writing this book, I often thought how lucky I was to share in the archetypal but also very personal experiences of the people at P.S. 86, experiences that came together in one joyous moment in the remote Aland Islands.

Memory is a fragile resource, but one that every reporter and historian is ultimately at the mercy of. Wherever possible, I have tried to corroborate events and their significance through multiple sources. Where I attribute thoughts or feelings to individuals, it is based upon conversations with them or on the recollections of participants.

I'd like to thank all of the children and families who made up the community of P.S. 86 in 2001. A few took a central role in the making of this book. The free-spirited Ileana Alvarez has lived her life as if it were theater, raising a daughter, Ashley, whose show-business drive and magnetism lit up the stage at P.S. 86 and in Aland. I am sure we will be hearing from Ashley again some day. Ileana and her proud Cuban mother, Ana, opened their homes and hearts to me. Ruth Gonzalez dedicated herself to protecting her only son, Vincent Maldonado, from the mean streets and poverty that surrounded them. Vincent's father, Ralph, came to the rescue of them both at the critical moment. Erica Davies shared her thoughts with a wisdom far beyond her years, a precocity nurtured by her attentive and trusting mother, Nila Cadornigara. I will never forget Candida Brito-Marquez trailed by her nine little ducklings. She and her husband, Pierre, have raised their eldest son, Pierre Jr., to be a person of humility and savoir faire. In his gravity, introspective nature, and maturity, Jamie Flores would stand out in any school, and is a tribute to his accomplished mother, Marie and step-father, Mike Muñoz. I will always remember Keshuana Sanders for her smile and sweetness, and for the fiercely protective loyalty of her mother, Janet.

Among the staff and wider community of P.S. 86, Margaret Bartelme, the arts coordinator who hired Johanna and nurtured her success at P.S. 86, provided valuable support and information throughout the reporting and writing of this book. Howard and Dorothy Pack, the school's surprise benefactors, detailed their memories with integrity and care, and were always hospitable.

Sheldon Benardo, the principal, extended himself to me from the first moment I visited his school. He patiently explained the difficulty of managing the conflicting personalities within a large urban school and of operating within the sometimes stifling constraints of the larger school system. I was impressed by his commitment to the children above all else, to the teachers secondarily, and to the bureaucracy last and least. That is, I thought, how it should be. I admired his intelligence and independence. I gained insights into education from his point of view, which was firmly rooted in one school building, that I never gleaned while covering education from the lofty vantage point of chancellors, politicians, academics, and experts.

From the first time I wrote about Shelly Benardo for the *Times*, I have tried to depict him in all his humanity, his flaws as well as his wonderful strengths. At some point, he felt wounded by my reporting, and stopped cooperating, for the reasons I have described in this book. I was therefore unable to discover whether he was the author of the Art Goodfellow email. Nevertheless, the thoughts attributed to Shelly Benardo in this book come directly from my conversations with him. Even though they are not in quotation marks, they are, in most instances, the words he used with me in conversation.

I also want to thank the many people who contributed to my reporting from outside the current confines of P.S. 86. Mindy Chermak, the principal of the Professional Performing Arts High School, showed compassion for children and gave me a window into the elite world of professional-quality arts education in the public schools. Ray Osinoff, the longtime principal of P.S. 86, shared his knowledge of P.S. 86 history as well as his analysis of the principal's role in running a school. Bernard Phillips, executive director of the Harlem School of the Arts, helped me understand the issues faced by children growing up in difficult circumstances. Irving Newman provided insight into Sheldon

Benardo's early career. Paula Simon, of the alumnae association at De-Witt Clinton High School, provided valuable fact-checking.

Schuyler Chapin, the former New York City arts commissioner, graciously traced the history of Project Arts. Christopher Gray, the author of the Streetscapes column in the *New York Times*, as well as the staff of the New York City Arts Commission and the staff of Mayor Michael R. Bloomberg, helped me research the history of P.S. 86 and its building. Jeremy Rosenholtz, an English teacher at Fieldston, provided information on prep school programs, and opened his own program to me. Cheryl Hemenway, Johanna Grussner's student-teaching advisor at Berklee, shared her memories of Johanna's early days. James Staffan was generous with his memories of the months he spent with Johanna before the trip to Finland. Rob Pape, a dedicated teacher, helped fill out the picture of P.S. 86 while Johanna was there. Elsa Coriano, another dedicated and fearless teacher, was forthright in answering often personal questions. Will Shortz, puzzles editor of the *New York Times*, verified crossword puzzle information. Katherine Damkohler, executive director of Education Through Music, discussed music education. Bernard Stein, editor and co-publisher of the *Riverdale Press*, enriched my understanding of political corruption in the Bronx. Maura McDermott, a dear friend and talented reporter, helped research the ballot-fraud scandal.

The people of Aland took an almost personal interest in the P.S. 86 chorus.

Johanna Grussner worked closely with me every step of the way, sharing the memories of her divided life in the Bronx and Aland with unstinting honesty and openness. She also paved the way for other people in her life to come forward.

Johanna's devoted family welcomed me back to their home and kitchen table for a second visit and extended themselves more than I could have hoped: Lillemor and Uffe, Cocki and Bodi, Martin Cromwell-Morgan, and Magnus Danielsson. Aland would not have been the same without the observant Helena Lundberg.

Tracy Nyholm, Tomas Lundberg, Maria Svenblad, and Siv and Anders Hallback extended the same hospitality to me that they had shown as host families to the Bronx children. Malin Jansson, Christoffer Blomqvist, Rasmus Kytomaki, Emil Sundberg, and their families helped shed light on what it means to be a child growing up in Aland. Esther Miiros and Anne-Charlotte Haggblom shared their knowledge and perspective on the educational system in Aland and in Finland. Peter Lindback, the governor of Aland, shared his insights into local culture and society.

My journalistic colleagues Stefan Randstrom and Kerwin DeVonish, documentary filmmakers, and Robert Jansson, a photographer based in Aland, were unfailingly professional and generous.

Here it seems appropriate to make a comment about the Swedish names and words used in this book. Although it may appear jarring to the many Swedish-speaking Alanders who assisted with this book, the text omits Swedish accent marks, for reasons of readability in English.

I have supplemented my reporting with written documents including: court records regarding the allegations of ballot fraud in District 10, some of which have been sealed but remain in the hands of people who obtained them in the 1990s; the report "From Chaos to Corruption: An Investigation into the 1993 Community School Board Election," by Edward Stancik, special investigator for New York City schools, on alleged political corruption in the community school districts; records of the city's Board of Education, since renamed the Department of Education, particularly the annual school report cards; news articles from the *New York Times,* the *Riverdale Press,* the *Christian Science Monitor,* the *New York Daily News, Newsday,* the *New York Post,* and the Associated Press; the autobiographical book *A Man in the Making: Grandfathers, Fathers, Sons,* by Richard C. Robertiello, M.D. (Richard Marek Publishers, 1979); and documents from the private files of Johanna Grussner and Margaret Bartelme.

I could not have written this book without seven years of experience as an education writer at the *New York Daily News, Disney,* and the *New York Times*. Along the way, my understanding was enriched by exposure to thought-provoking people within the education field, including a succession of chancellors, from Rudy Crew to Harold Levy; Randi Weingarten, president of the United Federation of Teachers; Carol Gresser, former president of the New York City Board of Education; and Seymour Fliegel, president of the Center for Educational Innovation—Public Education Association.

At the *New York Times*, I am thankful to Jon Landman, an inspiration as Metropolitan editor; his deputy and successor, Susan Edgerley; and Anne Cronin, the display editor and a model of grace under pressure. I was privileged to work with Ethan Bronner, the former education editor, and Joe Berger, his deputy. A special nod to Jacques Steinberg, my irrepressible colleague on the education beat. Connie Rosenblum helped liberate my writing voice through the Coping column. Joyce Purnick has been a mentor since Room 9.

Peter Osnos, the book's publisher, has been unfailingly supportive. Kate Darnton, my editor, was the soul of patience, discretion, and discernment. Liza Dawson, my agent, held my hand.

Lastly, I would like to mention my three children, who are everything a mother could want, and my husband, Josh Barbanel, who is my best critic and strongest supporter.

PublicAffairs is a publishing house founded in 1997. It is a tribute to the standards, values, and flair of three persons who have served as mentors to countless reporters, writers, editors, and book people of all kinds, including me.

I. F. Stone, proprietor of *I. F. Stone's Weekly,* combined a commitment to the First Amendment with entrepreneurial zeal and reporting skill and became one of the great independent journalists in American history. At the age of eighty, Izzy published *The Trial of Socrates,* which was a national bestseller. He wrote the book after he taught himself ancient Greek.

Benjamin C. Bradlee was for nearly thirty years the charismatic editorial leader of *The Washington Post.* It was Ben who gave the *Post* the range and courage to pursue such historic issues as Watergate. He supported his reporters with a tenacity that made them fearless, and it is no accident that so many became authors of influential, best-selling books.

Robert L. Bernstein, the chief executive of Random House for more than a quarter century, guided one of the nation's premier publishing houses. Bob was personally responsible for many books of political dissent and argument that challenged tyranny around the globe. He is also the founder and was the longtime chair of Human Rights Watch, one of the most respected human rights organizations in the world.

.　　　.　　　.

For fifty years, the banner of Public Affairs Press was carried by its owner Morris B. Schnapper, who published Gandhi, Nasser, Toynbee, Truman, and about 1,500 other authors. In 1983 Schnapper was described by *The Washington Post* as "a redoubtable gadfly." His legacy will endure in the books to come.

Peter Osnos, *Publisher*

JUV
PS
613
.08   The Other side of a
              poem

DATE DUE
